INSTRUCTOR'S RESOURCE

to accompany

BECOMING A MASTER MANAGER
A COMPETENCY FRAMEWORK
SECOND EDITION

Robert E. Quinn
University of Michigan

Sue R. Faerman
State University of New York at Albany

Michael P. Thompson
Brigham Young University

Michael R. McGrath
Personnel Decisions International

LAURIE DiPADOVA
University of Utah

John Wiley & Sons, Inc.
New York • Chichester • Brisbane • Toronto • Singapore

Copyright © 1996 by John Wiley & Sons, Inc.

This material may be reproduced for testing or instructional purposes by people using the text.

ISBN 0-471-13064-8

Printed in the United States of America

10 9 8 7 6 5 4 3 2 1

PREFACE

Writing the *Instructional Guide* for **Becoming A Master Manager** has been a most exciting and energizing project. The textbook conveys a meaningful expression of the Competing Values approach, a theory which appeals to academics and practitioners alike. Further, the text's ALAPA learning model format enhances management/business education. We are living in times of immense social and political changes, and of growing urgent concerns for the physical environment. These changes and concerns pose momentous challenges for business, industry, and goverment that will only accelerate during the coming decades. However, I am convinced that the resources--many of these being creative resources in the individuals who work in organizations--are available to meet those difficulties successfully. This text represents a superb effort to educate our future--and current--managers to face these challenges.

In addition, this text represents efforts to enhance learning and to affirm the student-teacher relationship. Because of the ALAPA learning model, the text is interaction-intensive. The traditional learning model, with the teacher-as-lecturer and student-as-note-taker format has its merits, but that format may reinforce distance between teachers and students. In contrast, the ALAPA model functions to reduce that distance, advancing more interaction in the classroom, and a more honest degree of sharing among students and teachers. As such, ALAPA affirms a student-teacher relationship which is at once candid and sharing, viewing all concerned as pilgrims together on a journey of discovery. It implicitly rejects one-way communication, which magnifies the already existing status barriers between students and teachers. The text, then, gives the student-teacher relationship the increased emphasis it deserves. ALAPA allows students and teachers to know, understand, and subsequently appreciate each other better.

I would like to express my gratitude to Bob Quinn, Sue Faerman, Michael Thompson and Michael McGrath for giving me this opportunity to write the *Instructional Guide*, and for their help and encouragement. A special thanks also goes to Ellen Ford at John Wiley and Sons. An additional debt of gratitude goes to Luke Hohmann for his work with the software.

I am grateful to those whose contributions appear in this (and the former) *Instructional Guide*: Dan Denison, University of Michigan; Bill Metheny, Montana State University--Billings; Larry Michaelsen, University of Oklahoma and Deborah Wells, Creighton University. In addition, I am grateful to Michael P. Thompson of Brigham Young University for his contribution to this edition. Also, I am very appreciative to those who contributed to the adult learning section of the *Instructional Guide*: Alan Belasen of SUNY-Albany and SUNY-Empire State College; Meg Benke of SUNY-

Empire State College; Andy DiNitto of SUNY-Empire State College; and David Hart of SUNY-Empire State College.

I am grateful to the Division of Developmental Services at the New York State Governor's Office of Employee Relations for permission to use materials from the Advanced Human Resources Development Program, now called the **Advanced Program**.

During my years as a student, I was particularly blessed to have gifted and talented teachers. They inspired me in numerous critical and subtle ways. There is no doubt that their fine examples helped shape my thinking regarding the entire enterprise of teaching at the college and university level. I am especially grateful to Sue R. Faerman and to John Rohrbaugh, at the Graduate School of Public Affairs and Policy, University at Albany, State University of New York. They not only demonstrated superb teaching skills and outstanding scholarship, but combined these attributes with a genuine concern for students. Sue is a fine mentor, wise advisor, and wonderful friend! I also wish to express special gratitude to Sterling M. McMurrin and Lowell L. Bennion, of the University of Utah. Although both are retired now, they continue to inspire thousands of their former students, myself included, with what they taught and how they taught it.

Also, a special debt goes to Michael V. Fortunato. While he was not one of my professors, I learned much from him. As Director of FORUM/East, he mentored me as I set about teaching organizational theory and behavior to experienced managers. Michael demonstrated for me remarkable sensitivities and insights which are needed in order effectively to teach managers and executives, and he modeled compassionate and effective leadership in every respect.

Finally, a special note of deep appreciation to my husband, Hugh Stocks, who assisted me in countless critical ways--and always with warmth and patience.

While I willingly take responsibility for the contents of the *Instructional Guide*, I am deeply grateful for the support and assistance that I've been granted to bring this effort to completion.

Laurie Newman DiPadova
Salt Lake City, Utah

TABLE OF CONTENTS

PART 1: OVERVIEW   PAGES 1-18

Organization of the **Instructional Guide**	1
Key features of the Quinn, et al. text	3
Using the Instructional Guide	8
Using ALAPA	8
Integrating Supplemental Texts	10
Chapter Organization	11
Activity Flow Sheet	11
Process Guide	12
Group Facilitation	13
Additional Suggestions for Classroom Management	16
Advice from the Authors	17
References	18

PART 2: TEACHING WITH THE TEXT   PAGES 19-50

"Notes on Teaching with *Becoming a Master Manager*" Daniel R. Denison	21
"Using Quinn, et al. in Large Management Classes" William M. Metheny	25
"Team Learning and Development of Leadership Competencies" Larry K. Michaelsen	29
"Experiential Learning in the Classroom" Deborah Wells	37
"Using the Competing Values Framework in the Classroom" Michael P. Thompson	41

PART 3: TEACHING CVF TO MANAGERS   PAGES 51-72

Teaching Managers with the Competing Values Framework	51

"Teaching Organizational Theory and Behavior to Traditional
    Students and to Mid-Career Managers"
    David W. Hart
	55

"Competency-Based Management Education: Challenges and
    Methods in Teaching Adult Learners"
    Alan T. Belasen, Meg Benke, and Andrew J. DiNitto
	59

Assessment By Others CVF Instrument, Instructions, Computational Sheet, and Profile	69

PART 4: THE CHAPTERS   PAGES 73-351

CHAPTER 1: THE EVOLUTION OF MANAGEMENT MODELS 73

Course Preassessment 75
Competing Values Skills Survey
    Robert E. Quinn and Daniel R. Denison 77
CVSS Software Instructions
    Luke Hohmann 79
Competing Values Management Practices Survey 87
    Computational Worksheet & Profile 88
Competing Values Self Assessment: Skills 90
    Computational Worksheet & Profile 93

CHAPTER 2: MENTOR ROLE 97

COMPETENCY 1: UNDERSTANDING SELF AND OTHERS

Assessment Activity Flow Sheet and Process Guide 99
Analysis Activity Flow Sheet and Process Guide 102
Practice Activity Flow Sheet and Process Guide 106
Application Activity Flow Sheet and Process Guide 108

COMPETENCY 2: COMMUNICATING EFFECTIVELY

Assessment Activity Flow Sheet and Process Guide 110
Analysis Activity Flow Sheet and Process Guide 113
Practice Activity Flow Sheet and Process Guide 120
Application Activity Flow Sheet and Process Guide 122

COMPETENCY 3: DEVELOPING SUBORDINATES

Assessment Activity Flow Sheet and Process Guide 126
Analysis Activity Flow Sheet and Process Guide 128
Practice Activity Flow Sheet and Process Guide 130
Application Activity Flow Sheet and Process Guide 132

CHAPTER 3: FACILITATOR ROLE 135

COMPETENCY 1: BUILDING TEAMS

Assessment Activity Flow Sheet and Process Guide 137
Analysis Activity Flow Sheet and Process Guide 139
Practice Activity Flow Sheet and Process Guide 141
Application Activity Flow Sheet and Process Guide 145

COMPETENCY 2: USING PARTICIPATIVE DECISION MAKING

Assessment Activity Flow Sheet and Process Guide 147
Analysis Activity Flow Sheet and Process Guide 149
Practice Activity Flow Sheet and Process Guide 151
Application Activity Flow Sheet and Process Guide 154

COMPETENCY 3: MANAGING CONFLICT

Assessment Activity Flow Sheet and Process Guide	156
Analysis Activity Flow Sheet and Process Guide	158
Practice Activity Flow Sheet and Process Guide	160
Application Activity Flow Sheet and Process Guide	162

CHAPTER 4: THE MONITOR ROLE — 165

COMPETENCY 1: MONITORING PERSONAL PERFORMANCE

Assessment Activity Flow Sheet and Process Guide	167
Analysis Activities Flow Sheets and Process Guides	170
Practice Activity Flow Sheet and Process Guide	175
Application Activity Flow Sheet and Process Guide	177

COMPETENCY 2: MANAGING COLLECTIVE PERFORMANCE

Assessment Activity Flow Sheet and Process Guide	179
Analysis Activity Flow Sheet and Process Guide	181
Practice Activity Flow Sheet and Process Guide	183
Application Activity Flow Sheet and Process Guide	185

COMPETENCY 3: MANAGING ORGANIZATION PERFORMANCE

Assessment Activity Flow Sheet and Process Guide	187
Analysis Activity Flow Sheet and Process Guide	189
Practice Activity Flow Sheet and Process Guide	191
Application Activities Flow Sheets and Process Guides	193

CHAPTER 5: COORDINATOR ROLE — 197

COMPETENCY 1: MANAGING PROJECTS

Assessment Activity Flow Sheet and Process Guide	199
Analysis Activity Flow Sheet and Process Guide	201
Practice Activity Flow Sheet and Process Guide	206
Application Activity Flow Sheet and Process Guide	208

COMPETENCY 2: DESIGNING WORK

Assessment Activity Flow Sheet and Process Guide	210
Analysis Activity Flow Sheet and Process Guide	212
Practice Activity Flow Sheet and Process Guide	214
Application Activity Flow Sheet and Process Guide	216

COMPETENCY 3: MANAGING ACROSS FUNCTIONS

Assessment Activity Flow Sheet and Process Guide	218
Analysis Activity Flow Sheet and Process Guide	220
Practice Activity Flow Sheet and Process Guide	222
Application Activity Flow Sheet and Process Guide	224

CHAPTER 6: DIRECTOR ROLE   227

COMPETENCY 1: VISIONING, PLANNING AND GOAL SETTING
Assessment Activities Flow Sheets and Process Guides	229
Analysis Activity Flow Sheet and Process Guide	233
Practice Activity Flow Sheet and Process Guide	235
Application Activity Flow Sheet and Process Guide	237

COMPETENCY 2: DESIGNING AND ORGANIZING
Assessment Activity Flow Sheet and Process Guide	241
Analysis Activity Flow Sheet and Process Guide	243
Practice Activity Flow Sheet and Process Guide	245
Application Activity Flow Sheet and Process Guide	247

COMPETENCY 3: DELEGATING EFFECTIVELY
Assessment Activity Flow Sheet and Process Guide	249
Analysis Activity Flow Sheet and Process Guide	251
Practice Activity Flow Sheet and Process Guide	253
Application Activity Flow Sheet and Process Guide	255

CHAPTER 7: PRODUCER ROLE   257

COMPETENCY 1: WORKING PRODUCTIVELY
Assessment Activity Flow Sheet and Process Guide	259
Analysis Activity Flow Sheet and Process Guide	261
Practice Activity Flow Sheet and Process Guide	263
Application Activity Flow Sheet and Process Guide	265

COMPETENCY 2: FOSTERING A PRODUCTIVE WORK ENVIRONMENT
Assessment Activity Flow Sheet and Process Guide	267
Analysis Activity Flow Sheet and Process Guide	269
Practice Activity Flow Sheet and Process Guide	271
Application Activity Flow Sheet and Process Guide	273

COMPETENCY 3: MANAGING TIME AND STRESS
Assessment Activity Flow Sheet and Process Guide	275
Analysis Activity Flow Sheet and Process Guide	277
Practice Activity Flow Sheet and Process Guide	279
Application Activity Flow Sheet and Process Guide	281

CHAPTER 8: BROKER ROLE   283

COMPETENCY 1: BUILDING AND MAINTAINING A POWER BASE
- **Assessment** Activity Flow Sheet and Process Guide   286
- **Analysis** Activity Flow Sheet and Process Guide   288
- **Practice** Activities Flow Sheets and Process Guides   291
- **Application** Activity Flow Sheet and Process Guide   296

COMPETENCY 2: NEGOTIATING AGREEMENT AND COMMITMENT
- **Assessment** Activity Flow Sheet and Process Guide   298
- **Analysis** Activity Flow Sheet and Process Guide   300
- **Practice** Activity Flow Sheet and Process Guide   303
- **Application** Activity Flow Sheet and Process Guide   306

COMPETENCY 3: PRESENTING IDEAS EFFECTIVELY
- **Assessment** Activity Flow Sheet and Process Guide   308
- **Analysis** Activity Flow Sheet and Process Guide   310
- **Practice** Activity Flow Sheet and Process Guide   312
- **Application** Activity Flow Sheet and Process Guide   315

CHAPTER 9: THE INNOVATOR ROLE   317

COMPETENCY 1: LIVING WITH CHANGE
- **Assessment** Activity Flow Sheet and Process Guide   319
- **Analysis** Activity Flow Sheet and Process Guide   321
- **Practice** Activity Flow Sheet and Process Guide   323
- **Application** Activity Flow Sheet and Process Guide   325

COMPETENCY 2: THINKING CREATIVELY
- **Assessment** Activity Flow Sheet and Process Guide   327
- **Analysis** Activity Flow Sheet and Process Guide   329
- **Practice** Activity Flow Sheet and Process Guide   331
- **Application** Activity Flow Sheet and Process Guide   333

COMPETENCY 3: CREATING CHANGE
- **Assessment** Activity Flow Sheet and Process Guide   335
- **Analysis** Activity Flow Sheet and Process Guide   337
- **Practice** Activity Flow Sheet and Process Guide   339
- **Application** Activity Flow Sheet and Process Guide   341

CHAPTER 10: INTEGRATION AND THE ROAD TO MASTERY   343
- **Assessment** Activity Flow Sheet and Process Guide   344
- **Analysis** Activity Flow Sheet and Process Guide   346
- **Practice** Activity Flow Sheet and Process Guide   348
- **Application** Activity Flow Sheet and Process Guide   350

PART 1

ORGANIZATION OF THE *INSTRUCTIONAL GUIDE*

This *Instructional Guide* accompanies the revised edition of *Becoming A Master Manager: A Competency Framework* by Robert Quinn, Sue Faerman, Michael Thompson, and Michael McGrath. The purpose of this guide is to empower instructors in using the text, rather than to prescribe ways of teaching from it.

The Instructional Guide as a Decision Making Tool: The text contains more material than can reasonably be taught in one semester. Thus the text provides flexibility, enabling you to tailor your course in a way you find comfortable. This *Instructional Guide* is designed to help you make necessary decisions in using the text. As such, effort has been made to exclude information which is probably on your bookshelves (such as more discussion on MBO), while including considerable detail on what may not be as assessable to you, such as specifics suggestions on processing each individual activity.

The *Instructional Guide* is divided into four parts:

Part 1: Discusses the key features of the text and its relevance for business and management education; how to use the ALAPA learning model; classroom management ideas; guidelines for group facilitation; and advice from the authors. It should be pointed out that the basic explanation of the Competing Values Framework and the ALAPA learning model is provided in chapter 1 of the text; explanations in Part 1 of this guide build on that discussion.

Part 2: Presents contributions from faculty who use the text, sharing how they use it in their classes. They share numerous excellent teaching suggestions including recommendations for setting up groups and for evaluating students.

Part 3: Discusses the use and applicability of this text to adult learners in general, and to adult learners who are *also* managers in organizations in particular. This section includes contributions from expert faculty who have been actively engaged in adult learning for many years, and who have also been using the Competing Values Framework in teaching managers at all organizational levels.

Part 4: Features specific assistance on the text chapters and on the processing of each activity. A 1-page Activity Flow Sheet and a complete Process Guide is provided for each of the 105 skill activities in the text.

If you have any questions or comments with regards to the activities and the *Instructional Guide*, please do not hesitate to contact me.

My address is:

Dr. Laurie N. DiPadova
Assistant Professor of Political Science
252 Orson Spencer Hall
University of Utah
Salt Lake City, Utah 84112
(801) 585-7985

dipadova@poli-sci.utah.edu

KEY FEATURES OF THE TEXT

Becoming A Master Manager: A Competency Framework
has a number of distinguishing features:

1. The grounding of competency-based learning in a solid organizational theory. One of the most compelling strengths of this text is that it incorporates competency-based learning in a theoretical context. The Competing Values Framework offers an approach which facilitates student comprehension of the major issues in organizational theory and their current relevance. Focusing on the paradoxes and tensions inherent in organizational life, this framework assists students in conceptualizing key managerial skills and competencies.

Although the need to include skills in management education has been widely acknowledged, it has been difficult to find a competency-based text which incorporates a recognized model of organizational theory. This text, based on the Competing Values Framework of Managerial Effectiveness, does precisely that. The organizational effectiveness model, roles and competencies have basis in research as well as in theory. References not included in the text can be found in Part 3 of this guide.

2. Use of a well-defined and proven learning model. Through the application of the ALAPA learning model, students are permitted to interact fully with the material for optimal learning, interest, and long-term retention. The ALAPA learning model, which is explained on pages 24-25 of the text, was developed (as PLAPA)[1] by Whetten and Cameron (1984, 3-5). In addition to its widespread classroom use, ALAPA has also been used extensively in management development education nationally and internationally.

This model enhances learning by providing students with opportunities to interact with and apply the concepts to their experiences. It approaches what is available to students in the physical sciences. Chemistry students, for instance, are expected to learn chemistry with the aid of experiences in the laboratory. In the lab they manipulate and test the chemical compounds and become comfortable with the world of chemistry. In much the same way, the ALAPA model permits students to find their laboratory in classroom activities as well as in their own life experiences.

While I am not implying that management is as discrete and precise as the physical sciences may appear, the point is that there are identified competencies than can be developed by students. The ALAPA model provides the structure through which the competency-based learning takes place.

3. Heightened perceived relevance of the text by students. Sometimes textbooks, as disseminators of data and information, can easily become regarded as valuable only for the duration of the course. In contrast, this text has explicit value to the student beyond the course requirements. This value is apparent for two reasons:

---

[1] *Parenthetically, it should be noted that the only difference between the Whetten and Cameron model and ALAPA is that PLAPA terms Preassessment as its first step, while ALAPA refers to it as Assessment. Conceptually the two are identical.

a) Relevance of the concepts is immediately discernible. Students will not have to wait until their first job to experience the pertinence of the ideas covered by the course content. For instance, most students will find immediate applicability of reflective listening skills; most will be able promptly to put stress and time management strategies into their lives; many will find current benefit from conflict management skills.

b) Experiencing course concepts as currently relevant adds to the heightened perception that the concepts are meaningful for their intended future use, as well. Any portions of the text not covered in class are more likely to be studied independently by students.

This textbook, by its interactive design, readily lends itself to being regarded by students as relevant after the course is completed. As such the text enhances the students' perception of the course as being relevant to their future as well as to their lives.

4. Flexibility of the text. This text is appropriate for use in a number of courses, including: Organizational Behavior, Principles of Management, Executive Skills, and various hybrid courses. Furthermore, it can be used as the main text alone, or in conjunction with another text. It can also be used in its entirety, or you may select chapters or competencies according to the needs of your students. As such, it permits greater reliance on your judgment, enhancing your freedom to tailor your courses without jeopardizing continuity.

Additionally, the text is so flexible that the ALAPA model does not have to be followed completely; the Competing Values framework is independent of the learning model. While ALAPA is the ideal, the text is organized in such a way that it easily accommodates to any level of approach to experiential education.

5. Skills-based learning and its value in American business education. Management skills is an issue facing business schools today. With the approach of the 21st century, American business faces new challenges, and so does American business education. The Porter and McKibbin study (1988), commissioned by the American Assembly of Collegiate Schools of Business, expressed concern that business education is deficient in several dimensions which may prove critical to American business into the next century. This textbook is a step towards meeting those needs. Students learn competencies that reflect the paradoxes and dilemmas of organizational life. As such they will begin to develop judgment and discretion, using critical analysis, creative thinking, and their experiences.

THE TEXT AS IT RELATES TO THE PORTER AND MCKIBBIN STUDY:

It is appropriate to consider briefly the major curriculum concerns highlighted in the Porter and McKibbin study, and how the text relates to them. According to the study, of the areas which were identified as undernourished in the American business school curriculum, six were specified by Porter and McKibbin to be the most important:

1. Breadth: There is a need to emphasize a broad education rather than too much business specialization. The concern is that business schools seem to be turning out focused analysts who are interested only with the "bottom line". Other consequences of outcomes are not seriously considered.

While the text does not address this point directly, it does so implicitly. Unlike the traditional management education approach, the content does not focus most heavily on the internal functions of planning, organizing, and controlling. Instead the text expands the managerial role to a balance of many competencies which are important for effectiveness. By doing so the text advances the need for a broad-based understanding of managerial effectiveness and expands what is considered necessary for sound management behavior.

2. The External Environment of Organizations: Related to the call for breadth is the call for a better balance in the curriculum between the "internal environment" and the external environment. Porter and McKibbin note that business education tends to focus on the internal functions of operational effectiveness. However, the reality of the situation is that the boundary between firms and their external environment is becoming more and more blurred. The competitive business environment, as well as government regulations, societal trends, and international developments, require that firms increasingly interact with their environment.

The text promotes this balance. In the Competing Values Framework, the importance of the external focus is recognized, balancing the internal focus. The boundary spanning roles of broker and innovator are given equal attention to the internal process roles of monitor and coordinator.

The importance of the balance in the text between internal and external process cannot be overstated. Students gain their understanding of what constitutes legitimate concerns for managers from the content of basic business/management courses. These courses provide for students the fundamental expectations of the managerial role. Of course students' programs of study may include additional courses in areas related to the external environment. However, the ability of such courses to address this concern of Porter and McKibbin is limited as long as the overriding definition of managerial effectiveness is confined to the traditional concepts. Only by broadening the definition of managerial expectations, as implicitly suggested by Porter and McKibbin, into basic management courses, can the concern of attention to the external environment be met.

3. The International Dimension: This point is a call for increased emphasis in the business school curriculum on a global perspective. It is a logical extension of the first two concerns, considered above. Recognized in this concern is the increasing competitiveness of other countries with U.S. businesses. As the decade of the 1990's begins, there seems to be heightened expectations that some of our future prime competitors are just now being born. Progress is being made on 1992 European Economic Community. New markets are rapidly developing in the Eastern Bloc. The probable economic unification of East and West Germany will present a formidable competitive force not only to Europe, but to the United States as well. Turning our attention to expanding markets and competition with Japan, China, and the other Asian countries, the need for internationalizing the business school curriculum becomes even more salient.

The U.S. business community tends to divide business into American business and international business. The Japanese have no such divisions: business **is** international business. Porter and McKibbin advance this more global perspective.

While the text appropriately does not directly address international and global issues, it does succeed in advancing concern for them in three ways:

1. The text advances this concern by redefining the managerial role in business education as having an external focus equal in importance to the internal focus. The recognition of the external focus as appropriate for the managerial role lends legitimacy to increasing the interest of the individual manager in global matters and international issues.

2. Many cases and examples in the text are based on multinational corporations, encouraging students to consider global matters.

3. The competencies in the text include many skills that managers need in order to function effectively in a world of intensifying change and innovation.

4. The Information/Service Society: This point recognizes the increasing information-intensive nature of society, as well as the related advancement of service industries. With regard to MIS, Porter and McKibbin advocate a halt to separate courses in information management, and an increased integration of these skills into the curriculum as a whole. No part of the organization - no manager - will be exempt from the need for skills in information management.

The text responds to this concern by incorporating information management into the managerial roles. This emphasis is found primarily in the monitor role and in the coordinator roles. Unlike Porter and McKibbin's first three concerns, which seem to advocate a decreasing emphasis on the internal organizational environment and processes, this point strengthens attention to internal process by advancing the need fully to integrate information management in the curriculum.

5. Cross-functional Integration: Porter and McKibbin emphasize here a need for an integrated approach. This point is beyond the generalist vs. specialist dichotomy. Instead, this concern addresses the issue of integrating specific functions into a coherent framework. As they point out, with increasing entrepreneurial trends, a specialized approach will not be adequate. Students must be aware of integration and how functional areas relate.

The Competing Values Framework, as discussed in the text, provides a basis for integration. The approach furnishes a graphic portrayal of how opposite roles are necessary, and how a number of specialized competencies are required to form an effective whole. For example, in becoming aware of the intricacies of the Broker Role, students are able to discern some of the qualities of the Monitor Role; in understanding the basis for the Mentor Role, they are assisted in understanding the dynamics of the Director Role. The framework makes clear that in managerial decision-making, the most troubling choices may be from among good alternatives. As they cognitively understand that the reality is one of paradox and dilemma, of tensions between important values, they can increase their discernment, their effectiveness, and their abilities to cope and adapt.

6. "Soft" People Skills: This last major concern is that people skills need to be advanced. The very nature of organizations as well as the composition of the workforce, is experiencing rapid change. Organizations are becoming less hierarchical and by extension are relying less on autocratic authority. At the same time, the workforce is becoming more diversified. It is estimated that by the year 2000, white males will comprise the definite minority. Managing a culturally diverse workforce poses tremendous challenges, and "people skills" are a must.

Porter and McKibbin point out that business schools have the challenge of incorporating more people skills without diminishing the necessary quantitative and analytical skills so valued by the corporate community. Several approaches are suggested, including greater utilization of interpersonal activities in class.

The text, with its basis in experiential learning, provides increased opportunities for students to advance their people skills. Not only is the development of such skills explicitly involved in 30-50 percent of the competencies, but often such interactive activities are used in learning the other competencies.

Summary: These six concerns seem to be grounded in a fundamental discrepancy between the expectancies of the managerial role taught in business education, and the expectancies of the role which are needed in the corporate and business world. The view traditionally espoused in business education is that the expectations of good managers are confined to the areas of internal organizational processes (planning, organizing, and controlling), as well as leadership. What Porter and McKibbin seem to be saying is that a broadening of those expectations is necessary. The needs of firms have changed, as the world has changed. The Quinn, et al. text penetrates the very definition of the managerial role, broadening it to an array of competencies, thereby materially addressing the concerns raised by Porter and McKibbin.

In sum, the text promotes a broadening of the definition of the effective manager from concern with internal process to concern with a number of different demands, roles, and perspectives. It places the management of information squarely within the managerial role, but integrated into a fuller dynamic system. And by virtue of its content and method, people skills receive considerable emphasis and modeling.

A final note is that the text has long-term value to students, preparing them for their changing roles in their careers. It is highly unlikely that graduates will stay in the positions in which they are initially hired. Further, the demands of the workforce are changing so rapidly that the content of specializations are sometimes quickly outdated; the content they learn in college may be quite different from the content they work with in ten years. Furthermore, job changes are likely, as buy-outs, take-overs and organizational restructuring become increasingly a fact of life for U.S. firms. Projections indicate that more business graduates may become entrepreneurs, requiring many diversified organizational and managerial skills. Indeed, we can expect that change will be the constant in the careers of graduates. Students need to be prepared for their changing work demands and their changing roles in their careers. The multifaceted and dynamic approach of the text can assist students as they face their future.

USING THE INSTRUCTIONAL GUIDE

Part 4 of the Instructional Guide is organized parallel to the text. The central 8 chapters (2-9) each address a key managerial role. As you have noticed from examining the text, 3 competencies are discussed in each role. Following the ALAPA model, for each competency there are 5 activities, 4 of which are skills-based and the other is the learning activity. The learning activity is the cognitive content for the competency.

Using ALAPA: ALAPA refers to five different activities: Assessment, Learning, Analysis, Practice, and Application.

Assessment: The assessment activities allow students to respond to scales and questionnaires and other activities, gaining a sense of their level of comfort with the competency. Please note that these activities are not included for the purpose of scientific measurement, but function instead to enhance student interest and awareness. As such the assessment activities provide natural transitions into the learning activity.

Learning: Learning activities involve conceptual content. After responding to the assessment activity, students read the learning activity to discover concepts relevant to concerns which may have been raised in the assessment. The content of the learning activities is supplemented by the instructor in class.

Analysis: After exposure to the concepts, the analysis activity allows students to work with the learning material, engaging in further learning and discovery.

Practice: The practice activity permits reinforcement of the learning through practicing the skill.

Application: Finally, the application affords students the opportunity of applying the competency to an appropriate personal or work situation.

It is important to note that assessment and application activities may be assigned as homework, or they may be completed in class if you prefer. If students complete the assessment activity and read the learning activity as homework, the basis is formed for class discussion the next session. After discussing the assessment and the learning portions, the analysis and practice activities can take place in class. Then students may be assigned to do the application as homework, along with the assessment and learning activities of the following competency.

A Possible Class Activity Schedule

If you follow the entire ALAPA model, you could anticipate taking a minimum of two 50-minute class periods to complete one competency, or two weeks to complete one chapter. Under such circumstances, a possible schedule would look like this:

Day 1: Students attend class having completed the assessment and read the learning activity. The assessment activity can be discussed as a warm-up. You could initiate discussion by asking the class questions such as:

> What did you learn from the assessment?
> What surprised you?

Then learning material could be presented, followed by the analysis activity and discussion.

Day 2: Summarize the analysis activity by asking questions such as:
What are we seeing with the results of the analysis?

This discussion may be used as a warm up before proceeding to the practice activity. Complete it and assign the application for homework, along with the next assessment and learning reading.

As you will recognize, this learning method constitutes an exploration/induction type of approach, which is variable depending on your emphasis. The activities vary widely according to the time it takes to do them and the time you choose to allot to their meaningful processing. Therefore I want to emphasize strongly that the above 2-day schedule is not concrete by any means.

As can readily be seen from the possible schedule of 2-days per competency, students have ample homework between Day 2 and Day 1. During this time they may be assigned to complete the application activity of the former competency, as well as complete the assessment activity and the reading for the upcoming competency. However, in between Day 1 and Day 2, there is no assigned reading. This is a good place to assign supplemental reading material related to the competencies.

INTEGRATING SUPPLEMENTAL TEXTS

BECOMING A MASTER MANAGER AND OTHER TEXTS TABLE

QUINN ET AL. CHAPS:	TEXT #1	TEXT #2	TEXT #3	TEXT #4
1: History/Models	Chap 1; Chap 9: 343-349	Chapter 2	Chapter 1	Chapter 1
2: Mentor	Chapters 4, 5	Chapters 12, 15	Chapters 9; 17	Chapters 4; 12
3: Facilitator	Chap 6; Chap 12: 406-413	Chap 16: 393-398; Chapter 17	Chapters 12; 14; in chap 16	Chap 8, 9; Chap 13: 203-208
4: Monitor	Chapter 2	Chapter 20	Chapter 8	Chapter 6
5: Coordinator	Chapter 9 Chap 12: 408-412; 415-425	Chapter 10: 239-249; Chap 11, 19	Chapters 5, 11	Chap 7: 94-102; Chap 14
6: Director	Chap 7: 210-241; Chap 12: 405-406	Chapters 6, 7, 9, 13	Chapter 6	Chapter 7: 102-108; Chap 11, 15
7: Producer	Chap 3; Chap 12: 439-442	Chap 14; Chap 16: 401-404	Chapters 7, 10; in chap 16	Chap 5; Chap 17: 275-278
8: Broker	Chapter 7: 206-210; Chapter 8	Chap 3, 4, 5; Chap 16: 389-393; 398-401	Chap 2, 3, 15; in Chapter 16	Chap 10; Chap 13: 208-214
9: Innovator	Chapters 10, 11	Chapters 1; 10: 250-255 Chapter 18	Chapter 18	Chap 16; chap 17: 269-275; 278-287.
10: Integration	Chap 12: 392-404; 425-439	Chapter 8	Chap 4 and 13	Chap 2 and 3

TEXT #1: Bowditch, James L. and Anthony F. Buono. *A Primer on Organizational Behavior.* Third edition. New York: John Wiley and Sons. 1994.

TEXT #2: Schermerhorn, John R., Jr. *Management.* Fifth edition. New York: John Wiley and Sons. 1996.

TEXT #3: Schermerhorn, John R., Jr. *Management and Organizational Behavior Essentials.* New York: John Wiley and Sons. 1996.

TEXT #4: Schermerhorn, John R., Jr., James G. Hunt, and Richard N. Osborn. *Basic Organizational Behavior.* New York: John Wiley and Sons. 1995.

Notice that while the competency of decision making was included in the director role in the original version of the Quinn, et al., text, it is not included as a competency in this revision. For those texts above which included decision making, I placed that with

Chapter 10: Integration, and there is always the issue of managers deciding which competency to use in which situations. Hopefully, the Integration will assist their decision-making processes.

Also, note that further readings in each role are included in the textbook at the end of each chapter, as well as in the chapter 10 summary of each role.

CHAPTER ORGANIZATION

A. The role and competency learning activities: Several pages of information on the role and its relation to the effectiveness model, and the three learning contents of the three competencies begin each chapter discussion of the guide. Other competencies which are a part of this role but not included in the textbook are identified, along with the rationale of why the authors chose these three specifically. Furthermore, since it is unlikely that you will be able to cover in your class each competency (they total 24), you can expect to be faced with the potentially troublesome decision of which ones to cover and which ones to omit. That question was posed to the authors, and their judgments of which one, or two competencies they would choose, are included. Additionally the relationship of this role to various issues in business and in organizations are noted here.

B. For each skills activity: After the above pages of discussion, you will find, for each activity (assessment, analysis, practice, and application), the following:

1. A 1-page Activity Flow Sheet. This is designed to give you salient information at a glance regarding the activity. For easy reference and identification, the Activity Flow Sheet is headlined with the chapter, role, and competency. This is followed by the type of activity (assessment, analysis, practice, and application). The format of the sheet, including an explanation of its information, is:

CHAPTER #	NAME OF ROLE
COMPETENCY #	NAME OF COMPETENCY

Type of Activity: Name of Activity
Activity Flow Sheet

PURPOSE: Abbreviated purpose of the activity as it relates to the learning section. This is designed to assist you in making the transition from the activity to your class lectures and discussions. An elaborate version of the purpose is included in the Process Guide.

KEY TOPICS: Specifies key topics from the learning section illustrated by the activity.

TIME ESTIMATE: Obviously time estimates are very imprecise. Much depends on how many students are in the class, and how you might choose to frame the activity. But experience provides some basis for estimating, so here is our best estimate. Please keep in mind that it is only a ball-park figure and you have considerable control as to how much time you wish to spend here. Also, whenever you assign part of an activity as homework, the class time is diminished.

FORMAT:	This is the group format of the activity, and includes whether it is an individual or group activity, size of groups, dyads, role-play, etc. **PLEASE NOTE:** observation sheets and other material related to an activity will be attached following the Process Guide.
SPECIAL NEEDS:	Things you may need to have on hand to complete the activity, such as observation sheets, diagrams, other instructional sheets, etc.
SEQUENCE:	A summary of the steps in process. These steps are further elaborated in the Process Guide.
VARIATIONS:	Variations in the activity format, including which parts can be assigned as homework, group sizes, etc.
KEY POINTS:	A summary of key discussion points.
WATCH FOR:	Discusses possible cautions such as the basis for anticipated student resistance, and suggestions of how to handle such resistance. Included only when needed.

It is hoped that this flow sheet will provide you at a glance with the most salient information you need in using the activities. Furthermore, we understand that you may have to decide which of the activities to omit from your course. Hopefully this flow sheet will assist you in making this decision efficiently by summarizing key information on one page regarding the activity.

2. Process Guide: Following the activity flow sheet is a 1 to 3 page process guide which provides the steps in the sequence in greater detail along with discussion questions. Effort was made to furnish many discussion questions, providing considerable choice. There is no intention implied that you use every question. Again, you can frame the process to your liking; this process guide is intended only to present ideas of how the activity has been done - not to prescribe how you should do it.

Additionally, this process guide may provide further information in deciding whether to use the activity. For quick reference and identification, it is headed in the same fashion as the activity flow sheet.

The following is the sequence of pages in Part 4, for each of the chapters.

1. Discussion of role, competencies and the learning sections
2. Competency 1:
    Assessment Activity
        One-page Activity Flow Sheet
        Process Guide
    Analysis Activity
        One-page Activity Flow Sheet
        Process Guide
    Practice Activity
        One-page Activity Flow Sheet
        Process Guide
    Application Activity
        One-page Activity Flow Sheet
        Process Guide
3. Competency 2: (same as above)

4. Competency 3: (same as above)

Any observation forms, diagrams, etc. which may be necessary for the activity are included between the Activity Flow Sheet and the Process Guide.

GROUP FACILITATION

As you know, the Quinn, et al. text is designed for the extensive use of group facilitation as a teaching method. Like many other current texts, it provides exercises to be used in class. In addition, using the ALAPA learning model, skills activities are integrated into the very learning fabric of the book.

It is recognized that many instructors already use group facilitation in classes; many believe that learning is enhanced with the use of such methods. However, some instructors may be hesitant to use experiential learning for a variety of reasons.

There are many excellent discussions of the value of process courses, or experiential learning, as compared with the traditional lecture approach. Especially in business education, the need for learning which more closely approximates situations in the real world is recognized. My intent in this section is not to reiterate these discussions in fine detail, but to acknowledge briefly some of the more salient points.

My purpose in this section of the **Instructional Guide** is to advance the use of group facilitation as a teaching method. To do this, some general guidelines will be summarized.

GUIDELINES FOR SUCCESSFUL GROUP FACILITATION IN THE CLASSROOM

1. Chapter 2: The Mentor Role and Chapter 3: The Facilitator Role. Fortunately an excellent source of information on the skills involved in group facilitation is chapters 2 and 3 of the text. Competencies in chapter 2 include Communicating Effectively and Developing Subordinates. Chapter 3 includes the competencies of building teams, using participative decision making, and managing conflict. Reviewing the points of these two chapters is recommended for those who wish to decrease their discomfort with the use of facilitation as a teaching method.

2. Provide clear instructions. Ambiguous instructions make it difficult for students understand what is expected of them. This is one of the more common hindrances to the successful completion of activities.. In order to be certain that students understand the instructions, you may not want to rely on their reading the directions in the text. Instead, read the directions to them. Procedural questions are more likely to be surfaced when the directions are read aloud.

3. Provide a safe environment for their responses. Structured classroom group experiences are in many ways *real* experiences emotionally. Students need to feel safe in this environment, not subject to condescension or ridicule by others. Only then can they risk their free expression of ideas. You, as the instructor, set the tone by how you respond to their questions, ideas, and concerns. Genuinely reflecting the attitude that "There is no such thing as a stupid question" is critical.

In addition, however, you may decide to set some ground rules, which could include how to respectfully disagree with someone else. One way is to suggest that students acknowledge the validity of the viewpoint or idea, or to express appreciation for that perspective, and then proceed to express specific disagreement and why. Too much attention to this detail may just stifle discussion, but a gentle reminder may be in order.

4. How to arrange small groups. Small group work within the classroom setting provides a real laboratory for learning. After all, much of what is work in organizations is accomplished in group settings. Further, in a real sense, the class is an organization.

One issue facing instructors using group facilitation as a teaching method is whether to set up permanent groups of students, or different groups for each activity. It is exciting to see classes formed into teams of 4-5 students who work on projects and engage in peer evaluation. While this text does not include long-term projects, instructors can include them, dividing the class members into long-term group teams. The contributors in Part 2 of the **Instructional Guide** address this issue and share their experiences.

If short-term groups are used, the optimum group size is 4-6 students, depending upon the task. Until the students seem to know one another well and are comfortable getting into groups, you may want to put them into groups, rather than have them do it. For instance, if you give the class members instructions to get into groups of 5, students typically will gravitate towards people they know. Some students may drift around, trying to find a group to join. These moments may be tense and awkward. When they do find a group, they may already feel that they are not equal participants, that somehow the others belong together.

One way to avoid these difficult moments, and to ensure that students who tend to sit together join different groups, is to divide the class by having everyone count off in turn. For instance, if there are 50 students, there can be 10 groups of 5. Have each student count themselves in turn, from 1 to 10. This will happen 5 times before everyone has a number. Then put all the one's together, all the two's, etc. In this way, every person comes to the group with an equal sense of legitimacy to being a part of the group.

More importantly, however, forming heterogeneous groups (age, work experience, major, etc.) is highly recommended. This requires that you take information from each student and assign them to groups. Sometimes professors have students fill out an index card, or a short form, gathering relevant responses from the students in order to form heterogeneous groups. Several of the contributors (Part 2 of this **Instructional Guide**) discuss in detail the mechanics of forming groups.

5. What to do during the group activities. Instructors sometimes feel hesitant to use group facilitation because they may feel awkward in the classroom which is filled with groups at work. They feel that they are not doing anything while the groups are involved. Several points should be made here.

a) Students need to know that you care very much about what happens in their groups. For at least the first part of the activity, it may be important to rotate among the groups, listening to be sure that they are on the right track, and being available to clarify any points.

b) Often facilitators report that their most successful groups are sometimes the ones where they "did the least". The key is the nature of the task, careful structuring of the activity, as well as clear directions. The point here is: don't be deceived into thinking that not much is happening just because you are not doing it. One of the most exhilarating moments in group work is to witness the excitement generated by groups actively engaged in dialogue and discovery.

6. Guidelines for role playing. Role playing is an activity format used frequently in the text. The technique is recognized as effective in helping students place themselves in a "real world" situation. Role plays permit students to apply and consider concepts beyond the cognitive environment of the traditional classroom. They also tend to be fun.

HINTS FOR CONDUCTING ROLE PLAYS

1) Consider how you wish to select the players. You may just call on individuals or ask for volunteers. Selecting individuals gives you some control, permitting a degree of "type-casting". If you ask for volunteers, there is always the chance that you may not get any. Some very effective role players may be too shy to volunteer. Sometimes the same people will always volunteer.

In small groups, how are role players and observers designated? At the beginning of the course, you may need to designate who does what. As students gain more experience with one another throughout the course, however, they will probably handle this themselves. When this happens is a judgment call on your part.

2) Give students prior notice. When possible, especially at the beginning of the course, let students know in advance that they will be role players in the following class.

3) Clarify your intentions. If you use the small group with observers, will everyone take turns playing the roles? If you use dyads, will students be able to switch roles? If so, be sure you have enough time. Its more important to have one role play, with observers, properly processed, than to have rotations so that everyone can play a role but the processing is compromised.

4) Set a time limit. Sometimes roles plays could continue for longer than you would like. Time limits frequently are helpful in role plays and in other group exercises for a variety of reasons, not the least of which is class management.

5) Give players a few moments to get into their roles before beginning. After assigning the roles and before starting the activity, allow the players a few moments to think about their role and some of the implications of it. In some cases there will be instructions for them to read, clarify their role.

6) Possibilities with the fishbowl. The fishbowl format provides numerous instructional possibilities. For instance, you can interrupt at any time and:

      a) allow the players to discuss their feelings.
      b) allow the class members to make observations.
      c) let other students step into the roles.
      d) make instructional points about what is happening.

ADDITIONAL SUGGESTIONS FOR CLASSROOM MANAGEMENT: The previous pages have covered a number of classroom management issues. Below is a summation and a few additional items you may wish to consider.

1. Explicit Course Expectations. The course design should be explained clearly to students on the first day of class, supplemented in writing on the syllabus. Expectations are different for a skills course, and they need to be explicit.

2. Class Attendance. Using group facilitation as a teaching method requires that students attend class on time. It is not unreasonable to make class attendance a requirement. This should be clearly stated on the syllabus.

3. Keeping a Journal. You may wish to have students immediately begin to keep the journal. The journal could include their skill application exercises as well as their feelings about the other activities. They will find this an invaluable source of data for learning about themselves at the end of the course.

4. Homework Activities. This is a reminder that the assessment and application activities can be used as homework. But of course you may use them in class if you prefer.

5. Guest Speakers. Guest speakers from the local business community may be a welcomed addition to the course. You may know some business people who have become known in the community for their performance in a particular role. This not only heightens relevance, but also serves to strengthen ties with the business community.

6. Evaluation of Students. There are a variety of ways to evaluate students in a competency-based course. Traditional testing is still an option; after all, there is ample content material in the text to allow for plenty of questions. Besides, in traditional lecture courses, instructors routinely grade for class participation. This course would be no exception.

Additionally, there are a number of discussion questions on the process guides for the skills activities. Obviously you will not want to use all of them; they are presented merely as a smorgasbord. However, some may be appropriate as test questions.

You may, of course, choose to evaluate student's on the completion of their activities; the most likely activities to be graded are the applications. It is recommended that, in so doing, instructors not grade students for successful application of the competency as much as for successful discussion of what they did, how it went, and the relation of the activity to the concepts. In this way there is a focus on the process of application and not on the content.

Parts 2 and 3 of the **Instructional Guide** includes essays from professors who are using the text, along with their evaluation methods.

ADVICE FROM THE AUTHORS

The question was posed to the authors: Pretend that a friend and valued colleague comes to you for advice on teaching from this text. This friend has never used experiential methods in teaching. **What advice would you offer to help your friend teach from this book?**

Responses from them include the following suggestions:

1. Review the first chapter of the text. Understand the Competing Values Framework.

2. Read what you plan to do a week or so in advance.

3. Make sure you think through what you need for the classes 2 days ahead.

4. Most important: Don't be afraid to trust the process. Its hard to let go of the straight lecture method. Trust that students learn from doing the exercises as much as they learn from listening to you.

5. Be flexible. If you find something is not working, don't keep going in that direction.

6. Remember that, as instructor, you are a facilitator. Be a good role model. Students will be frustrated if they do not see the principles they are learning being followed. This may sound negative, but I've seen this happen, where an instructor teaching the facilitator role never once asked students to respond to questions of other students and always gave the "expert advice."

7. Balance small group discussions, large group discussions, and group exercises. It is important for students to get feedback, whenever possible, from their peers as well as from the instructor. Try to structure exercises to allow for feedback.

8. Value and affirm students' experiences in organizations, whether they are work experiences, or experiences in student organizations, community or religious groups, sports teams, etc. Whenever possible, students should draw from their experiences.

9. Recognize the importance of the application exercise as more than an opportunity to assign a grade. I think that this is one of the most important parts of the students' learning experience. Encourage students to use this opportunity to grow and develop as managers (or managers-to-be).

10. As we have gone into organizations, the common complaint is that communication is too often one-way, from the top down. All too often this experience mirrors the classroom. When we use facilitated learning in the classroom, we model what organizations need, and thereby train future managers in these important skills.

REFERENCES

Bowditch, James L. and Anthony F. Buono. *A Primer on Organizational Behavior.* 3rd edition. New York: John Wiley & Sons, 1994.

Cameron, Kim S. "Effectiveness as Paradox: Consensus and Conflict in Conceptions of Organizational Effectiveness." *Management Science*, Vol. 32, No. 5, May 1986, pp. 539-553.

Cheit, Earl F. "Business Schools and Their Critics." *California Management Review*, Vol. 27, No.3, Spring 1985.

Dumaine, Brian. "What the Leaders of Tomorrow See." *Fortune*, July 3, 1989.

Faerman, Sue R., R. E. Quinn, and M. P. Thompson. "Bridging Management Practice and Theory." *Public Administration Review*, 1987, 47 (3), 311-319.

Getting Work Done Through Others: The Supervisor's Main Job. Advanced Human Resources Development Program, New York State Governor's Office of Employee Relations and CSEA, 1987.

Guzzardi, Walter. "Wisdom from the Giants of Business." *Fortune*, July 3, 1989.

Main, Jeremy. "B-Schools Get a Global Vision." *Fortune*, July 17, 1989.

Miles, Raymond F. "The Future of Business Education." *California Management Review*, Vol. 27, No. 3, Spring 1985.

Nelton, Sharon. "Molding Managers for the Tests of Tomorrow." *Nation's Business*, April 1984.

Porter, Lyman W. and Lawrence E. McKibbin. *Management Education and Development: Drift or Thrust into the 21st Century?* New York: McGraw-Hill Book Co., 1988.

Quinn, Robert E. *Beyond Rational Management.* San Francisco: Jossey-Bass Publishers, 1989.

Schermerhorn, John R., Jr. *Management.* Fifth edition. New York: John Wiley and Sons. 1996.

Schermerhorn, John R., Jr. *Management and Organizational Behavior Essentials.* New York: John Wiley and Sons. 1996.

Schermerhorn, John R., Jr., James G. Hunt, and Richard N. Osborn. *Basic Organizational Behavior.* New York: John Wiley and Sons. 1995.

Weisbord, Marvin R. *Productive Workplaces: Organizing and Managing for Dignity, Meaning and Community.* San Francisco, CA: Jossey-Bass, 1989.

Whetten, David A. and Kim S. Cameron. *Developing Management Skills.* Glenview, Illinois: Scott, Foresman and Company, 1984.

Woditsch, Gary A., Mark A. Schlesinger, and Richard C. Giardina, "The Skillful Baccalaureate" *Change*, November-December 1987.

PART 2

FIVE CONTRIBUTORS SHARE IDEAS AND INSIGHTS
FOR TEACHING WITH *BECOMING A MASTER MANAGER*

**Page 21: "Notes on Teaching with *Becoming A Master Manager:*
A Competency Framework"**
Dr. Daniel R. Denison, University of Michigan.
In this contribution, Dan describes his use of the Quinn, et al. text in a hybrid course of OB content and OB skills. He discusses specific readings, films, and class activities for each quadrant of the competing values framework and demonstrates how materials which are familiar to instructors may be incorporated.

Page 25: "Using Quinn, et al. in Large Management Classes"
Dr. William M. Metheny, Montana State University--Billings
Bill shares a strategy for using the Quinn, et al. text in large principles of management classes. He addresses the issue of evaluating students in an experiential course and describes using Quinn, et al. to enhance experiential learning through assessments, cases, and applications.

Page 29: "Team Learning and Development of Leadership Competencies"
Dr. Larry K. Michaelsen, The University of Oklahoma.
This contribution describes the use of Quinn, et al. with the Team Learning method. Larry describes how to build a class into an organization, the Team Learning Instructional Activity Sequence, and evaluation procedures for a competency-based course. He also includes several integrative application oriented exams.

Page 37: "Experiential Learning in the Classroom"
Dr. Deborah Wells, Assistant Dean,
College of Business Administration, Creighton University.
This contribution explores a number of ideas for using the Quinn, et al. text in various courses. She provides a discussion of handling experiential learning in the classroom.

Page 41: "Using the Competing Values Framework in the Classroom"
Dr. Michael P. Thompson, Brigham Young University
This contribution, excerpted from Michael's previously published article, presents the results of his interviews with ten faculty who use the Quinn, et al. text. Ample ideas for classroom use as well as advice for teachers are included in this article.

Notes on Teaching with
BECOMING A MASTER MANAGER: A COMPETENCY FRAMEWORK

Dr. Daniel R. Denison
University of Michigan

For several years I have taught organizational behavior as a "hybrid" - a mix of OB **content** and OB **skills**. For this reason, I was particularly pleased to see this new text. It is, from my perspective, the best attempt thus far to bringing these two approaches together in the classroom.

By OB content, I mean traditional topics in OB such as leadership, motivation, group process, culture, work and organization design, organizational development, and so on. The classic difficulty with teaching this material, particularly with students who have not had much work experience, is the lack of common experience that can be used to illustrate the theories. To overcome this, I typically grouped students into project teams and had them do diagnostic projects with organizations. This gave us two common points of reference: the groups that they had worked in and the organizations they had studied.

This worked well, but did not include what I consider to be the other important component of a successful OB class: an experiential approach to interpersonal, group, and leadership skills. To incorporate this, I typically tried to introduce a series of exercises that focused on forming groups, establishing group norms, analyzing group process, and so on.

The problem with this approach is that many students have trouble integrating it all: The skills exercises are great, but how do they fit together? The experiential learning is exciting, but how does it relate to "content" of the course? Analyzing a case or an organization is terrific, but what should I study? Leadership? Culture? Work design? Motivation?

The beauty of this text and the competing values framework is that it integrates these approaches and resolves many of the problems of teaching such a "hybrid" class. By doing so, the "content" sections become a way of understanding a particular management role, the exercises build skills in an area where the student may be weak or strong, and the diagnosis of a case or company can rely on the model. Slowly it begins to come together.

The following sections describe in some detail the approach I've taken recently with a large (N=60), required MBA class at the University of Michigan, titled **Human Behavior and Organizations**. The class used the text as a base, but often included other materials as supplements. In general, for each quadrant of the model, I went through some variation of the following sequence:

1. Present some of the background research supporting the perspective;

2. Discuss the managerial skills emphasized in that quadrant;

3. Do an exercise or two to build those managerial skills;

4. Present a case that shows a manager or situation emphasizing those skills;

5. Analyze a video clip of a manager with respect to those roles and skills.

Introduction and Overview of the Model

The fundamental point to make in an overview of the model and the book is the centrality of paradox and balance to the leadership role. Bob Quinn, in his classes, shows video clips from the films Patton and Ghandi and then discusses leadership. We've also used a video tape of Allan Gilmour, Executive Vice President of Ford Motor Company in which he says, "You ask which is more important, cost or quality?" "The answer is yes." "Timeliness or customer service?" "The answer is yes." A presentation of the model, a discussion of the roles, and a discussion of paradox and balance makes the framework for the course very clear to most students. If additional material is needed to elaborate any of the theoretical perspectives in Chapter One, I suggest drawing from a reader like Shafritz and Ott's *Classics of Organizational Theory*. Introducing students to the Competing Values Skills Assessment software package at this stage also helps them to personalize the roles and model. Once they get data about themselves, they are highly motivated to understand and apply the model and the skills presented in the book.

The Open Systems Model

As background for the open systems model, I discussed Kanter's *The Change Masters* (particularly her ten rules for stifling innovation) and Katz and Kahn's *The Social Psychology of Organizations*. Material on intrapreneurship (Pinchot or Burgelman, for example) or the 3M "post-it" clip from the first **"In Search of Excellence"** video could also be used to make the point. These materials or others can be used to describe both the innovator and broker roles and the open systems model.

A creativity exercise is a must. One of my favorites is to ask students to answer the questions, "When was the last time you did something creative?" "What was it?" One time a manager answered this question by saying that the last time he was creative was six months ago when they found a new way to **drive home from work.** The message of this exercise is that the simple finding that people who **think** that they are creative, are creative. I sometimes follow this with a lateral thinking exercise described by Van Oech in his delightful little book, *A Whack on the Side of the Head*. My colleague Poppy McLeod often asks her students to work in groups to design products that would be in high demand if people doubled their height and weight. The textbook also contains several excellent exercises on creativity.

A case on entrepreneurship, such as People Express Airlines or an excerpt from *Odessey* by John Sculley, will continue to drive the message home. The People Express video clip is available from the Harvard Business School. At Michigan, we used a case study on People Express that is in my book *Corporate Culture and Organizational Effectiveness*, and a paper by Cameron and Quinn on organizational life cycles ["Organizational Life Cycles and Shifting Criteria of Effectiveness: Some Preliminary Evidence" *Management Science*, 1983] that uses the competing values approach. This usually allows for an excellent discussion of the changing balance that occurs as firms develop and the need for a different mix of skills at different points in their evolution.

Another Harvard case, the **Center for Machine Intelligence**, focuses on a joint venture between General Motors and EDS to develop computer-aided conference room technology. This case allowed for simultaneous discussion of organizational innovation and group process in meetings. By presenting background, skills, exercises, and video, students get a thorough exposure to this first quadrant.

The Human Relations Model

The Human Relations Model is often what students expect to hear about in an OB class. Our course began with several classes on culture, human resource management, managing diversity, and the contribution of these factors to creating competitive advantage for a firm. We read my paper, **"Bringing Corporate Culture to the Bottom Line,"** Dave Ulrich's work on **"Human Resources as a Source of Competitive Advantage"**, and the **Workforce 2000** report. Coupled with the description of the human relations model in Chapter One of the text, these readings help give the student the necessary perspective.

After an introduction to the mentor and facilitator roles and their associated skills, we did two exercises in class: a Human Synergistics exercise called **The Project Management Situation**, which serves as a great example of the facilitator role, and the exercise on facilitating conflict management in the text. We closed this segment by discussing the **Suzanne de Passe at Motown Productions** case, along with the Harvard video.

The Internal Process Model

This segment began by looking back to the introductory chapter and reviewing the origins and nature of bureaucracy, and then going on to discuss the design of control systems and organizations in general. David Halberstam's discussion of Ed Lundy and the McNamara "Whiz Kids" at Ford Motor Company in *The Reckoning* makes a great supplement to this material. A reading from *Classics on Organizational Theory* might also be useful here.

After discussing the monitor and coordinator roles, I focused primarily on organizational design as a key skill. It is a subject that I like to teach, so I integrated some material on design and structure at this point in the course. As an exercise, we used a very short case, **The Dashman Company**, that required groups of students to design a control system and then present their plans to the class.

We then discussed the Citibank A&B cases, which focus on John Reed's role in restructuring the Citibank back office during the mid-1970's. The case addresses control systems and organizational design issues, leadership styles, strategies for managing change, and even leadership succession. We also made a video of a recent presentation Reed made at Michigan to contrast his style in this case with his development as a manager.

The Rational Goal Model

For the final section, we focused first on the concept of economic rationality, and contrasted the assumptions of neo-classical economics with Simon's concept of bounded rationality. I found Etzioni's new book, *The Moral Dimension*, to be useful both in presenting a clear statement of what economic rationality **is**, and to provide examples that contradict economic rationality.

The discussion in the text of the producer and director roles and related skills focused primarily on goal setting, delegating, and the expectancy theory of motivation. I did two exercises to try to build an understanding of these skills: One concentrated on motivation and asked students to compare the job design, goal setting, and expectancy theories of motivation, and then write down their own theory of motivation. It was surprising how few students had a confident answer to such a central question. The second question asked students to think of a time when they had tried to delegate work and then comment on what worked well and what did not. It focused their attention on an area that they all felt quite uncertain about.

The case that we discussed in this section was the HBS Hercules case. Included along with this case was a video of the CEO. The CEO tends to emphasize a task and control approach to managing the organization and has fundamentally restructured the company over the past decade. He has a clear vision for the organization, but, unfortunately, it is less clear if it is the right vision, or if the rest of the organization is behind him.

A few final comments:

As the reader can see from my description, I used the textbook for three purposes:

1. A framework for discussing organizations and managerial leadership.

2. A set of roles and skills that operationalize leadership in a highly specific way.

3. A source of cases and exercises that parallel the model.

Many other resources were incorporated into the class and allowed me to teach the OB "content" in a way that was familiar and worked best for me. Fitting this content into the framework generally strengthened it; contrasting one perspective with another or personalizing the content by relating it to a managerial role all helped to pull things together.

My initial apprehension about this book was that much of the OB content that I valued so highly (and knew so well!) would be lost in taking a skills approach. After trying it once, I see it quite differently: there are many ways in which familiar materials can be incorporated into the competing values framework, and doing so tends to give greater integration to that material and link it directly to managerial skills.

USING QUINN, ET AL. IN LARGE MANAGEMENT CLASSES

Dr. William M. Metheny
Montana State University--Billings

Introductory management classes provide an excellent opportunity to share the excitement of management with a diverse group of students. The Principles of Management course is required of all business students in most schools. Students from disciplines other than business are also required to study management or are allowed to take the course as an elective in many institutions. In my classes, for instance, I teach students from all of the business disciplines, political science, psychology, art, music, and other departments. With limited resources, serving all these constituencies often requires the use of large classes (mine have ranged in size from 120 to 220 students, though some are much larger). The anomie of such large classes, added to the diversity of backgrounds, can be a challenge to an instructor.

To take advantage of the differing strengths and interests of such a varied group of students, I ask them to actually use the principles they are studying throughout the semester. The procedure is to break them into heterogeneous groups, then assign tasks which require them to both study and practice management as a team. Managing this small organization is their real introduction to the topics of management. Texts help them understand the processes they are experiencing and explain reasons for their successes or disappointments. This reinforces their learning.

The Quinn text assists this process in two ways. First, the **competing values framework** helps students appreciate others in the group who enter the management class with a different perspective than theirs. Over the semester, different tasks will also allow group members to experiment with an assortment of management models and roles. Varying levels of success give them an incentive to compare their experiences with the theories presented.

Second, the Quinn, et al text provides a rich source of material to enhance experiential learning. **Assessments** allow the students to measure their attitudes and discuss them with other group members. **Cases** offer concrete examples of the managerial actions being discussed. The chapters provide **specific suggestions** on developing particular competencies. **Applications** help shorten or eliminate the lengthy process of designing exercises which offer students new ways to learn.

SOME SPECIFICS

Textbook

Most recently, I have been using Stephen Robbins' text, *Management*, 4th ed., from Prentice-Hall. This offers a functional approach to the study of management. The Quinn approach blends well with the Robbins approach and an emphasis on experiential learning.

Conduct of the Class and Evaluation

In the first two sessions of the semester, the instructor assigns students to groups. Students fill out a questionnaire listing their major field, personal background, weaknesses, and strengths. The instructor and teaching assistant assign students to groups by selecting a mix of their backgrounds, interests, and abilities. Groups have from 5-7 students each. After the groups take a few minutes to get acquainted, then send representatives to determine the grading system for the semester. Within limitations set in advance, the class may elect any mix of the following grade components:

Individual Performance	_____ %
Examinations	
Group Performance	_____ %
Examinations	
Group Projects	
Peer Evaluation	_____ %
(Ratings by team members)	
TOTAL	100%

Individually, and in groups, students study assigned reading material. There is no formal lecture. After studying a block of material, students take a brief test. When all individuals have completed the test, the group takes the same text. Exams are mechanically graded, and returned as soon as the last group has finished. While the groups write appeals on those answers which they disagree, the instructor analyzes the overall results. If there are areas of misunderstanding, then an immediate mini-lecture is presented on that material. The individuals receive the grade they made on the test. Also, each group member receives the group grade on that exam as a component of the group grade for the semester.

During subsequent class periods, groups work together on assignments which give them an opportunity to apply the material they have studied. These assignments could be an analysis of a case, an interview of a practicing manager, or a description of their experience with one facet of managing a small group. All group members receive the group grade on the project. Members whose performance is exceptional in either direction are rewarded through their peer evaluation grades.

Using Quinn, et al. As A Supplement

The first reading assignment in the Robbins text is normally chapters one through four. To many students, "The Evolution of Management Thought" is an exercise in memorization. Yet the topic is crucial to the understanding of management. Adding Chapter 1 of Quinn will help the students integrate the large amount of information without reducing their study to rote memorization.

As an introductory exercise, the group could be asked to turn in their written responses to the following exercise:

ASSIGNMENT: Throughout this semester, your group will be required to hand in answers to exercises concerning your readings. This is the first exercise. Your group should turn in **one paper** for each exercise. All of you will receive the same grade for that paper.

You are now beginning the management of a small organization. At this point, there is probably no single manager in your organization; you are sharing the managerial tasks. Like other organizations, yours has ultimate goals. In the case of your group, ultimate goals might be to learn the basics of management and to receive good grades for your efforts. There are always intermediate goals that must be accomplished in order to attain the ultimate goals. This assignment is one of those.

Quinn lists a number of the roles performed by managers.

   a. What part will these roles play in the management of your group this semester?

   b. Which roles do you feel will be the most important?

   c. Which roles will be the least important?

   d. Did you have difficulty getting some members to agree on the most or least important roles? Could it be that they subscribed to competing models of management? If so, try to explain the competing models.

   e. Now look at Mintzberg's managerial roles in your Robbins text. Some of these have different names than the roles described by Quinn. Compare Mintzberg's roles with those in Quinn.

A Second Use

The first example used the first chapter of Quinn to supplement the first chapter of Robbins. Of course that simple pattern doesn't follow. The Quinn section, **Seeing Things As We Really Are** (chapter 2), ties in with Robbins' chapters on decision making or communication, depending on instructor preferences. I would assign this section during the communication chapter. At this point in the semester, many of my students are beginning to wonder about the value of all the "behavioral stuff." Quinn does an excellent job of focusing on the importance of communication in the decision making process. Rather than writing an assignment this time, the instructor could assign the practice section, **Argument Mapping**. That would reinforce the study of communication from a managerial perspective.

Assessments

The group development process, of course, includes one or more stages of "Storming." To many of our students, this confrontation portends the imminent demise of their team. In the past, I've worked in some form of personal style assessment in weeks five and fifteen to help them understand the sources of conflict. Copying costs for the instruments and explanations, alone, were very high. The Quinn text is a rich source of instruments which point to the uniqueness of individuals. This reduces costs to the school, offers a wider variety of instruments, and frees up class time that was spent in distributing and administering the assessments.

SUMMARY

This section has briefly discussed how one professor might use the Quinn text in conjunction with the Robbins text on management. It discussed, briefly, one approach to teaching management experientially. Within that framework, one specific example was presented showing the integration of the Quinn text. A broader example showed the flexibility of the text. Finally, this section explained how the assessments in the Quinn text could save money and classroom time.

TEAM LEARNING AND DEVELOPMENT OF LEADERSHIP COMPETENCIES

Dr. Larry K. Michaelsen
The University of Oklahoma

In recent years, there has been an increasing interest in group-oriented instruction. This probably stems from a number of factors. These include: an increased use of teams and task forces in the work place, the growing recognition of the deficiencies of business school graduates' interpersonal and group skills (e.g. see Porter and McKibbin, 1988), an increased awareness of the usefulness of group interaction in the development of higher level learning and problem solving skills (e.g. Kurfiss, 1989), a growing number of students who are critical of professors who waste their time by going over material that they can read in a text. When the primary instructional objective is to increase students' mastery of leadership competencies, however, the simple fact is that the opportunity to work in small groups is an absolutely essential part of the process. They can't become better leaders if they don't have the opportunity to practice leading.

Unfortunately, simply having students work in groups is no guarantee that either they will learn more or that they will be more satisfied with the instructor. In fact, just the opposite can occur. Unless the groups are structured properly and group activities are designed and managed effectively, they ban both be an obstacle to learning and a source of considerable student frustration.

One of the ironies of group oriented instructional formats is that, as group interaction becomes more intensive, the potential for both positive and negative outcomes also increases. As the groups become more "real" they provide an increasingly valuable source of data from which students can learn about themselves and about the way they interact with others. The danger is that the learning comes from making mistakes and the pain can be so great that the learning never occurs. The key is providing students with the opportunity to experience working in an "organization like" situation that promotes successes but also provides support when the inevitable failures occur.

Two Approaches for Bringing the Organization into the Classroom

There are two basic approaches for providing students with the opportunity to practice using the leadership competencies in a classroom setting. These are:

1. Engaging in activities that, in effect, bring a "slice" of the organization into the classroom. Some of the most common of these types of activities are cases, role plays and simulations.

2. Organizing the class in a way that causes it to take on the properties of a real organization. This approach requires the use of:

    - "Permanent" groups
    - A grading structure in which group work really "counts".
    - Activities that ensure individual accountability to the groups.

There are significant advantages and disadvantages to both approaches. For example, bringing the organization into the classroom through the use of cases, role plays and simulations can be very effective in helping students to develop a cognitive understanding of specific leadership competencies and learn from observing and experiencing the impact of specific leadership competencies in a low-risk situation. On the other hand, they may experience the activities as a series of "games" to be played. When this occurs, the intensity of students' involvement is usually so low that students may not become introspective enough that they seriously examine their own strengths and weaknesses. In addition, focusing on competencies can inhibit students' ability to see the "big picture" issues such as how the organizational context affects the appropriateness of the various competencies.

WHAT IS AND ISN'T IN THE QUINN, ET AL. BOOK

In my judgment, the Quinn, et al. book contains:

1. Excellent cognitive material on the various models of competent leadership.

2. Well presented material about some of the key theoretical approaches that relate to the leadership competencies.

3. An effective model for aiding students in the development of leadership competencies.

4. A wide variety of examples, short cases, and role plays to help students:

    - develop a cognitive understanding of specific leadership competencies.
    - learn from observing and experiencing the impact of specific leadership competencies in a low-risk situation.

In my judgment, the Quinn book does **not** (and should not) contain two items that are critical from a teaching perspective. These are:

1. An approach to managing the instructional process so that the class itself provides a real-life opportunity for students to experience the concepts they are learning about.

2. Material and/or activities that will allow students to actively struggle with the "big picture" issues of:

    - how competencies relate to each other.
    - how the organizational context affects the need for different leadership competencies.

USING TEAM BUILDING TO BUILD THE CLASS INTO AN ORGANIZATION

The Team Learning format (see Michaelsen, Cragin, Watson & Fink, 1985) seems to me to be a near ideal way to meet the instructional needs of a course whose primary objective is to increase students' mastery of leadership competencies and also utilize the strengths of the Quinn book. Team learning, by its very nature, ensures that:

1. Students will develop a working familiarity with key course concepts and terminology using an absolute minimum (approximately 20%) of class time.

2. The class will quickly become very much like an ongoing organization due to the fact that the vast majority of groups will take on the characteristics of highly effective task teams (i.e. they become a very powerful source of motivation for students to complete reading assignments, attend class and participate in group activities.

3. Virtually all of the class time will be spent in group activities in which students will have the opportunity to observe and practice using specific competencies and to experience the relationship between the competencies in a wholistic way.

Essential Elements of the Team Learning Model

The team learning model has been used with many subjects in a wide variety of settings. The degree of success you can achieve by using the model, however, depends on:

1. Availability of appropriate reading material. (The Quinn book is key here. It provides most of the material I would use the first time through, although I would probably use some additional readings in specific topics later on.)

2. Immediate feedback on both individual and group performance. (*See* instructional activity sequence below.)

3. A grading system that provides incentives for group work. (I would use the "Setting Grade Weights" -- see Michaelsen, Cragin & Watson, 1981 -- to establish a grading system for the class. This exercise is a highly effective way to build group cohesiveness, clearly demonstrates that both the teacher and student roles in the class will be different from most other courses, and ensure that both group performance and a peer evaluation are an important part of the grading process.)

4. Individual accountability for pre-class preparation. (This is largely accomplished through a combination of an appropriate grading system and the individual mini-tests -- see instructional activity sequence below.)

Key questions in developing a course using Team Learning:

*1. What do I want students to be able to **do** when they have completed this unit of instruction (or course, program of study, etc.)?* This identifies the desired outcome(s) of the instructional process. In the case of a Leadership Competencies course they would include making sure that students were able to do such things as:
 - Describe each of the key leadership competencies and the kinds of situations in which they would be critical to organizational success.
 - Observe others' behavior and correctly identify their strengths and weaknesses with respect to the leadership competencies.
 - Gain a sufficient level of self understanding that they can correctly identify their own strengths and weaknesses with respect to the leadership competencies.
 - Use the learning model as a means of improving degree of mastery of one or more of the leadership competencies.

2. What will students have to know to be able to do #1? This questions the content that will have to be covered in the readings or in some other way. (Fortunately, the Quinn book does a terrific job on this one.)

3. How can I tell what students have already learned on their own so I can build from there (rather than assuming that they don't know anything and starting from scratch)? This question guides the development of:

- Mini tests (see instructional activity sequence below).
- Application exams and projects (see instructional activity below).

Forming groups

I always form groups and, in doing so, attempt to ensure that: 1) they are as heterogeneous as possible and 2) both the key members assets (e.g. full time work experience) and member liabilities (e.g. limited fluency in English) are evenly spread across the groups (see Michaelsen et al., 1985 for additional information). In my judgment, allowing class members to form their own groups is asking for trouble for a variety of reasons (see Fiechtner & Davis, 1985).

Team Learning activity sequence

Team Learning employs a six-step instructional activity sequence that is repeated for each major unit of instruction (see Michaelsen et al., 1985). These steps are shown in Figure 1. With the Quinn book, I will probably divide my course into five instructional units (a unit on the introductory chapters plus a unit on each of the four models in the framework). Thus I will go through the sequence five times.

Probably the most unique overall feature of this sequence is that there is no input from the instructor until very late in the instructional process. This is possible because of the mini tests, steps 2-5 (see the discussion on Informative Tests in Michaelsen et al., 1985). This sequence, which takes approximately an hour to an hour and a half to complete (thus consuming approximately 20% of the total available class time) virtually eliminates time that is often wasted in "covering" material. The instructor can be certain whether or not students have mastered the key concepts by designing appropriate test questions. Furthermore, by providing immediate feedback, he or she can correct any misconceptions before students move on to other activities or material for which they are inadequately prepared (see Michaelsen et al., 1985).

In addition to ensuring that students develop a sound understanding of course concepts, the mini tests also accomplish two other important objectives with respect to the management of the class. One is that they are extremely effective at building cohesiveness. As a result, you can count on group norms to provide a motivation for individual study and class attendance. The other is that, due to the fact that the individual and group scores have an impact on both course grades and group status, the mini tests provide multiple opportunities for students to engage in group decision making and conflict resolution in a situation that **is** real life. Every question provides an opportunity to practice a wide variety of interpersonal and group skills while, at the same time, developing an understanding of the course content.

Due to the efficiency of the mini test process, approximately 80% of the class time can be spent on application oriented class activities (e.g. role plays, case discussions, etc.) which should be designed and executed so that they:

1. Provide a structured situation that is focused on the application of specific competencies.

2. Ensure that students have the opportunity to gain both a cognitive and an affective understanding of the leadership competencies.

3. Provide vehicles that allow students to examine the relationship between the cognitive and affective aspects of the leadership competencies.

Effective application oriented activities, projects and exams:

A factor that has a tremendous impact on the success or failure of group work is the nature of what they are being asked to do. (Fortunately, the Quinn book has many excellent application oriented activities.) In case you decide to create some of your own, the following general guidelines should be helpful. Group activities are likely to be very effective if they:

1. Require participants to produce a visible product (preferably one that could be graded even though you may not actually grade it).

2. Can **not** be successfully completed unless participants understand the concept(s).

3. Are difficult enough that they can not be successfully completed by any of the group members working alone.

4. Require the groups to do things they do well (collect and process information) and minimize the effort they have to put into things they do very poorly (e.g. create a polished written document while sitting together as a group).

5. Simulate as closely as possible the kind of activities participants will experience in their work situation.

INTEGRATIVE APPLICATION ORIENTED EXAMS

In addition to the integration oriented activities that focus on specific competencies, in my judgment, it would be extremely important to use two or three major application oriented exams that give students the opportunity to focus on the relationship between the competencies. In general these would be based on "cases" that portray a complex organizational situation over time and in which organization members exhibit a wide range of leadership competencies. The purpose of these integrative exams would be to:

1. Help students to develop a sound understanding of the leadership competencies by observing and classifying a variety of contrasting approaches to leadership behavior.

2. Ensure that students have the opportunity to observe the impact of the organizational context on the need for different leadership competencies.

In most cases, I use case examples from either novels or full-length feature films (in which case I show the entire film so that students are exposed to the entire context and have to learn to separate the important from the unimportant). These are open-book exams and I typically allow the groups at least two hours of class time to work on the exams. I also hand out the exams a week or so in advance so that they can work on them longer if they want. Most groups get so involved that they work on the exam 6-8 hours outside of class in addition to the designated class time. Three examples of integrative application exams are shown below.

The Bridge Over the River Kwai

I would give a group exam over this movie following the introductory unit of the course. My primary objective would be to ensure that students had a basic understanding of the four models of the competing values framework. In addition, this movie provides two special bonuses. One is that it does an excellent job or portraying the organizational costs of having an unbalanced set of competencies (most of the principal characters are nearly one-dimensional). In addition, it clearly shows the personal cost of having a rigid view of what is appropriate.

The "Bridge Over the River Kwai" is an Oscar-winning movie that portrays the lives of a group of British POWs in a Japanese prison camp in Burma during W.W.II. The principal characters of the movie are:

- Colonel Saito: the Japanese camp commander
- Colonel Nicholson: the British POW commander
- Captain Reeves: Nicholson's immediate subordinate; a trained engineer
- Major Hughes: Nicholson's immediate subordinate; an excellent administrator
- Major Clipton: Nicholson's immediate subordinate; an M.D.
- Commander Warden: the leader of a British Commando team that was sent to destroy the Kwai bridge

In general terms, the movie is a story about Nicholson's initial refusal and subsequent adoption (for the POWs) of the project of building a Japanese railroad bridge over the Kwai River. Each of the British officers plays a consistent role throughout the film. In contrast, Saito, who fails to make progress on the bridge using the director role (because of Nicholson's stubbornness), later shifts to the role of supporting Nicholson in his role of directing the building of the bridge.

In the exam, I would ask the following:

1. Identify the principal competency quadrant(s) for each of the principal characters in the film. (Please provide specific examples to justify your conclusions.)
2. In what way, if any, is the effectiveness of the organizations portrayed in the film affected by an imbalance in the competencies of their leaders? (Please provide specific examples top justify your conclusions.)
3. In what way, if any, are the individuals portrayed in the film personally affected by an imbalance in their own leadership competencies? (Please provide specific examples to justify your conclusions.)

The Golden Gate (a novel by Alistair MacLean, Fawcett)

The Golden Gate is an adventure novel about an incident in which a bus, containing the President, several Cabinet members and a couple of oil sheiks is kidnapped and held for ransom in the middle of the Golden Gate Bridge. The principal characters in the novel are:
- Branson: the leader of the hijackers
- Hagenbach: the head of the FBI
- Revson: a top FBI agent who is on the bridge posing as a reporter
- The President
- General Cartland: the President's chief of staff

I would give this as an open book exam near the end of the term. As with the earlier integrative exam, I would give the exam out in advance and also give the groups at least two hours to work on the exam in class. In the exam itself, I would ask the following:

1. Identify the principal competency quadrant(s) for each of the principal characters in the book. (Please provide specific examples to justify your conclusions.)
2. In what way, if any, is the effectiveness of the organizations portrayed in the book affected by an imbalance in the competencies of their leaders? (Please provide specific examples top justify your conclusions.)
3. In what way, if any, are the individuals portrayed in the book personally affected by an imbalance in their own leadership competencies? (Please provide specific examples to justify your conclusions.)
4. In what way did changing circumstances affect the appropriateness of relying on different leadership competencies? (Please provide specific examples to justify your conclusions.)

There are two principal differences between this and the Kwai Bridge assignment. One is that several of the characters are much more well rounded. The other is that the organizational conditions change dramatically over the course of the book. Also, by the time the exam is given, I would expect the groups to be able to do a much better job of dealing with the first three questions. In addition, I think it would be important to ask a question that causes the groups to think through the relationship between the organizational situation and the appropriateness of various competencies.

The Flight of the Phoenix

This feature film is about the survivors of a plan that crashed in the Arabian Desert, who rebuilt the plane and flew it to safety. The principal characters in the film are:

- Captain Towns: the pilot, played by Jimmy Stewart
- Lou Moran: the co-pilot
- Heinrich Dorfman: an aeronautical engineer who is among the stranded passengers

I would probably use this film as an individual final exam. This would give me the opportunity to evaluate how well the individuals in class had been able to develop competencies in working with the course concepts. In this case the three principal characters are adept at different competencies and very poor in most of the others. In the exam, I would ask:

1. Identify the principal competency quadrant(s) for each of the principal characters in the film. (Please provide specific examples to justify your conclusions.)
2. In what way, if any, is the effectiveness of the organizations portrayed in the film affected by an imbalance in the competencies of their leaders? (Please provide specific examples top justify your conclusions.)
3. In what way, if any, are the individuals portrayed in the film personally affected by an imbalance in their own leadership competencies? (Please provide specific examples to justify your conclusions.)
4. In what way did changing circumstances affect the appropriateness of relying on different leadership competencies? (Please provide specific examples to justify your conclusions.)
5. Given the fact that no one in the group was very balanced with respect to leadership competencies, how do you explain the fact that the group was able to make it back to safety? (Please provide specific examples to justify your conclusions.)

A unique contribution of this film is that it dramatically portrays the fact that group effort can overcome obstacles that are created by individual members' weaknesses but not without considerable cost. In addition, it clearly portrays the importance of having someone who is skilled at handling the interpersonal conflicts that keep threatening to blow the group apart.

TEAM LEARNING RESOURCE READINGS

1. Fiechtner, S. B. and Davis, E. A. Why some groups fail. <u>The Organizational Behavior Teaching Review.</u> 1985. 9 (4), 58-73.
    Helpful in thinking through the implications of utilizing different types of group activities and grading strategies.
2. Mallinger, M. A. and Elden, M. Improving the quality of working life in the classroom: QWL as self-managed learning. <u>The Organizational Behavior Teaching Review.</u> 1987, 11(2), 43-45.
    A description of the Team Learning process using QWL terminology and examples.
3. Michaelsen, L. K., Watson, W. E., and Cragin, J. P. Grading and anxiety: A strategy for coping. <u>Exchange: The Organizational Behavior Teaching Journal.</u> 1981, 6(1), 8-14.
    Describes the "Grade Weight Setting" activity that we use to get the groups started off on the right foot.
4. Michaelsen, L. K., Watson, W. E., and Schraeder, C. B. Informative testing: A practical approach for tutoring with groups. <u>The Organizational Behavior Teaching Review.</u> 1985, 9(4), 19-33.
    The key article on Team Learning. It outlines the theoretical rationale for the process, what to do to get started, and what to watch for along the way.
5. Hackman, R. E. The design of work teams. In <u>Handbook of Organizational Behavior</u>, J. W. Lorsch, ed. Prentice-Hall, Englewood Cliffs, N. J., 1987, pp. 315-342.
    Provides a conceptual rationale for and research evidence which supports the value of many aspects of the Team Learning process.

OTHER REFERENCES

Kurfiss, J. G. (1988). Critical Thinking: Theory, Research, Practice, and Possibilities. Washington, D.C., ASHE-ERIC Higher Education, Report No. 2.

Porter, L. W. & McKibbin, L. E. (1988). *Management Education and Development: Drift or Thrust into the 21st Century.* New York: McGraw Hill.

EXPERIENTIAL LEARNING IN THE CLASSROOM

Dr. Deborah Wells, Assistant Dean,
College of Business Administration, Creighton University

Some General Comments and Ideas:

First, let me say that I really like this book. Its greatest strength is its organization around four management models, the roles associated with those models, and then the competencies that might logically accompany each role. That is an excellent structure, and so rational! In fact, I could imagine a whole course for non-traditional students (typical adult night class students, for example) that progresses through this entire book. My fear is that if you use bits and pieces of it as supplements to a regular text in a lecture format course, you'll destroy the effect that this excellent organizational heuristic creates.

The second really nifty thing about this book is its inclusion of critical thinking, analyzing information, writing, and oral communication skills as important competencies. Thanks to the authors for doing that! It's about time those skills were directly addressed as an integral part of a management text (and thus a management course) instead of saying, "Hey, that's a problem for the English department."

The third strength of this book is its presentation of background material on each of the competencies in the "learning" section (the L in ALAPA). This will make the professor's job easier because it has already pulled together for him or her theoretical and conceptual material most relevant to each competency. It also reinforces for students why and how this competency would be important for them as practicing (or potential future practicing) managers. Because of this, Quinn would not only make an excellent supplement, but a "stand alone" text as well.

I can actually see Quinn used three different ways: as a supplement to *Management for Productivity* by Schermerhorn, as a supplement to *A Primer on Organizational Behavior* by Bowditch and Buono, or alone. Because it provides background on each topic, it could be used in a second management course for undergraduate students (assume they've already had a principles course) as either a supplement to Bowditch and Buono or even to a Schermerhorn, Hunt, and Osborn. Or, it could stand alone as a text. Here at Creighton all juniors take MGT 301 (Management and Organization Behavior) and then all management majors must take MGT 341 (Advanced Organizational Behavior). Nonmanagement majors may also choose this as a management elective course. I could use Quinn alone as the text for 341 (Advanced OB) because it does provide background on each topic. In fact, it would be super to be able to do that because there is so much redundancy in management principles and OB texts. Quinn stands in contrast to the experiential paper I currently use (*Experiences in Management and Organizational Behavior* by Lewicki, Bowen, Hall, & Hall; John Wiley) in the advanced OB class because it does have some readings included (the learning sections that accompany each competency).

How I teach my courses:

The principles of management course is basically a lecture course. I talk about all of the substantive topics; students listen and take notes. But I have to break the monotony of constant lecturing with activities that involve the students in some way other than note taking, so I try to use appropriate and relevant self-tests, exercises, and cases. I haven't asked students to buy two books for that class - just the Schermerhorn text, and then I hand out or verbally direct exercises. Because this is a first course and there is so much material to cover, I'm not sure that I would attempt to use the Quinn book in my class the way I teach it, but if an instructor wanted to, there are lots of things in Quinn that would be good complements for lectures.

The organizational behavior course (MGT 341) really de-emphasizes lecturing (although I've had to do more of it than I wanted to set up the experiential exercises in Lewicki, et al.). I do use Schermerhorn, Hunt, and Osborn's *Managing Organizational Behavior* in that class, but I wouldn't have to if I used Quinn. To have students really benefit from experiential exercises they need some background information to anchor the exercise to whatever topic it was relevant. Otherwise, experiential stuff is like eating cotton candy: "Gee, that was fun, but I didn't really get anything out of it." The questions you ask afterward and the discussion do this, too.

Another strength of Quinn is the number of self-assessment instruments it provides. Students really like self-assessment, because it answers "Who am I -- what am I like compared to other people?" (Some norm). Because a lot of my students are very competitive, self-assessment goes over well.

What roles and competencies I'd use and why:

Korn/Ferry International, an international headhunting firm, conducted a survey of international executives in 1988 to explore the traits that CEO's of the future will need. Among those skills that will be needed and demands that will be placed on future execs are visionary leadership, rather than traditional managerial skills, the need to communicate frequently with employees, promotion of management training and development, concern over planned management succession, and a global outlook ("How the next CEOs will be Different," Lester B. Korn, *Fortune*, May 22, 1989).

There is no doubt that all eight roles presented in the Quinn text are important. The first four are historically important and present some very basic skills all managers must have. With an eye toward the future, however, the last four roles presented by Quinn become very important. If you look back to the paragraph above, the results of Korn/Ferry's survey indicate that vision, good relationships with subordinates, communication, negotiation, and so on will be increasingly important. So will the Mentor, Facilitator, Innovator, and Broker Roles, and all 12 competencies associated with them.

How to mesh a traditional text with experiential learning and tips on how to handle what's likely to happen:

The chart on page 10 of this **Instructional Guide** addresses the how-to question from the standpoint of what to use with what topics. In general, try to make sure the experiential exercise you choose is closely related to the subject it is supposed to illustrate so that students see the relevance. You'll have to set up almost every exercise by providing some lecture-type instruction, although this can often be fairly brief especially in an advanced course where what you're doing is essentially reviewing material presented once before (in an OB class, for example, for topics covered in a previous principles of management course). Also, be sure to follow up exercises with a discussion or questionnaire or some other form of evaluation to make sure that the point came across. In some ways, the follow-up is the most important part, and the hardest part, because it is tempting to say to yourself, "Well, we've done that - now it's over" or to cut the follow-up short for exercises that the class really gets into or that are time consuming.

If you use any experiential or self-assessment type activities in a class, students tend to become impatient on the days that are mostly lecture. Warn them at the beginning of the semester that the course format will require a good deal of input, cooperation, and participation from them but that they will also have to take notes some days as they would have to do in a more traditional class. You have to be able to count on your students to behave maturely and truly participate or the whole class can become just a "blow off" for them. Crack down on goof-offs very early in the semester to set an example, if you have to.

How to adapt exercises:

Much of Quinn won't require adaptation, with the exception of the assessments and exercises geared toward practicing managers and students with lots of work experience. For these assessments and exercises, you'll have to tell students to think of the roles they've played that involved management or management-related skills in some form or another; groups in school, clubs and organizations, part-time jobs, sports teams, hobby groups, scouting, church activities - whatever.

How I would evaluate my students on their grasp of the material:

I have been giving exams composed of multiple choice and short essay questions. I would like to get away from that. In fact, I can envision teaching a very experiential course that doesn't have traditional exams at all. The problem with that is getting students to read if you don't test them over the material. One approach might be to have them be the teachers - after all, training or teaching is a part of managing people - and make them present the brief "learning" section to their classmates. This would reinforce the "Presenting Ideas Orally" competency that appears in the Broker Role and would give them more practice at that. The more involved projects suggested in the text would be good substitutes for exams. They are very experiential in nature and will cause students to do some first hand exploration of management in action.

I've wrestled with the problem of how to acknowledge participation in experiential activities from semester to semester when I have taught the OB course. I have tried awarding points for each exercise assigned. That gets to be a clerical nightmare is you have a lot of students and you do a lot of exercises, particularly when you try to deal with students who miss class and then need to do some kind of make up. This semester, I decided to award a "bunch" of points (50 points total) for attendance and participation in the assigned experiential exercises. Some students didn't buy the experiential book as a consequence, because they didn't need to study it directly to do well on exams (the primary determinant of final course grade). After trying it both ways, I really believe you do have to award points for every exercise or you just don't get much effort out of students. Get clerical help in keeping track of points and who was absent, etc.

How could students evaluate themselves?

The last chapter of Quinn (Total Integration and Mastery) provides a ready answer to this question. The assessment exercise asks students to return to previous chapters and reevaluate their profiles, putting the result into a convenient matrix that will reveal their strengths and weaknesses. What could possibly be a more fitting cap for the course than such a comprehensive self-evaluation? The application appearing at the end of this chapter is also excellent and takes students to the final step. After all, it isn't enough just to know their own weaknesses, they need to plan to do something about the,. The final overall project for the course should be writing an improvement plan and long-term improvement strategy, as the authors suggest. This is another illustration of the way in which Quinn, et al. succeed in personalizing the management experience (and why I maintain the whole book is really a simulation) for students.

Long-term or short-term groups:

I tend to favor short-term groups for two reasons: first, they give students a chance to get to know and work with many more classmates than do permanent groups assigned for the entire semester. Secondly, you may by chance or by design (if you don't use a seating chart and students sit by friends) end up with a group that is particularly hard to manage and non-functional. This has happened even when there is just one students in the group with a bad attitude. Bad attitudes seem to be infectious, and pretty soon the whole group has a "This experiential stuff is stupid and isn't teaching me anything" attitude. The opposite can happen, too. A group of really high-powered "get in there and give it all its worth" students will form. It is better to spread these energetic, insightful, and bright students out through the rest of the class so they can enthuse their classmates.

Another reason for not using permanent groups for the exercises in the Quinn text is that the activities require different sized groups. For example, the Broker Role practice section task force role play requires groups of 6; the Facilitator conflict management role play requires groups of 5, and so on. Assigning students randomly to groups by asking them to "number off" about 50% of the time, and then allowing them to self-select into groups about 50% of the time seems to strike a good balance between forcing them to meet and work with new people and letting them work with people they know and like.

Business Games or Projects:

Becoming a Master Manager is so loaded with experiential "stuff" that a professor really need not include a business game as well. That would be overkill, in my opinion. In fact, I would characterize the entire Quinn book as a simulation of the role of a manager because of the systematic way it takes students through all these needed competencies. After all, a game is just one format for presentation of experiential learning.

There are great project ideas sprinkled throughout Quinn in the application (the last A in ALAPA) section associated with each competency. If instructors are using Quinn as a second book with a primary text as well, they should pick their favorite of these projects and assign one or two. In a way, there are more projects in Quinn than you could possibly assign in a semester unless you make it the focus of the course and use it as the stand alone. Many of these projects require a 3-5 page written report following an interview or some other form of in-organization data gathering. Instructors will have to be judicious in balancing the demands placed upon students as the select potential projects to assign, as well as the grading and evaluation demands they place upon themselves.

Excerpts from: **USING THE COMPETING VALUES FRAMEWORK IN THE CLASSROOM**[1]

Michael P. Thompson
Brigham Young University

This paper is intended to aid instructors in thinking about how to use the Competing Values Framework (CVF) more effectively in the classroom. Over the past decade, CVF has been used extensively in research on organizational and leadership effectiveness, and has become a major implement for teaching management and leadership in universities across the nation. With the publication of Robert Quinn's *Beyond Rational Management* in 1988, and the appearance of a textbook, *Becoming a Master Manager* by Quinn, Faerman, Thompson, and McGrath in 1990, the resources became available for use of the framework in the classroom.

In this article the major themes discussed in interviews with ten professors of organizational behavior who use the framework extensively in their teaching are presented. The comments cited here are by instructors who indicated they had made extensive use of the framework in their teaching and would be willing to be interviewed. The goal of the interviews was to allow professors to tell their own story. They are presented here in the following order:

1. Adopting the CVF: What needs did it fill, or problems did it solve?
2. Introducing the CVF: successful approaches
3. Making the CVF relevant to managerial work and life in real organizations
4. Applying the CVF in theory courses
5. Reacting to the CVF: students

WHY WAS THE FRAMEWORK ADOPTED?

The major reasons cited for adopting CVF were its comprehensiveness and visual clarity. Most professors were attracted to what several called the framework's "maplike qualities," while others described it as both visually and cognitively comprehensive. More than half of the people interviewed said they found the efficiency of the CVF appealing. It enabled them to retain most of the material they had successfully taught in courses, while injecting that material with a tighter focus and internal consistency. Here are some representative statements:

> I teach an MBA class designed around the CVF. One of the major themes of the course is that conflicts, paradoxes, and tensions need to be encompassed and exploited, not denied. The CVF is ideal for making this point. When I chose to use the CVF, I didn't need to change much of what I was already doing in the course. I still use many of the classic OB nuggets in the course, but the nuggets are integrated better by the CVF than by any other

---

[1] This article is previously published, in its entirety, in *Human Resource Management*, Spring 1993, Vol. 32, Number 1, pp. 101-119. Copyright by John Wiley and Sons, Inc. Used with permission.

approach I've used thus far. Most of the classic dilemmas and traps of management can be located somewhere on the framework.

I use the framework in an introductory management principles course that is offered to business management majors in the beginning of their junior year. For several years I used the Bolman and Deal model (1991) which includes the four quadrants of "structural," "human resources," "political," and "symbolic." I liked this framework because most of the managerial activities and organizational dilemmas I could imagine seemed to be encompassed by those quadrants. But a major limitation was that these four quadrants seemed to have little connection to each other; there was no tension, no interconnectivity across them. I require my students to explore the implications of putting a lot of emphasis in one area, such as structural change. What happens to people in the wake of major restructuring, or what connection is there between the symbolic work of organizations and their structure--the way they are organized to work? It seemed I had to do much of that myself.

The CVF makes those connections more explicit, and I find that students can get into those issues more quickly. It has "lines" drawn across the quadrants and you see quickly that the tensions and conundrums of managerial work are built into the framework. The CVF is visual; it has a kind of face validity and coherence to it that many models or frameworks lack.

Many of those interviewed said that adopting the CVF did not require major changes in the content of their courses, but provided a more coherent integration of that content. About half of the instructors interviewed use the textbook, *Becoming a Master Manager* (Quinn, et al.). The other half use material on the framework found in Robert Quinn's *Beyond Rational Management* and other discussions of the framework such as that found in Richard Daft's textbook, *Management* (Daft, 1991).

SUCCESSFUL APPROACHES TO USING CVF

The specific approaches used to introduce and integrate the framework vary widely. Most of the approaches are inductive in that they create problems or dilemmas with which the students must wrestle. In many cases the students are exposed to the dilemmas before seeing the framework. One professor said, "I have learned that students need to contract the disease before being given the antidote." The framework is often introduced as a way of mapping or charting the dilemmas and seeing how they relate. In other cases, the framework is introduced after the students create a long list of activities or tasks managers typically perform. The point made is that the complexity of managerial work needs some kind of organizing schema.

The following is a characteristic approach described by **Bob Marx of the University of Massachusetts**. Marx uses the CVF in a modular course on managerial principles. He teaches a four-week module within a 12-week undergraduate course in managerial behavior.

I introduce the framework by asking the question, "What do managers do?" I have the class describe the organizational activities they have engaged in, or have observed over the past several years. We construct a list, a huge list. and stand there in front of it for awhile. It looks pretty bewildering. We then talk about Mintzberg's work, which helps us see how truly bewildering and disjointed a typical manager's day can be. At that point I introduce the model. I should add that I seldom move through the model in all of its complexity. When all of the roles and descriptions are attached to all of the quadrants, the framework can be pretty overwhelming.

Joseph Whorton at the University of Georgia uses the CVF in a public management course in the University's graduate Public Administration Program. He finds the CVF especially helpful with public management topics because the role of public managers is so "conflicted" by competing values and demands, many of them from stakeholders outside the organization. Whorton's approach to introducing the CVF could be applied to managers in the public or private sectors.

Whorton, along with half of those interviewed, prefers to use a historical perspective (similar to that found in the first chapter of *Becoming a Master Manager*). Whorton traces the evolution of major schools or developments in managerial thinking and the social context which fostered these developments. He demonstrates how our conceptions of organizations have changed in only 75 years. "Our students have no idea how recent a social invention the large institution really is (Vickers, 1973, p. 13). In two generations we have become a culture dominated by huge institutions. How we deal with them is a more recent question than how we can build them."

Whorton then uses the CVF to trace the origin of organizational structure in societal values. The complexity of organizations is explained by the intersections and tensions of values, which is the central point made by CVF. Every program, every unit of an organization, was created originally to satisfy some value. Whorton believes that the behavior of an organization can openly be understood by mapping (historically) the values it has tried to enact. Values (provided by society) lead to the creation of structures that then determine the fabric of relationships within the organization.

> It is not enough to map the existing systems of an organization; we have to build them from a historical perspective, understand why they came to be, and then study how they interconnect. This task becomes immensely important in studying public organizations that have so many conflicted norms working on them simultaneously (Powell & Dimaggio, 1991, pp. 183-203). We have a system for hiring and retaining employees that will assure equity and fairness in distributing employment opportunities. However, we have another system driven by an efficiency value that demands we reward performance. We have systems that monitor the workplace and the provision of public services, but others designed to enhance innovation and flexibility. All the values that drive the organization are "good," but they can converge in the same work unit, in the jobs of the same people, and create some classic tensions and paradoxes. The CVF helps me show those tensions. My students can then account for the complexity and paradox they see around them.

Joe Weiss of Bentley College uses the CVF in both undergraduate and graduate courses, Weiss also uses the historical perspective with the CVF in both an advanced undergraduate and an MBA class in Organizational Behavior. Weiss spends one full class session moving through the history of managerial thought. Only when that historical grounding is in place does he proceed to the applications of the CVF similar to those outlined in the first chapter of *Becoming a Master Manager*. He administers some of the assessment instruments on the various competencies included in the CVF. Weiss uses the instruments included in the *Instructional Guide to Accompany Becoming a Master Manager* (DiPadova, 1990).

After the students have completed all the questions, Weiss has them plot their own profiles on blank forms. This process gives the students immediate feedback from the instrument, helps them become more familiar with the CVF, and triggers a lively discussion on what the data might mean. Weiss reminds students that the profiles are merely provisional sketches, and that far more observation and work will be required to understand their own aptitudes and dispositions of managers. They like to discuss what the data might mean and how to adjust to and compensate for lack of experience or discomfort in certain competencies.

Alan Bluedorn of the University of Missouri has experimented with the use of self-assessment instruments in teaching the CVF, but has chosen to discontinue using the assessment instruments in courses offered to students with little organizational experience.

> I found that the inexperienced students almost always plotted themselves as too high on their profiles. They would average a 6 on each role out of a possible 7...This lack of self awareness and lack of appreciation for the complexities of managerial life is a massive challenge for us in the classroom. I try to at least simulate behavior the students can observe in each other and themselves and then evaluate or observe in a supportive, but discerning way.

Bluedorn also requires his students to keep a log for three consecutive days on how they spend their time. They then write a memo on how effective or ineffective that self-monitoring device was for them. They repeat the assignment later in the semester and evaluate it again. Bluedorn also assigns group presentations on managerial topics. These assignments have several benefits. The students have to work in teams; they have to study some relevant topics together, and they have to manage the entire process of designing, presenting, and evaluating their projects. They grade one another, and they mentor one another. As in many organizations, the team fails or succeeds together, so there is considerable motivation for cooperating. Bluedorn says:

> A point of all this is to demonstrate that we all do a fair amount of informal managing: we coach, we direct, we coordinate, we monitor, and we broker. I think we place too much emphasis on formal learning experiences and do not recognize out informal learning experience--which is often much more powerful. The language of the CVF helps me make this point. Students don't know they are mentoring or brokering until their exposure to the CVF and out discussion in class helps them see it.

Paula Caproni of the University of Michigan has used the CVF in a 13-week course entitled "Managing Personal Relationships." Caproni holds the CVF in abeyance until the final four weeks of the course. The first eight weeks on the course are devoted to micro issues: interpersonal relationships, intergroup relationships, culture, and socialization. The CVF is then used to relate human behavior to macro issues of organizational culture, strategy, work design, innovation, etc. Caproni likes the CVF because it draws the attention of the class back to macro issues.

For each quadrant in the CVF, Caproni completes three tasks with the class:

1. read a complex case;
2. read articles from the business press that offer examples of effective or ineffective leadership in the quadrant being studied;
3. complete individual assessment instruments to help students examine their strengths, weaknesses, and interests within a given quadrant.

Caproni finds that delving deeper into the implications of the CVF makes the framework far more beneficial to students. The eight managerial roles, and the ways in which they compete for attention and energy in the same leader, must be discussed in detail. Caproni says that early in the discussion of the CVF, one or more students will make the point that the so-called tensions that build up between roles or across the quadrants are predictable but manageable. "Can't we assume that smart people who run the organization will just make sure they strike a healthy balance?" That works in the abstract. No one can argue with the principle that we have to allow for flexibility and still have some predictability and control. The difficulty is in working out the details.

> The person with the high need for structure and control gets put in charge of the accounting system, and the people who can't tolerate control, and love to exploit ambiguity, are working in the product development unit. Both groups have a very different recipe for achieving a healthy balance. When we turn to cases, the differences become even more intense.

In a final lecture, Caproni summarizes the four week section of the course with these observations:

Organizations are paradoxical
Simple solutions are suspect
Effective leaders see the contradictions in organizational norms
Effective leaders struggle for self-awareness

Caproni believes that using the CVF late in the course makes its relevance more apparent.

MAKING THE CVF RELEVANT TO MANAGERIAL WORK

Most of those interviewed use the CVF in skills-oriented courses. These faculty talked about having a "bias for performance." **Gary Coombs, of Ohio University**, says the following about his concentration on managerial competencies:

> I notice that the Quinn, et al. text, is often used as a secondary book to one of the blockbuster texts in Organizational Behavior. I flip that approach on its head and use the skills book and the CVF as the primary focus and assign the big OB textbook as background reading. The OB texts are huge, and they focus primarily on theoretical work, and examples taken from practice. But the implications of the theory are often unclear, and theory seems to get the lion's share of the attention. I seem to do much more for my students with the opposite approach.

The instructors try to have students on their feet, giving presentations, and involved in simulations or discussion. Most of the classes require students to observe and evaluate the behavior of other people--classmates or managers in other organizations. The CVF provides a functional language for describing and evaluating what leaders do. The challenge of making the CVF, and the course in general, more relevant to managerial work seems to be met in three ways:

> Requiring students to interview and observe "key informants," practicing managers, and supervisors.
> Requiring students to "perform" some of the roles or competencies included in the CVF, such as mentoring other students or brokering for a specific business decision in an assigned case.
> Requiring students to observe the behavior of others in light of the competencies included in the CVF and to record and discuss those observations.

Alan Bluedorn of the University of Missouri integrates the CVF with the use of key informants or professionals with extensive managerial experience whom the students interview several times during the semester. Students are responsible for contacting their own key informant. The students study the CVF, as well as other documents on organizational culture and structure. After discussing the material in groups, and after at least three interviews with their key informants, they write a ten-page paper on the informant's organization. The paper addresses the question: "Would I find this organization's culture compatible with myself?"

The CVF provides the focus for the interviews. The students often take graphics depicting the framework into the interviews and present the CVF in broad outlines to their key informant. "The process makes the interviews much more focused and detailed," says Bluedorn. Students are able to ask: "What kind of mentoring do you do in your work unit? Do you believe your unit is placing too much emphasis on any of the four quadrants of the framework? If so, what are some examples?" Bluedorn believes that his students, armed with the lens of the CVF, come out of the interviews with a better analysis of an organization and a better feel for the organization's culture--as seen through the eyes of a key informant.

Richard Blackburn of the University of North Carolina believes that the CVF is brought to life through the application of cases that are sufficiently current and complex. Blackburn believes one of the greatest needs students have is to think simultaneously about the roles and quadrants of the CVF while examining real managerial problems. Blackburn likes to demonstrate nonlinear managerial thinking; he does this by examining cases that offer detailed narratives of decision making and managerial choice.

> Managerial problems don't come bundled as operations problems or finance problems, and they are always interrupted and complicated by a deeper context. Richard Wagner (1991), who has followed up the kind of work that Mintzberg (1973) and later Isenberg (1984,1986) have done on managerial work, uses the term "convoluted action" to describe how interrelated and turbulent the playing field is in organizations. Managers don't follow the linear, rational models for making decisions and taking action. They make little decisions while they study problems, and they usually do an immense amount of conferring with other people. To use the language of the framework, they direct while they monitor, and they mentor while they broker. Complex cases, discussed in light of the CVF, help my students see this more clearly.

Blackburn also uses the CVF to address specific business problems. Discussing innovation is of little value, says Blackburn, if the discussion is not grounded in context--the efforts of a specific organization to spur innovation in a particular service or product line. Blackburn will discuss such an effort by an organization, put the CVF back up on the overhead and ask: "Now, what's going on in this organization in light of the Competing Values Framework?"

Another strategy for making the course managerially relevant is the use of observation and discussion. **Larry Michaelsen of the University of Oklahoma** uses this strategy extensively.[2] He also assigns students to teach various competencies from the CVF, but requires them to use a format other than lecturing. Says Michaelsen: "The only thing worse than a professor lecturing a group of students is another student lecturing to students." The students offer a workshop that usually takes an hour of class time. They work in teams, each team taking a different competency and deciding how to involve the class in the process, but much of the learning takes place within and among the groups behind the scenes. Michaelsen says most of the discussions about leadership principles draw upon the experience of groups, not what the class as a whole is doing. The groups become a laboratory for doing the things leaders do. Students have to broker ideas and mentor group members who are shy or who lack a meaningful group role early in the group's life cycle. Someone has to monitor the group's progress and coordinate its work with other groups or the instructor. Michaelsen's students are thus using the CVF not only to describe leadership behavior, but to enact it themselves.

---

[2] See pages 29-36 of the **Instructional Guide** for a complete discussion by Larry Michaelsen of his strategies for making his courses managerially relevant. Because that detail is available there, this section of Michael Thompson's article is omitted.

Bob Marx of the University of Massachusetts has developed a major video component into an undergraduate class on managerial principles. Marx and several colleagues have developed *Management Live: A Video Book* (Prentice-Hall, 1991). This is a videotape of scenes from feature films, talk shows, and segments from documentaries that depict leaders in action. Some of the people featured include David Letterman, Hyman Rickover, and Patricia Carrigan who is manager of a GM plant. The class observes these clips and then discusses these leaders' behaviors in light of the CVF.

The skills courses are thus less focused on conceptualizing than on performing. The assignments and projects require students *to be managers* and not simply to discuss or observe managers. **Alan Bluedorn** describes his efforts to create a managerial environment in the classroom:

> I try to model some of the competencies I'm teaching. I have them coach one another instead of doing all the coaching myself. I ask them to try things more than once whenever I can, after they have received some kind of feedback. I have them write their own questions for the final exam. They write the questions and then come in and write essay-type answers to those questions. I grade them quite rigorously, and not everyone is up to an A. I think this process helps them understand how to provide a buy-in strategy for being effective in the facilitator and mentor roles. I push away from "one best way" approaches, but I also try to demonstrate that they, as managers, have to listen to the perceptions of the people they work with, no matter how much they disagree. The CVF, by featuring roles and competencies, has helped me to make the course student-centered, instead of teacher-centered. I think a good OB course is student-centered.

Not all of the courses revolve around skill building. **Ray Zammuto of the University of Colorado** uses the CVF in an organizational theory course. Zammuto focuses on organizational effectiveness, The course revolves around a major project in which the students choose an organization, analyze the industry in which it is nested, and then study the organization's strategies and conclude by making recommendations for change. Zammuto says he "doesn't use the CVF to look at paradoxes as much as many instructors do." He is more interested in the alignments or misalignments between an organization's strategies and its culture. For example:

> If you look at a lot of organizations that are doing Total Quality Management, you quickly see that many, if not most of them, are failing in their efforts. When we use the CVF to examine the culture (in terms of where it places its emphasis from day to day), we see that we usually have a mismatch between the organization's culture and the very changes it is trying to make. Organizations that exert high, centralized control often fail in implementing quality improvement programs that require lots of local autonomy. The same is true of efforts to create high-performance work teams. Many of these organizations can't get what they need without changing their cultures.

> Organization A is talking alot about the need for flexibility, but it is not becoming more flexible. There is a misalignment between the behavior the organization needs and the behavior it continues to use. The design of the course pushes the students to look at where the organization is really placing its emphasis.

The students use both the data from the culture profile and the conceptual map provided by the CVF to write their audit reports on their organizations.

Sue Faerman of the State University of New York at Albany also requires her students to do performance audits of organizations. Faerman teaches a graduate seminar in Organizational Development and a graduate class in Organizational Behavior. She uses the CVF in both courses. Her OD course focuses on instruments and methods for doing organizational assessments. Faerman has used the CVF extensively in research on individuals performance assessment, and she presents it as one of many instruments and approaches her students can use in analyzing organizations. Most students use the CVF in group interviews with people from diverse positions in an organization. They respond to written instruments based upon the CVF, but also answer questions in live interviews conducted by Faerman's students in a kind of focus group. "This approach," says Faerman:

> enables us to see how diverse performance is in the same organization across the quadrants of the CVF. Bureau chiefs or division directors may do things as brokers or monitors that are very different from people in front-line supervisory positions, though supervisors also perform very effectively in the same roles. So the CVF is helping us understand in more precise terms how leadership is exerted at different levels in the same organization.
> Students also gain a feel for action research. While gathering a lot of information on how the organization is performing, they are conducting interviews and asking questions that are actually changing the way the organization performs. In their audit reports, students often discuss the theme of "interviews as interventions."

SUMMARY AND IMPLICATIONS

All of the professors interviewed felt that a major, if not *the* major strength of the Competing Values Framework is its capacity to accommodate and visualize the tensions and paradoxes that contemporary leaders face. Most faculty indicated that the framework is an economical or efficient tool for teaching because it accommodates the best material they have been using to teach management and leadership concepts. Choosing the CVF does not require jettisoning something else.

The framework, in spite of its visual lucidity, is complex. Of those who teach skills courses, most professors said they had decided not even to attempt to teach all 24 competencies in the Quinn, et al., text, but to concentrate on the four quadrants and deal with selected competencies in each quadrant. This was, in fact, the major piece of advice for faculty who are considering adopting the CVF: move slowly and incorporate the things you are already doing successfully. Don't attempt to teach all 24 of the competencies. Most faculty commiserated on the difficulties of teaching management topics to full-time students with little organizational experience, especially students at the undergraduate level. Some even volunteered the thought that undergraduate courses in management might represent a futile effort because it is so difficult to "simulate" a meaningful context for managerial tasks. Not one faculty member said it is easier to teach the framework to full-time students than to practicing managers and executives.

The CVF appears to be helpful in "complexifying" students' thinking. After students had worked with the framework, faculty believe they (students) can frame problems in a more sophisticated way and tend to think about such phenomena as the unintended consequences and systemic effects of decisions. If the framework is taught well, students usually change their perceptions of their own capacities as managers and leaders, understanding that most people are not equally strong in every quadrant and must compensate for weaknesses in some areas and capitalize on strengths in others. Through the CVF students acquire a functional language for observing and describing behavior. The vocabulary of the CVF enables them to observe nuances in organizational behavior they might not have noticed without that vocabulary.

The CVF seems to help organizational behavior faculty teach concepts related to organizational culture. It appears to be used increasingly in organization theory and organization development classes which deal with macro issues of strategic competitiveness and redesign. There is also growing evidence that faculty who use the CVF in teaching are also using it in research projects related to topics they cover in courses. That research/teaching interface is making the CVF more relevant to current issues in management and leadership.

REFERENCES

Bolman, L. and Deal, T. 1991. *Reframing organizations: Artistry, choice and leadership*. San Francisco: Jossey-Bass.
Daft, R. 1991. *Management* (2nd ed., rev.) Ft. Worth: Dryden.
DiPadova, L. 1990. *Instructional guide to accompany becoming a master manager*. New York: John Wiley & Sons.
Isenberg, D. 1984. "How senior managers think." *Harvard Business Review*, 62, 81-90.
Mintzberg, H. 1973. *The nature of managerial work*. New York: Harper & Row.
Powell, W. and Dimaggio, P. 1991. *The new institutionalism in organizational analysis*. Chicago: University of Chicago Press.
Quinn, R. 1988. *Beyond rational management: Mastering the paradoxes and competing demands of high performance*. San Francisco: Jossey-Bass.
Quinn, R., Faerman, S., Thompson, M., and McGrath, M. 1990. *Becoming a master manager: A competency framework*. New York: John Wiley & Sons.
Vickers, G. 1973. Making institutions work. London: Associated Business Programs.
Wagner, R. 1991. "Managerial problem solving." in *Complex problem solving: Principles and Mechanisms*, R. J. Sternberg and P. A. Frensch (eds.). New Jersey: Lawrence Erlbaum Associates.
Whetten, D. and Cameron, K. 1991. *Development management skills* (2nd ed.). Illinois: Scott, Foresman.

PART 3

TEACHING MANAGERS WITH THE COMPETING VALUES FRAMEWORK

This section features two contributions from professors who have been teaching with the CVF to experienced managers:

Page 55: "Teaching Organizational Theory and Behavior to Traditional Students and to Mid-Career Managers"
David W. Hart, Ph.D. candidate

Dave shares his personal experience of teaching mid-career managers about organizational life. Since many of his students are considerably older than he is, he developed strategies for overcoming what some would regard as a credibility gap. His course is organized around the CVF.

Page 59: "Competency-Based Management Education: Challenges and Methods in Teaching Adult Learners"
Dr. Alan T. Belasen, Dean Meg Benke, Dr. Andrew J. DiNitto

Alan, Meg, and Andy discuss the basic differences in adult learners and traditional students, and how the CVF is used to meet the needs of adult learners who are managers in organizations.

The fastest growing student population in higher education today are adult learners--non-traditionally aged students who are returning to school. These adults are from a wide variety of backgrounds and bring to the classroom a wealth of experience, as well as independent thinking.

Many adult learners are also managers in corporations, private agencies, and other organizations. A number of executive programs exist today in MBA and MPA programs alike. These programs may hold classes during evenings and weekends, and attract experienced managers who are still working in demanding positions. These manager-students are striving to achieve their educational goals while still maintaining their work and family responsibilities. They tend to be very bright, achievement-oriented, and highly motivated. They want their education, and they want it to be relevant. They are willing and able to test classroom ideas with their own experience, as well as to reframe their experiences using theories and concepts gleaned in class.

Perhaps the "acid test" of the Quinn, et al. text is how it fares among experienced managers in organizations. Faculty who were interviewed by Michael Thompson, as reported in his article, excerpted in this **Guide** (see pages 41-50), often reported that teaching the CVF to managers is quite a different experience from teaching traditional-aged undergraduates. This is likely true of teaching most courses dealing with organizations and management.

While we know that the CVF and the text are used with a variety of managers in many organizational settings, the contributors to this section are from the State University of New York-Empire State College in Saratoga Springs, New York--a leading institution in adult learning. These authors are in the college's FORUM/East program, a highly reputed baccalaureate degree program for mid-career managers and executives. Drawing on their vast experience, these faculty members give us a useful picture of teaching adult learners in general, and with the competing values framework in particular.

I should perhaps point out that Empire State College, founded by Ernest Boyer[3] in 1971 when he was Chancellor of the State University of New York, began with his vision of individualized education. Empire State College has since become one of the premier institutions in the country--indeed in the world--specializing in adult learning. Empire State College's FORUM/East program is a specialized, dynamic and innovative program designed to serve the needs of managers in organizations who are returning to school to complete their baccalaureate degrees. FORUM/East developed a competency-based management degree for manager-students; the degree program is centered on the Competing Values Framework and uses the Quinn, et al. book as its core text. This program is highly successful, and very well received by experienced managers who are enrolled.

With regard to the differences between teaching the Competing Values Framework to full-time students and to experienced managers, the following is observed by Dr. Joseph Whorton at the University of Georgia:[4]

> I use the analogy of a disease and its antidote. I feel like I'm walking around with vials of antidotes for deadly diseases, but the students have not yet contracted the disease--so they have little appreciation for the antidote. Give me thirty minutes in a room with practicing managers, allow me to use the framework and I'll have them leaning forward, waving their hands in the air, ready to discuss the implications of the framework for hours. Full-time students can look at the CVF and shrug their shoulders. I have to get past the shrug and demonstrate how this stuff can be applied.

---

[3] Ernest Boyer, former U. S. Commissioner of Education, publically counted the founding of Empire State College as his proudest achievement.

[4] Quoted in: Michael Thompson, "Using the Competing Values Framework in the Classroom." *Human Resource Management*, Spring 1993, Vol. 32, Number 1, p. 116. Copyright by John Wiley and Sons, Inc.

HINTS FOR TEACHING MANAGERS FROM THE QUINN, ET AL. TEXT

1. **Recognize the unique situations of manager-students.** They come to class with a vast array of rich organizational experience. Many may also come from turbulent organizational downsizing situations. In addition, as we know, organizations are not always friendly to personal autonomy, and so some managers may work in environments where their sense of individual worth is assaulted in a myriad of ways. What we offer them in class, explicitly with the CVF, is a way to reframe and reinterpret their organizational experiences. This can be very healing for many managers.

2. **Adjust the activities in the text to the organizational setting, as appropriate.** The text is a generic text, written primarily for full-time students. Many of the activities, however, can be conducted in the organizational setting or using the manager-student's work as the base of the activity. Be alert to these possibilities. Often your manager-students will point them out to you!

3. **Adjust the CVF Leadership Self-Assessment.**
Note that I have included in this section an instrument which is NOT included in the software **(see page 68-71)**. This instrument is found in Robert Quinn's *Beyond Rational Management*.[5] In addition to the self-assessment instruments included in the software (a hard copy is provided in the **Instructional Guide**, pp. 87 - 95), experienced managers-students often see the value of seeking feedback from peers, subordinates, and bosses. With this instrument, they can ask designated individuals to complete a questionnaire regarding their (the students') CVF role strengths. Students then compare this information from others with the profiles they generated when they responded to the self-assessment questionnaires on themselves. This provides a rich dimension to the self-assessment process.

4. **Encourage manager-students to tell you what is happening in their organizations.** Frame your exam questions and written assignments to allow manager-students to share with you aspects of their organizational work experience. Teaching managers is often a tremendous learning experience for teachers who are interested in organizations! Encouraging them to apply the CVF to their work experience not only helps them to reinterpret and reframe their organizational life, but also allows them to share important information with you, the teacher.

---

[5] San Francisco: Jossey-Bass. 1988. See pages 175-176.

I taught an Executive MPA course recently, using the Quinn, et al. text along with Bolman and Deal.[6] The final examination was designed to help students analyze their organization from different perspectives and perhaps to come to see their experiences in different ways. Some of the following questions were included:

A. INTRODUCTION: Briefly describe your organization and your association with it, in several paragraphs.

1. Summarize some of the major elements of the structural frame/Rational Goal and Internal Process Models and discuss some of the theoretical underpinnings of the frame/models. Why are these underpinnings important to the understanding of this frame? *[Any of the quadrants and frames can be substituted in this question.]*

2. Write a brief description of your organization from the structural frame/Rational Goal and Internal Process Models. What are the major components of the organization from the perspective of this frame/models? In your view, in which ways do these components contribute to the effectiveness of your organization, and in which ways to they detract? *[Again, any of the quadrants and frames can be substituted in this question.]*

3. Describe some ways in which these components influence your life in this organization.

4. Choose any supervisor that you have or have had and describe her/his activities in terms of one of the Competing Values roles which relate to this frame/these models, and discuss which you observe to be helpful, and which you consider to be a hindrance, and why. *[Again, any of the quadrants and frames can be substituted in this question.]*

5. Describe a problem situation facing you in your organization, and how the principles of the structural frame/Rational Goal and Internal Process Models, or the competencies in the CVF roles which are associated with this frame, can assist you. . *[Again, any of the quadrants and frames can be substituted in this question.]*

6. Describe the use of the symbolic frame in your organization, in terms of organizational control and stability, and in terms of organizational flexibility and change.

One very important note here: If you encourage manager-students to be open with you about their organizational experiences, it is critical that all information they give you be kept in strictest confidence. This is worth noting on the syllabus, and also a good idea to repeat on exams.

---

[6] Lee Bolman and Terrence Deal. *Reframing Organizations: Artistry, Choice, and Leadership.* San Francisco: Jossey-Bass. 1991.

TEACHING ORGANIZATIONAL BEHAVIOR AND THEORY TO TRADITIONAL STUDENTS AND TO MID-CAREER MANAGERS

by David W. Hart[7]

INTRODUCTION

As a part of my graduate assistantship as a doctoral student in Public Administration at the University at Albany, State University of New York, I was given the responsibility for teaching an introductory course in Organizational Behavior and Theory to traditional undergraduates. The approach that proved to be quite successful was the Competing Values Framework. I used that framework to introduce students to the complexities of organizations. Most undergraduates have had little experience in "traditional" organizations, and much of the course was therefore devoted to introducing students to basic issues inherent in the interactions within and between organizations.

After having taught the course for several semesters, I was offered the chance to teach a similar course for SUNY-Empire State College. More specifically, I was to be involved in a growing program that catered to mid-career students, most of whom were middle-managers in large corporations. After quickly accepting what appeared to be an exciting and interesting opportunity, I began to realize that the challenge was greater than I had originally envisioned -- teaching mid-career managers about organizations was significantly different than teaching traditional undergraduates.

I had two major strikes against me. First, I was a "professional" student. Having gone straight from a bachelor's degree into graduate work, I had few opportunities for "real-world" experience. This, I suspected, would not garner much respect from seasoned managers. Second, I was young, 28 at the time, but looked even younger. So, students entering the course for the first time would see a "kid" with no "real" experience attempting to tell them about organizational life. Middle managers do not suffer fools gladly -- and I was a prime candidate.

---

[7] David Hart, a Ph.D. candidate in Public Administration at the Graduate School of Public Affairs and Policy, State University of New York at Albany, has been teaching experienced managers in a baccalaureate program for mid-career managers at FORUM/ East, SUNY-Empire State College. He is, indeed, considerably older than he looks!- LND

TEACHING MID-CAREER STUDENTS

Recognizing this problem, I struggled to structure the course in a way that would offset the potential difficulties that might arise out of this situation. The only solution I saw was to exploit the strengths of both the students and the instructor. Most students in the program were middle managers with anywhere from 5 to 35 years of experience in large corporations. This experience is a vast and critical resource and I wanted to utilize it as such.

I, on the other hand, had little traditional organizational experience. My strength, however, consisted of coursework, study, and research in organizational theory and behavior. My hope was to fuse theory with experience -- a fundamental component of the learning process. The division of labor was clear, then. I would present students with pertinent theories of organizations and the behaviors within them in a systematic and logical manner. The students were expected to understand those theories and apply them to their rich experience--and I in turn would be able to learn from their experiences, as well. This process was to be reflected in a series of papers that focused on pertinent areas of the field (by quadrant in the CVF). In these papers, students were asked to demonstrate their comprehension of the theories presented, apply them to their experience, and discuss why (or why not) those theories helped them to make sense of or at least better understand that experience. This, of course, would require a good comprehension of the theories and the ability to articulate those perspectives in light of one's own experience.

I have found this approach to be quite successful. Mid-career students do not need to be told what life is like in organizations -- in fact, as of this writing, many of my students have worked in large organizations longer than I have been *alive*. Therefore, students are not looking for broad (but superficial) overviews or cursory introductions to organizational life. They want to substantively discuss organizational issues that have a direct impact on their lives. Early on, many students may not possess the vocabulary and theories of the discipline, but they do possess valuable insights from personal experience. It is important to not only seek out that insight, but to value it as well. Mid-career students bring as much knowledge to the course as the instructor.

COURSE STRUCTURE

Structuring a course as broad as organizational behavior and theory is always a challenge. The problem of striking a balance between breadth and depth are well-known to anyone that has taught introductory courses. With so many theories and their accompanying approaches, it is difficult at best to include an adequate survey of the field without becoming too superficial.

Fortunately, I had been using the Competing Values Framework in other courses and decided to structure the course around the four quadrants.

As such, the course was divided into four broad sections: the literature and theories that fall under each of the four quadrants. I used the rational goal quadrant to discuss traditional classical/rational approaches. The internal process model was used to discuss structure, hierarchy, and organizational processes. The human relations model served as a medium for presenting theories of human interaction in organizations which included traditional and contemporary theories from this perspective. Innovation and change, among others were discussed in the open system section. Finally, to wrap up the course, the framework as a whole was used to introduce organizational culture (i.e. culture emerges from the interaction of the quadrants within [and without] an organization). This includes areas such as meaning and symbolism in an organizational context as well. The required papers for students focused on each of these areas.

CONCLUSIONS

The benefits of using the Competing Values Framework in this way are several. First, it provides the students with a model for understanding the discipline while avoiding the encyclopedic approach so common in introductory courses. A theoretical base (such as the CVF) gives students a context into which mainstream organizational behavior fits, thereby diminishing the need to "cover everything" in one semester. Also, because of its relative simplicity, the Competing Values Framework provides an excellent foundation for further coursework in related areas as well.

The major benefit of the framework, however, comes from its original purpose: It is a conceptual model that reveals and categorizes contradictory expectations that individuals have of organizations. By providing a systematic typology of behavioral roles within organizations, the CVF also serves as a medium for discussing organizational behavior at the individual level as well. The result is a model that can systematically address organizational issues at the macro- and micro-levels, with relative conceptual ease.

The Competing Values Framework has proved to be exceptionally helpful in working with managers. For one, and this should be taken lightly, the model is easy to understand and easy to remember. I have had countless instances of students calling or writing to talk about how the CVF had helped them to work through some situation at work. Nearly all mentioned, however, that the best part about it was that the model was already in their head at the time.

Finally, the unpredictable environment in today's business world, with rampant downsizing, globalization, and emphases on innovation and change, has also made the CVF particularly relevant to managers. The philosophical foundation of competing or contradictory values in organizations seems to ring more true among mangers than ever. And by emphasizing those contradictions and competing values in the workplace, the Competing Values Framework provides a manageable framework that will help individuals to make sense of, or at least better understand, their often chaotic and uncertain organizational experience.

"The presence of so many different racial, ethnic, age, income and experience groups promises much vitality; it also means very little can be taken for granted. Approaches that once seemed at least adequate need to be rethought and restructured as faculty members are challenged to reach students who differ both from their predecessors and from one another. In the long run, education should be enhanced as faculty members experiment with an increased variety of styles, contents and pedagogies to support students' full participation in learning communities."
--Challenge of Connecting Learning

Competency-Based Management Education: Challenges and Methods in Teaching Adult Learners

Alan T. Belasen, Ph.D.,[*] Meg Benke, Ph.D.,[**] Andrew J. DiNitto, Ph.D.[***]

THE PEDAGOGICAL CHALLENGE

Effective instructors know that understanding the context and frame of reference of all of their students is important for effective instructional design and delivery. When their students are adult learners, instructors take steps to adjust their styles, contents, and pedagogies to support adult learners both emotionally and psychologically. Instructors must recognize that often, adult learners return to school after a considerable hiatus and with a self-perception of a relatively large intellectual gap between themselves and traditional-aged students. Instructors must also recognize that adult learners come with significant amount of knowledge, managerial and job skills, as well as a practical approach to problem solving, intuition, and common sense. Regardless of the rich experience that adult learners bring to the classroom, instructors must recognize that adult learners nonetheless come into the academic world full of trepidations and anxieties.

Adult learners bring with them a vast array of philosophical assumptions, personal biases, and values which are built from their extensive personal and work experience. They may also bring with them images and metaphors that often are incompatible with what is presented in academic environments. While they realize the importance of getting a college degree, they have been justifying the lack of the degree for many years. They may know the relative value of education as applied to their jobs and organizations, but they are not sure how to go about realizing it. They are good at writing a detailed technical report or executive summary, but do not know how to approach the writing of a research paper or how to critique a scholarly work.

We should not be surprised, then, that although these adults may manage hundreds of people, and be responsible for millions of dollars, and in all likelihood earn more than their instructors, they still feel insecure when they enter the classroom. Assuring them that we as instructors value their knowledge and experiences is the kind of validation which could help them reduce their anxieties and put them on the track to success. Encouraging adult learners who are managers in organizations, to draw on their experiences in their engagement with the course material, is a way to validate the significance of their work experience for their academic endeavors. It also becomes a way for us, as their instructors, to keep learning about the "real world" or life in organizations.

---

[*] Assistant Professor of management, Empire State College and Department of Communication, University at Albany, State University of New York.
[**] Assistant Dean, Collegewide Programs, Empire State College, State University of New York.
[***] Assistant Professor of political science, Empire State College, State University of New York.

There are significant fundamental differences in the experience of operating in the academic world and the business world. Surfacing these differences is important for people who are trying to function in both arenas. Dr. Michael V. Fortunato, Director of the FORUM/East Degree Program for mid-career executives at SUNY-Empire State College, devised the following conceptualization to orient managers who are returning to school. This figure presents a comparison of the business and academic environment which might help adult learners to shape their pedagogy and instructional design.

BACK TO SCHOOL

Hints for Reducing Culture Shock

BUSINESS	COLLEGE
Focus is on getting the job done: the results are what count	Focus is on process: what matters is how you got there and whether or not you could repeat it
Work is expected to be relatively error-free	Errors are essential--we learn more from our mistakes than from our successes
Learning is often by "apprenticeship": explicit directions are customary	Learning is by "self-discovery": ambiguity is thought to be essential to the learning process
Solutions are formulaic: results can be described in a policy manual	Solutions are heuristic: creative inspiration is often needed to put knowledge to use
Gather just the facts necessary to make a good decision: redundancy is discouraged as "inefficient"	Research standards demand that "all" available evidence be considered: redundancy is encouraged as "comprehensive"
Solicit opinions of others "who have been there before"	Seek out other methods for approaching this or similar problems
Delegation is encouraged as "effective management"	Sensitivity to taking ownership of one's work and giving credit to whomever it is due
Tolerance for variety of processes/ workstyles that lead to correct results	Tolerance for a variety of results that follow from correct processes: a tolerance for a variety of informed opinions
Risk acting on imagination without knowledge	Risk acting on knowledge without imagination

Adult learners use a frame of reference and mental constructs that are based on their intuition and common sense of what works well and what fails. They were trained and developed requisite skills that conform to the need to become highly proficient and productive in fulfilling their tasks. They were taught to think critically, be decisive, initiate actions, and add tangible value to their work units and organizations. As the figure indicates--while in the business world managers are expected to optimize results, in the academic world they are expected to satisfy process requirements. The academic world allows for unresolved arguments to coexist and for dialectical notions to surface and be respected. For adult learners, these contradictions are a source of frustration and ambiguity--they represent equivocal issues that are not easily reconciled with their views of the world.

Effective instructors must anticipate these reactions and be prepared to deal with these issues and help adult learners rebuild their confidence and trust in the system of management education. Notably, effective instructors must be familiar with contextual factors that uniquely affect adult learning, such as socio-economic, psychological, perceptual, and cognitive factors.

The pedagogical challenge for us as instructors of adult learners is to realize that the cognitive map of adult learners is different and unique. Adult learners bring their own complex set of values, beliefs, and perceptions about the world to the educational environment. The challenge for instructors, then, is to shift away from the traditional, functional approach and move toward a more critical perspective that recognizes the richness of the world of adult learners. At minimum, instructors are expected to reconcile the two approaches by using a flexible and adaptive approach that is experientially-based. The challenge faced by instructors is designing a flexible course that gives attention to both individualization and previous learning. Instructors must give up or "sacrifice" some of their autonomy to create a learning environment that is flexible enough to accommodate the psychological, cognitive, and behavioral needs of adult learners.

In examining the challenges faced by instructors of adult learners and in proposing a set of pedagogical options to deal with these challenges, we opted to structure this paper as follows: First, the factors that shape the frame of reference of adult learners are highlighted and discussed. Second, we suggest enabling mechanisms or strategies that instructors can use to create effective learning environment. Third, we describe the tenets of the competency-based approach to learning and the expected outcomes of using such an approach. Finally, the use of the Quinn, et al. text is demonstrated through the lenses of the competency-based approach. This approach was applied successfully at FORUM-Empire State College management development degree program.

ADULTS AS UNIQUE LEARNERS

Adults returning to school come from all levels of social and economic backgrounds. In earlier years of adult education, the focus was on the man returning from the military on the GI bill, the higher-level manager who could afford to pay tuition, or the displaced homemaker with the need and time to complete a degree. Today, however, the student in a management education program may often be a person who has through the ranks of an organization and perhaps has attained a lifestyle that goes beyond class dimensions. Regardless of their social and professional background, adult learners require academic as well as emotional support through validation, individualization, and involvement.

Combined, the above concepts simply suggest that as college teachers of older students, we must recognize that, though seeking validation and involvement may be universal human needs, they are especially significant to students who may have perceived themselves as academic and even social failures in the past. As the demographics of the student population continue to change, we need to keep reminding ourselves the higher educational institutions were originally created with privileged white male as the model student. That was the profile of the college student; but while the student population has changed, the traditions, the culture and so on are still grounded in that old model.

Thus, we as instructors of adult learners must tailor our instructional design and methodologies to the unique frame of reference, psychological differences and needs, aptitude and perceptions, and cognitive abilities of adult learners. The sections below examine each of these factors.

PARTICULAR FRAME OF REFERENCE

Adult learners bring to the classroom an ample supply of experientially-based knowledge and a practical prism through which they judge the utility of the process and content of learning. They measure theoretical constructs and conceptual models against their intuition and common sense that is both pragmatic and concrete. They use an inductive approach in explaining and relating to their surrounding and they expect instructors to have working assumptions and interpretations about the world that fit with their own. While instructors normally use a functional perspective for teaching and explaining organizational factors (e.g., factors in organizational communication may include information flow and networking, breakdowns, managerial responses to information overload/underload, etc.), most adult learners develop interpretations of organizational reality on the basis of shared meaning. They employ behavioral/intuitive criteria to judge the success of deliverables and the utility and relevance of material. Since they view the world from their own frame of reference, they also expect their instructors to reconfirm their assumptions about the world. Hence, adult learners expect their instructors to use a reflective approach, rather than a deductive one to help them reconstruct images of their organizations and management practices.

How one frames professional problems and the range of solutions available is what differentiates the education of an expert from the education of the novice. Schon (1987) highlights the importance of reflection in learning and suggests the importance of the "right kind of telling" that takes place when students work closely with faculty, learning to frame questions and responses. His explanation for reflection in learning begins with knowing in action which is presumed knowledge. He follows this with reflection in action which considers the possibility of surprise or an unexpected finding. Reflection about action is done through experimentation which is particularly important for adult learners in the protection of an education program. An experiential approach to learning also allows students and practicing managers to reflect on the results of decisions and actions, a luxury not always evident in the business environment. Downplaying the importance of universal principles helps them interpret events through the narrow prism of their experiences and understanding — it reinforces their preconceived ideas of what is working and what is not.

PSYCHOLOGICAL DIFFERENCES/NEEDS

Adult learners may have different goals and different motivation in going back to school. Some return to school in order to gain new skills or to get a promotion, while others enroll to meet a personal goal or because it is the requirement of continued employment. Whatever the reason, instructors should realize that adults differ from one another in their motivations and expectations. Some students need more direction and support than others, and may place considerable claim against the time and attention of their instructors. These students are also influenced by their own perceptions of their weaknesses and lack of capacity to learn, requiring counseling and constant guidance. Learning activities which enhance self-confidence as well as personal competencies are valuable. Yet, instructors should recognize adult learners' personal limitations and use flexible instructional design to respond to the psychological needs of the students.

Successful teachers of adult students with managerial experience seek to understand the prior experience, skills, and competencies of their students and to apply this understanding to the design of the assignments. The study of management is enhanced by the experiences which managers bring. As instructors, it is important that we have an understanding of the background and competencies of the adult learners--we should be able to diagnose their learning needs and why they are participating in our course.

APTITUDE AND PERCEPTIONS

Adult learners might have different needs and goals in going back to school than young, full-time students. Adult learners may select and organize learning stimuli based on their perceptions of what is important and relevant to their work and what is not. Thus, they may respond differently to the context of learning (e.g., group activities versus independent learning), the type of communication used (e.g., verbal explanations versus visual aids), level of conceptualization (e.g., abstract versus concrete concepts), and problem solving orientation (e.g., intuitive versus logical reasoning). It is therefore important that instructors tell learners in advance what the format and mode of learning are and how they are expected to demonstrate mastery of instructional objectives. Adults expect explicit instructions, reasonable deadlines, and realistic assignments because they often are juggling through multiple expectations. For example, group assignments should only be given in a time period which recognizes that adults may have difficulty scheduling time outside of class with other students.

COGNITIVE FACTORS

The adults in your course may have a great deal of prior knowledge in selected areas of the study ("positive depth"), but almost no knowledge in other key areas ("negative breadth"). This may require tailoring specific assignments to reflect the level of this knowledge, but also redirecting the adults toward the basic concepts or principles they need to know to be successful. Adult educators such as Friere (1992) and Cervero (1988) have long investigated the relationships between learning and the changing patterns of knowledge within a profession. Cervero advocates the need for a shift from a functionalist perspective to a critical view. Functionalism views professionals as a group who use knowledge to address problems that are important to society. The work of the manager is technical or specialized, so that more knowledge provides a basis for solving problems more effectively. When the functionalist approach is applied to education, deficiencies are corrected by expanding the knowledge base through training.

The functionalist (instructor) uses reasoning and logic to explain managerial and organizational dynamics. He or she supports the explanation with theoretical constructs and empirical models, using a deductive approach to generalize, infer, and draw conclusions. The result is often gross simplification of organizational and social reality. The interpretivist (adult learner) is less concerned with validity and reliability of measurement and about studies supporting general assertions about organizational behavior and/or managerial dynamics. Instead, the interpretivist is more likely to draw on his/her stories, organizational saga, rites, rituals, dynamics, and so on to draw conclusions about what is working. For example, the interpretivist is less concerned with the argument that feedback is crucial for establishing effective communication across levels, and is more concerned with the reflections and uses of feedback in his/her organization—from his/her own frame of reference. Therefore, when working with adults, it is important to use a critical approach to clarify the sources of adult learning and if necessary change the actual knowledge. Instructors must have impact on how knowledge is shaped by working with adults.

ENABLING MECHANISMS AND STRATEGIES

Adults with management experience present a challenge for the instructor using the Quinn, et al. text. Recognizing and expanding on the previous learning which has been acquired through practical experience takes significant design and individualization. In addition, instructors must help students to unleash the business learning which must be shaped for the academic environment.

There are a number of ways by which instructors can create a high energy learning environment that is both stimulating and appropriate for adult learners. We suggest that instructors shift away from "understanding by learning" edification to "learning by doing" pedagogy by considering the following strategies:

1. **Validation**
   - Make students comfortable enough to tell you and the class what they know and think. This may not happen right away, but small advances will make the adult learner more confident about application of new ideas.
   - Get to know your students by name and job/personal experiences which will allow you to design more specific and targeted examples.
   - Open up the communication channels by provide them with more opportunities to participate and have access to you as a resource.
   - Give specific and clear directions about your expectations.
   - If the work submitted does not meet your expectations, identify first what was good or acceptable in the work, then make specific and brief suggestions on how to improve the rest; give them an opportunity to redo the work.
   - The gap between the time they submit their work and they receive your comments should be as short as possible, but never more than a week.

2. Strike a balance between soft, value-loaded skills (e.g., mentoring, leadership, communication) and hard, analytically-driven skills (e.g., decision science, math, statistics).

3. Integrate students' on the job training into the instructional design by using an "executive development" style of short courses combining both work and study. Instructors should create opportunities for communication outside the class and via the electronic media (e.g., e-m).

4. Turn instruction into more issue-based, focused approach using students' work experiences and organizational (or social) images as living cases to examine the issues.

5. Present knowledge and provide reasoning and analysis from a multiple perspective and integrative framework. Rely on cross-functional synergies by encouraging students to share their views from different perspectives (e.g., macro, micro, internal, external) and different levels of analysis (e.g., interpersonal, organizational).

6. Use the case method to teaching by preparing data, arguments, and expectations in advance, and provide adult learners students with full ownership of the discussion. The activities involving the case analysis must be driven by the students and particularly their images of what works and what does not work. Let them reason and explain the causes and effects of their diagnosis and action plan regarding the case. You should also use questions in rather provocative way in order to elicit different perspectives on the focal points under discussion. The trade-off between depth and breadth of discussion will need to be managed. Remember, however, to maintain mutual respect and a supportive climate by constructively manage intragroup dynamics and conflicts. You might want to use humor to relieve tension or overcome barriers to group communication and turn the learning process into an enjoyable process..

7. Use a competency-based approach to learning (CBAL) with built-in helping mechanisms to facilitate teaching and enhance learning. Center on application and the realization of skills essential for building cross-functional synergies, while also emphasizing cognitive learning and the internalization of skills necessary for situational management. When used appropriately, CBAL can become a powerful teaching tool!

COMPETENCY-BASED APPROACH TO LEARNING[8]

Unlike traditional approaches to management education which are pedagogically input based—relying on the functional orientation and specialized knowledge of instructors—CBAL is individually-focused, value-added, and outcome-oriented. We will discuss each in turn.

INDIVIDUALLY-FOCUSED

CBAL is individually-based in that the students' values, knowledge, abilities, and needs are incorporated into the pedagogy of management development through an experiential approach to learning. This experiential approach involves cognitive as well as applied learning. Using diagnostic instruments, students are able to identify their special managerial and professional needs. They then pursue competencies in areas where they are relatively weak, or in areas where they have a special interest. A student is encouraged to construct a personal model of self-directed learning which is matched to his/her particular needs. These needs can be immediate, emergent, or anticipated, and are triggered by the demands of the position or task environment, organizational or technological changes, as well as career and professional opportunities. Since the student is at the center of learning, he or she becomes involved in determining learning priorities and in establishing the boundaries for the learning process. For example, if the student wants to improve her conflict management skills (objective), so she can become more proficient in facilitating group processes (need) in the near future (anticipated), she will initiate action learning in that direction which may include interpersonal communication, resolution strategies, etc. (boundary). Much of the learning draws on personal experiences and real work situations and integrates these within a theoretical framework of concepts and approaches. Students are encouraged to use their office desk as a laboratory where they are engaged in applying concepts to practice.

VALUE-ADDED

CBAL assumes that knowledge is acquired and skills are developed through action learning. As such, the emphasis is on adding value to the students' capacity to act through anticipating changes in their task environments, adapting to these changes through the development of new behavioral skills, reflecting on the outcomes of this adaptation through insights and cause/effect analysis, and leveraging the new learning to create high value for themselves, their organizations, and their customers.

The value that is added through action learning is then reflected practically through the realization of important abilities and skills that are essential for effective management, and cognitively through internalizing methodologies and knowledge necessary for reasoning and evaluation of the work environment. Thus, CBAL provides students with a unique opportunity to apply their knowledge and to conceptualize new frames of reference, replicate managerial experiences in individualized, structured learning environments, and to utilize real-life events in learning situations.

---

[8] This section is adapted from Belasen, A., "Competencies and Learning in Management Education-- FORUM/East Case Example," *FORUM Chronicle*, Spring, 1995, pp. 71-81.

OUTCOME ORIENTED

The focus of CBAL is on the needs, expectations, and objectives of students. It is an approach with a built-in bias toward an outside-in perspective. The structure of the program, its strategy, goals and processes as well as rewards for faculty are driven directly by the values of the "end users"—those who are affected by the learning process. A CBAL creates a commitment structure in which the educational system becomes more responsive to the needs of individuals adapting to the changing needs of their work environment. It runs counter to the traditional, control structure approach in which predetermined disciplines and functions both constrain and define the boundary of learning. As such, CBAL is anchored in meeting and/or exceeding students' needs, values, and expectations.

PROGNOSIS

Possessing a cognitive map of the competencies required for joint performance enables learners to quickly translate theories into applications, conceptual constructs into pragmatic approaches, and model managerial situations in a familiar and meaningful way. Thus, CBAL helps adult learners achieve what traditional methods of teaching have failed to accomplish—to deliver instructional modules and learning units that are both critical and relevant. The stimulation comes from the instructor and learning activities, but also from the practical knowledge and observations as well as the cognitive processes (i.e., critical thinking, reasoning) of the learners. CBAL is thus a method that is enriching, engaging, rewarding, and value-adding for the adult learner.

Within this context, the role of the instructor is to become a facilitator in helping the student move back and forth from a normative or mental mapping and abstraction to practical, concrete, or applied environment. The instructor must be able to assess the current skills and abilities of students, familiarize them with important concepts and methods of analysis, help them apply knowledge gained in examining parallel issues, move them through action learning to practice new ways of thinking and adjusting new behaviors. The idea is to facilitate their learning by doing or applying the new knowledge and skills effectively.

Using the above as a baseline for a new approach to teaching, instructors will be able to optimize the balance between cognitive and applied learning, respond to the psycho-sociological needs of adult learners for relevance and pragmatism, and reduce anxiety by increasing validation. This approach also helps expand a student's internal locus of control—the student ultimately identifies his/her needs and engages in any adaptive learning process which adds value and maximizes the outcome of learning. The instructor is more involved at the beginning of the process, particularly in the transference of knowledge. As the student's control over the learning becomes crucial, the instructor gradually reduces his/her involvement. The instructor becomes a facilitator who guides the learning environment by utilizing real-life events and replications of managerial situations.

INSTRUCTIONAL DESIGN -- SPECIAL APPLICATION

FORUM, a management development degree program at SUNY-Empire State College, employs CBAL which draws on the Competing Values Framework of leadership. The program, essentially a competency-based management concentration, consists of three sequential key components: pre-assessment, 8 x 3 core competencies, and post-assessment. Credit by evaluation (CBEs) can be generated at the core component. See Figure 2.

Figure 2: The Sequence of the Competency-Based Management Concentration

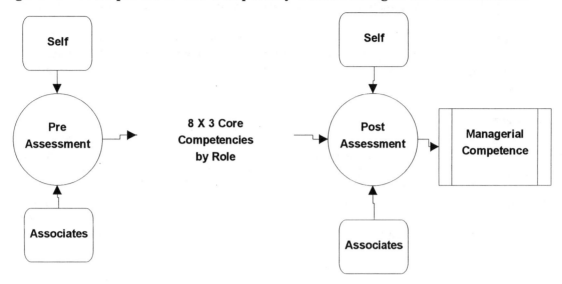

The pre-assessment, core competencies, and post assessment together constitute the essence of the study for a total of 13 credits. The rest of the credits typically come from "complementary" courses such as quantitative (e.g., math, statistics), socio-behavioral (e.g., organizational behavior), performance (e.g., operations management), etc. The pre-assessment and/or core competencies can also be taken as stand-alone courses to satisfy the requirements for a degree. However, students are advised to complete the entire sequence to legitimize the competency-based management as their major area of study.

PRE-ASSESSMENT

The underlying assumption of this learning contract is that via the process of self-assessment, students identify managerial values and attitudes, determine their capabilities and needs, and guide themselves through a process of self-directed learning which ultimately should lead to self-improvement. The purpose of this learning contract, therefore, is to learn a method for self-assessing students' management related knowledge and abilities, diagnose strengths and weaknesses, and formulate plans for skill development. Students coming into the competency program complete assessment instruments and engage in some guided activities. The assessments include input from self and associates which results in a composite profile highlighting the students' managerial strengths and weaknesses within the Competing Values Framework of leadership.[9]

8 X 3 COMPETENCIES BY ROLE

Eight learning contracts (independent, guided learning activities) paralleling the eight leadership roles comprise the core of the competency management concentration. Each role has 3 interrelated competencies and together, all 24 (8 X 3) define the core content of the concentration. The objectives of these learning contracts are:

- To appreciate both the values and the weaknesses associated with the particular role.

---

[9] The instrument used to elicit input from others/associates is included at the end of this article. For their own self-assessment profiles, students use the competing values instruments in this **Instructional Guide** (the 36-item Competing Values Management Practices Survey and the 117-item Competing Values Self Assessment: Managerial Skills Survey) and in the software.

- To acquire and use the competencies associated with the particular role.
- To integrate dynamically the competencies associated with the particular role in managerial situations.

Each learning contract is a series of short assignments involving elements of the competency approach: learning, analysis, practice, and application as discussed above. The assessment instruments help identify areas of weakness and strength in students' abilities and skills.

POST-ASSESSMENT

This is the capstone component of the competency-based management concentration. Essentially, students who participate in the concentration are expected to replicate the same procedure suggested in the pre-assessment, except here, the intention is to verify whether the gap between the initial profile and the desired one has been narrowed, or whether the desired goal or target-profile has been attained. Students will also engage in learning and applying a series of strategies aimed at helping them sustain the results of their self-improvement effort and achieve higher levels of competence.

IMPLICATIONS

Instructors can use examples of content applications that relate to learner's work experiences or career goals. They should encourage students to illustrate course points with relevant experiences from work. This, however, may need to be balanced against expanding breadth of learning to other environments. The approach of the text to assess competencies can be used as an important step in validating the learning which managers have gained through the business environment. Research on learning has shown that learning is improved when the learner is actively engaged in the study activity and when content mastery is important to the learner. Hence, assignments will be most successful when built on the experiences of the students.

It should also be noted that assignments relating the manager-students' work experiences to the course content are a wonderful window into organizational life for instructors. This, of course, is no small benefit.

Using the competing values framework as the theoretical basis for learning, instructors of adult learners have a well defined domain that is normatively exhaustive and practically rooted in the criteria of organizational effectiveness. The framework makes learning stimulating, critical, and relevant. Moreover, learning becomes continuous and self-directed. The framework reinforces the need for a built-in learning process that allows one to develop on-line skills and abilities. At the instructional/pedagogical level, the use of the CBAL leads to ownership of the skills and internalization of the knowledge essential for self-learning and self-improvement. At the institutional level, the use of CBAL is expected to lead to more innovative approaches to management education that are both value-added and outcome oriented.

REFERENCES

Association of American Colleges. *The Challenge of Connecting Learning*. Liberal Learning and the Arts and Sciences Major, *Vol. I*. Washington, D. C.: Association of American Colleges. 1991.

Cervero, R. M. *Effective Continuing Education for Professionals*. San Francisco: Jossey-Bass. 1988.

Freire, P. *Education for Critical Consciousness*. New York: Continuum. 1992.

Schon, D. A. *Educating the Reflective Practitioner: Toward a new design for teaching and learning in the professions*. San Francisco: Jossey-Bass. 1987.

INSTRUCTIONS FOR COMPLETING THE

COMPETING VALUES LEADERSHIP INSTRUMENT
Assessment by Others[10]

The first step is to decide on the individuals from whom you would like to have feedback regarding your leadership profile. These individuals may be bosses, peers, or those who work for you in your organization. Make as many copies of the instrument (page 68) as is necessary. Assure the individuals you ask that you want their honest responses, and that you will be combining the responses of a number of people.

Once you have their returned responses in hand, use the computational worksheet (page 69) as a basis for computing a number score for each of the eight roles. The number for each role should be between 1 and 7. Compute each response and then average all of the responses for each role. Once you have the number for each role, you are ready to chart your profile (page 70).

On the profile, consider the small inner circle to carry a value of one, and count out from there, along the lines on each role. Place a small "x" on the role-line, at the nearest point that matches the number you wish to graph. Simply connect the "x" marks and you have a visual profile of responses from others.

This profile may be very useful as you compare it with your own self-assessment responses to the **Competing Values Management Practices Survey** instrument in the software, also found on page 87 of this **Instructional Guide**.

It is the case, of course, that few people see themselves as others see them. However, if there seems to be a significant discrepancy between your view of yourself and the views of others towards you, then you might find this to be a rich area of exploration and discovery.

---

[10] In Robert E. Quinn, *Beyond Rational Management: Mastering the paradoxes and competing demands of high performance.* San Francisco: Jossey-Bass, 1988. pp. 174-176.

COMPETING VALUES LEADERSHIP INSTRUMENT
Assessment by Others

Listed below are some statements that describe managerial behaviors. You are asked to respond to this instrument, giving your best judgment of the behaviors of _____ (name of the person who gave it to you to complete). Indicate how often this manager engages in the behaviors, using the scale below to respond to each statement. Please place a number from 1 to 7 in the space beside each question.

Very infrequently   1   2   3   4   5   6   7   Very frequently

In doing the job, this manager:
_____ 1. Comes up with inventive ideas
_____ 2. Protects continuity in day-to-day operations
_____ 3. Exerts upward influence in the organization
_____ 4. Carefully reviews detailed reports

_____ 5. Maintains a "results" orientation in the unit
_____ 6. Facilitates consensus building in the work unit
_____ 7. Defines areas of responsibility for subordinates
_____ 8. Listens to the personal problems of subordinates

_____ 9. Minimizes disruption to the work flow
_____ 10. Experiments with new concepts and procedures
_____ 11. Encourages participative decision-making in the group
_____ 12. Makes sure everyone knows where the unit is going

_____ 13. Influences decisions made at higher levels
_____ 14. Compares records, reports, and so on to detect discrepancies
_____ 15. Sees that the unit delivers on stated goals
_____ 16. Shows empathy and concern in dealing with subordinates

_____ 17. Works with technical information
_____ 18. Gets access to people at higher levels
_____ 19. Sets clear objectives in the work unit
_____ 20. Treats each individual in a sensitive, caring way

_____ 21. Keeps track of what goes on inside the unit
_____ 22. Does problem solving in creative, clever ways
_____ 23. Pushes the unit to meet objectives
_____ 24. Encourages subordinates to share ideas in the group

_____ 25. Searches for innovations and potential improvements
_____ 26. Clarifies priorities and direction
_____ 27. Persuasively sells new ideas to higher-ups
_____ 28. Brings a sense of order to the unit.

_____ 29. Shows concern for the needs of subordinates
_____ 30. Emphasizes the unit's achievement of stated purposes
_____ 31. Builds teamwork among group members
_____ 32. Analyzes written plans and schedules

COMPUTATIONAL WORKSHEET FOR ASSESSMENT BY OTHERS

The Facilitator

\# 6 ____
\# 11 ____
\# 24 ____
\# 31 ____

Total ____ / 4 = ____

The Mentor

\# 8 ____
\# 16 ____
\# 20 ____
\# 29 ____

Total ____ / 4 = ____

The Innovator

\# 1 ____
\# 10 ____
\# 22 ____
\# 25 ____

Total ____ / 4 = ____

The Broker

\# 3 ____
\# 13 ____
\# 18 ____
\# 27 ____

Total ____ / 4 = ____

The Producer

\# 5 ____
\# 15 ____
\# 23 ____
\# 30 ____

Total ____ / 4 = ____

The Director

\# 7 ____
\# 12 ____
\# 19 ____
\# 26 ____

Total ____ / 4 = ____

The Coordinator

\# 2 ____
\# 9 ____
\# 21 ____
\# 28 ____

Total ____ / 4 = ____

The Monitor

\# 4 ____
\# 14 ____
\# 17 ____
\# 32 ____

Total ____ / 4 = ____

ASSESSMENT BY OTHERS: COMPOSITE PROFILE

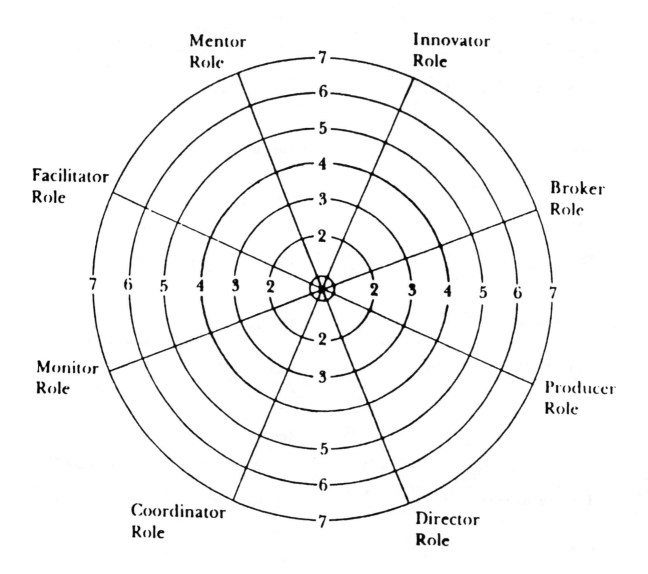

| **Chapter 1** | **THE EVOLUTION OF MANAGEMENT MODELS** |

Chapter 1 begins the text with two very important tasks. First, it traces the historical development of management theory and details the emergence of the Competing Values Framework. As such the Competing Values Framework, and its eight key managerial roles, are integrated into an historical-theoretical context. The second task is that the chapter explains the ALAPA learning model. This learning model is further discussed in the **Instructional Guide**.

The Competing Values Framework acknowledges the value of the previous management models which have emerged in this century. While affirming that rich heritage, the framework also introduces the concept of paradox as a fundamental context in which organizations and individuals operate and thrive.

While the idea of paradox may be new to some, it is familiar to those acquainted with Eastern thought. The co-existing of opposites is considered basic to reality, and in fact they serve to define one another and to facilitate each other's existence and distinctness. It has been argued that the advancement of the metaphysical notion of paradox has been difficult in Western culture due to the dichotomous structure of the language structure. Western languages tend to be built around a framework of subjects and predicates, nouns and verbs, actors, actions, and the acted upon. Such language structure implicitly espouses a separated view of reality characterized by an "either-or" orientation. In contrast, many Eastern languages are noted for their more integrated view of reality.

Paradox, however, is more than a passing philosophical interest. Reflection affirms that it makes a good deal of common sense. We recognize that the universe is at once characterized by order and chaos, strength and weakness, energy and entropy.

We encounter paradox in our everyday existence. People ordinarily experience opposite feelings and reactions to the same event. For example, we can approach the prospect of marriage with anticipation and trepidation; parenthood with elation and dread; death of a suffering loved one with grief and gratitude. Rather than ask ourselves why we are experiencing such different intense feelings, we are well advised to acknowledge paradox as fundamental to the very nature of existence, including human existence. Such recognition assists us in accommodating the competing demands of the managerial role in organizations.

Each of the competing values not only has legitimacy but is critical to the functioning of organizations. As we learn to live in a world of paradox, of competing values, we find ourselves taking the first steps toward mastery. The textbook provides students with essential and timely assistance to that end.

Topics included in this chapter are:

    1900-1925: The Rational Goal Model and the Internal Process Model
            Social Darwinism
            Scientific Management
            Taylor's four principles of management

1926-1950: The Emergence of the Human Relations Model
    Fayol's General Principles of Management
    Characteristics of Weberian Bureaucracy
    Human Relations Model
1951-1975: The Emergence of the Open Systems Model
    Contingency Theory
    Open Systems Model
1976-The Present: The Emergence of "Both/And" Assumptions
The Four Models in a Single Framework
    Competing Values Framework
    The Use of Opposing Models
Becoming A Manager: The Need for New Competencies
    Eight Roles
        Rational Goal Model: The Director and Producer Roles
        Internal Process Model: Monitor and Coordinator Roles
        Human Relations Model: The Facilitator and Mentor Roles
        Open Systems Model: Innovator and Broker Roles
    Identifying the Core Competencies
Organizing the Learning Process: ALAPA
Conclusions

| Chapter 1 | THE EVOLUTION OF MANAGEMENT MODELS |

Assignment: Course Preassessment
Activity Flow Sheet

PURPOSE: This activity allows students to develop a pre-course profile of their managerial strengths. **SPECIAL NOTE:** At the end of the course, students will have the opportunity to take this assessment again and develop a post-course profile to compare with this profile.

KEY TOPICS: The eight managerial roles and their key competencies.

TIME ESTIMATE: In class set up: 15 minutes; outside of class: 45 minutes; in class follow up discussion: 20 minutes.

FORMAT: Individual activity followed by large group discussion.

SPECIAL NEEDS: Students will need either the software package that accompanies this **Instructional Guide**, or a hard copy of the instruments and blank copies of the profile graphs. Complete software instructions as well as the hard copies of necessary sheets follow the process guide.

SEQUENCE: 1. Introduce the activity.

2. Remind them that there are no right or wrong answers to this instrument.

3. Explain that the resultant profile is for their use, and will be used again at the end of the course.

4. Conduct a large group discussion after they have finished with the instrument and have their profiles.

5. Summarize.

VARIATION: If students wish to compare their profiles with how others view them, the CVF Assessment by Others instrument is provided on pages 69-72 of the **Instructional Guide**. It is **NOT** in the software.

KEY POINTS:
1. People are not born managers; the competencies are learned skills.
2. Identifying competency weaknesses is important to the process of self-improvement.
3. One can self-improve even in areas of strength.

| Chapter 1 | THE EVOLUTION OF MANAGEMENT MODELS |

Assignment: Course Preassessment
Process Guide

PURPOSE: This activity allows students to develop a pre-course profile of their managerial strengths.

> **SPECIAL NOTE:** At the end of the course, students will have the opportunity to take this assessment again and develop a post-course profile to compare with this profile. This activity has the effect of generating excitement for the course, as students readily see the application of the course content to their behavior.

STEP 1. Introduce the activity by directing students to the assignment on page 26 of the text. Note that there are two instruments to complete: the 36-item Managerial Practices Survey (which measures responses to the 8 managerial roles) and the 117-item Managerial Skills assessment (which measures responses to the 24 competencies within all eight managerial roles). Give them either the software, or the hard copy of the instrument. Complete instructions for use of the software follow this process guide.

For using the hard copy of the questions, instruct students in the use of the computation sheet for the 36-item Management Practices Survey. Direct them to compute the mean for each role, and locate themselves on graphic Competing Values Skills Assessment Leadership Role Profile. Note that each role has a line which goes to the center of the circle. The slash in the line nearest the center has a value of 1; the outer edge has a value of 7. After students have placed their score on each role line, they can connect the marks to gain a graphic profile. Also note that their individual scores from the Managerial Practices Survey can be used to fill in the role bar graphs.

A computation sheet is also provided for the 117-item Self-Assessment: Managerial Skills instrument. The profile is graphed in the same way as for the Leadership Role Profile.

STEP 2. Remind them that there are no right or wrong answers to this instrument. Although they may have little or no experience in managerial positions, instruct them to think about group experiences where they might have used these skills, or to anticipate as clearly as possible how they would respond.

STEP 3. Explain that the resultant profile is for their use, and will be used again at the end of the course.

STEP 4. Conduct a large group discussion after they have finished with the instrument and have their profile. Ask for volunteers to share what surprised them about the instrument and about their profile. What did they learn form this experience?

A key component of personal growth and development is the ability to share the results of an assessment with others, to discuss the results and to try to understand the results within a context. Students should be encouraged to think about what the results mean for them within an organizational context.

STEP 5. Summarize their major points, and the key points on the activity flow sheet.

COMPETING VALUES SKILLS SURVEY:
A Suggested Exercise to Accompany the Text

Robert E. Quinn and Daniel R. Denison

One of the unique features of this textbook is the **Competing Values Skills Survey**, a software system designed to assess students' managerial skills with respect to the competing values model. At the end of chapter 1, the book mentions that the instructor may have students complete this assessment. Again, in the last chapter of the text, the book mentions that the instructor may want students to complete the assessment again.

The software has two distinct parts; Part One consists of 36 items that assess student's ability to perform each of the eight managerial roles outlined by the model; and Part Two consists of 117 items that assess student's abilities with respect to three skills associated with each of the eight roles, for a total of 24 skills in all. Indexes are created for each of the roles and skills and the results are then plotted as a profile on the competing values model.

The software requires Windows 3.1. The program can also be set up on a computer network or student computer lab to allow for easier access. It provides students with a quick diagnosis of their managerial abilities as they begin your class.

One copy of the software accompanies the **Instructional Guide**, as does a hard copy of the instruments.[1] It is designed for the use of students who have purchased the textbook and are using it in your class. Permission is granted to instructors to make copies or other arrangements so that CVSS is available to each student. Any other use of the CVSS software is a violation of copyright. If the instructor chooses to use the CVSS it is the responsibility of the instructor to determine how the software will be made available.

---

[1] For directions hand computation of the instruments and graphing the profiles, see the instructions for the computing the CVF *Assessment by Others*, found on page 69 of the **Instructional Guide**. Also note that computational sheets and blank profiles for the CVSS instruments are found, along with the isntruments, on pages 87-95 of the **Instructional Guide**.

FOR THE INSTRUCTOR: How To Use the Software for Teaching

We've found that the most effective way to use the software is to diagnose students' abilities **as they begin the class**. In the first few classes, when the competing values model is initially presented, students can be instructed to answer the questions in the package and to obtain a skill and role profile about themselves. This accomplishes three key objectives in the course:

It Personalizes the Model. When a student receives personalized data, the model hits home. An abstract presentation of a framework suddenly becomes a statement about their abilities. The data also serve as a very personal statement of **what the book is about**, and force each student to begin building a leadership agenda that they want to pursue in the course. This objective can be effectively underscored by requiring a brief paper in which students comment on their data and whether or not it is consistent with their past experience.

It Provides Diagnostic Data. Once a student has the data, certain parts of the textbook and the course become highly salient. Suppose I discover that I'm a terrible broker because I can't build an influence network, or make good presentations. The broker chapter and the skills described within it suddenly become very important to my future as a manager. In contrast, supposed that I find out that I'm a great monitor: I'm an immediate "expert" in this area and view it as a strength that I can rely upon. In our experience, recognizing either strengths or weaknesses increases motivation to understand and build upon the content of the course.

The Data Can Be Used as a Baseline. The data can be used as a diagnostic baseline and compared to data collected later in the course. One simple way is to have students answer the role and skill items a second time at the end of the course to measure their progress.

It should be noted that this current release of the software does **not** support aggregation of the data from multiple respondents.

CVSS SOFTWARE INSTRUCTIONS

by Luke Hohmann[2]

GENERAL INFORMATION	79
NAVIGATING THROUGH CVSS	80
CREATING A NEW SURVEY	81
SAVING YOUR WORK	83
SAVING YOUR WORK TO A DIFFERENT FILE	84
USING A SAVED SURVEY	85
GRAPHING AND PRINTING YOUR RESULTS	86

NOTE: A hard copy of the instruments and blank profile sheets are found on pages 87-95 of this *Instructional Guide*.

GENERAL INFORMATION

Welcome to the Competing Values Skills Survey!

CVSS is a companion software system to *Becoming a Master Manager: A Competency Framework*, a textbook based on the Competing Values model, written by Robert Quinn, Sue Faerman, Michael Thompson, and Michael McGrath.

CVSS evaluates
1. your managerial skills with respect to the eight roles defined by the Competing Values model
2. skill sets essential to each of these managerial roles

CVSS evaluates managerial skills through the use of two question sets that measure specific personality traits. The first set of questions relates to the managerial roles defined in the Competing Values model, while the second set of questions measure specific skills essential to these roles.

---

[2] Independent consultant and author of forthcoming book: *Journey of the Software Professional: The sociology of software development.* Prentice-Hall.

The questions presented in the two sets measure different personality traits. Take enough time to completely understand the question before answering it.

If you do not have enough time to finish all the questions in one sitting, answer as many as you can and then write the results to your data file. The next time you use CVSS you can then read in the previous information and continue to answer questions until you have finished all the questions in the survey.

Navigating through CVSS

CVSS uses standard Windows navigation keys for most operations. In addition, a mouse can used to maneuver through CVSS.

To select an item from the menu using the keyboard, press and release the <ALT> key. This will allow you to use the arrow keys to maneuver through the menu. To get to the survey screen, press the <ESC> button.

To select a specific menu item from a menu, you may press the key that corresponds to the underlined letter in the menu item. For example, to select the "Exit" item from the File menu, press <ALT+F> then press <X>.

In addition to the "hot keys" for the menu, some menu items have a "short-cut" key. Items with a short-cut key will have the key displayed in the menu. Here are the available short-cut keys.

<CTRL+N>	New Survey
<CTRL+O>	Open a saved survey
<CTRL+S>	Save the current survey
<CTRL+P>	Print the graphs for the current survey
<CTRL+X>	Exit CVSS
<F1>	Help
<ALT+F4>	Exit CVSS

To select a response to a survey question on the short form, use the mouse to click on one of the responses or press the number key corresponding to the response you wish to select.

To move to another question, use the mouse to click one of the arrow buttons or press <Page Up> to move to the previous question, or <Page Down> to move the next question.

Creating a New Survey

1. Press <CTRL+N> or use the mouse to select New Survey from the File menu.

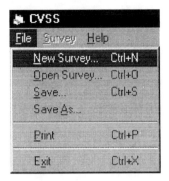

2. You will be prompted for your name.

Note: If you do not enter a name, CVSS will not let you continue the new survey.

3. A new form will be displayed for you to enter answers. Click on an option from 1 - 7 and then click on the right arrow to move to the next question. You may change previous answers by clicking the left arrow button to move back.

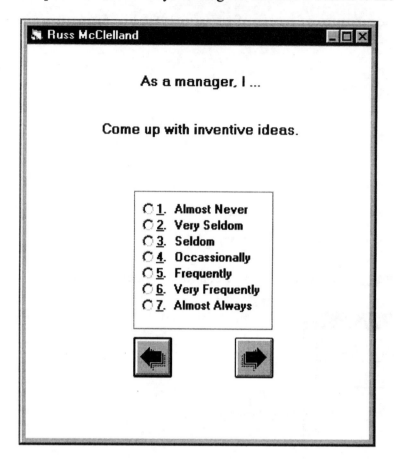

Saving Your Work

Press <CTRL+S> or use the mouse to select Save from the File menu.

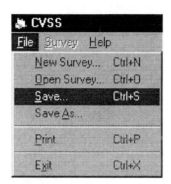

1. If this is a new survey, you will be prompted to enter a file name.

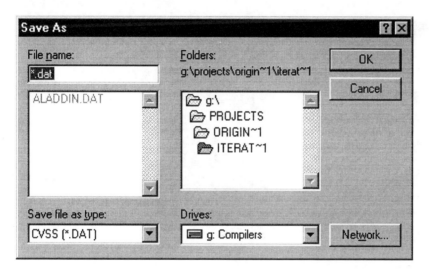

2. The survey will be saved into this file until you save it under a different name.

Saving Your Work to a Different File

1. Use the mouse to select Save As from the File menu.

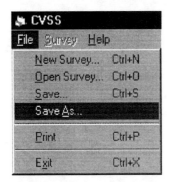

2. You will be prompted to enter a file name for the survey.

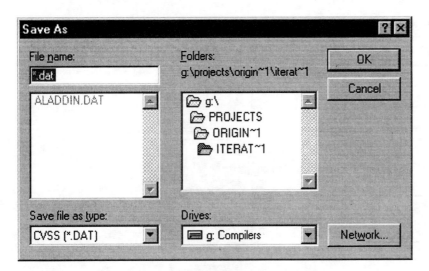

3. Use the mouse to select OK.

Using a Saved Survey

1. Press <CTRL+O> or use the mouse to select Open Survey from the File menu.

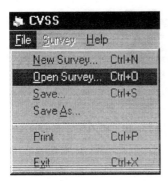

2. You will be prompted to enter the name of a survey file.

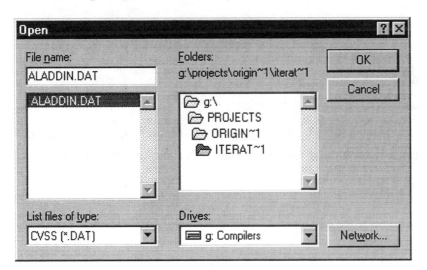

3. After selecting the file to use, use the mouse to click OK.

Graphing and Printing Your Results

To graph your results, use the mouse to click on either

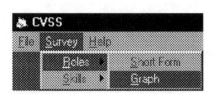 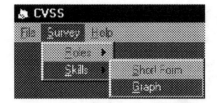

To print your results, press <CTRL+P> or use the mouse to click on

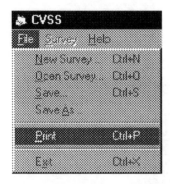

Note: To graph an assessment, you must have completed at least half of all questions in the assessment. Additionally, you must answer at least half the questions in each topic of the assessment.

NOTE: IF YOU ENCOUNTER TECHNICAL PROBLEMS THAT YOU CANNOT RESOLVE, PLEASE CALL THE JOHN WILEY & SONS COLLEGE SOFTWARE HELPLINE AT 212-850-6753.

COMPETING VALUES MANAGEMENT PRACTICES SURVEY

Listed below are some statements that describe managerial practices. Indicate how often you engage in the behaviors, using the scale below to respond to each statement. Please place a number from 1 to 7 in the space beside each question.

Almost never 1 2 3 4 5 6 7 Almost always

As a manager, how often would you

_____ 1. Come up with inventive ideas.
_____ 2. Exert upward influence in the organization.
_____ 3. Clarify the need to achieve unit goals.
_____ 4. Continually clarify the unit's purpose.
_____ 5. Search for innovations and potential improvements.
_____ 6. Make the unit's role very clear.

_____ 7. Maintain tight logistical control.
_____ 8. Keep track of what goes on inside the unit.
_____ 9. Develop consensual resolution of openly expressed differences.
_____ 10. Listen to the personal problems of subordinates.
_____ 11. Maintain a highly coordinated, well organized unit.
_____ 12. Hold open discussion of conflicting opinions in groups.

_____ 13. Push the unit to meet objectives.
_____ 14. Surface key differences among group members, then work participatively to resolve them.
_____ 15. Monitor compliance with the rules.
_____ 16. Treat each individual in a sensitive, caring way.
_____ 17. Experiment with new concepts and procedures.
_____ 18. Show empathy and concern in dealing with subordinates.

_____ 19. Seek to improve the workgroup's technical capacity.
_____ 20. Get access to people at higher levels.
_____ 21. Encourage participative decision making in the group.
_____ 22. Compare records, reports, and so on to detect discrepancies.
_____ 23. Solve scheduling problems in the unit.
_____ 24. Get the unit to meet expected goals.

_____ 25. Do problem solving in creative, clear ways.
_____ 26. Anticipate workflow problems, avoid crisis.
_____ 27. Check for errors and mistakes.
_____ 28. Persuasively sell new ideas to higher ups.
_____ 29. See that the unit delivers on stated goals.
_____ 30. Facilitate consensus building in the work unit.

_____ 31. Clarify the unit's priorities and direction.
_____ 32. Show concern for the needs of subordinates.
_____ 33. Maintain a "results" orientation in the unit.
_____ 34. Influence decisions made at higher levels.
_____ 35. Regularly clarify the objectives of the unit.
_____ 36. Bring a sense of order and coordination into the unit.

COMPUTATIONAL WORKSHEET FOR SELF-ASSESSMENT

The Facilitator

\# 9 ____
\# 12 ____
\# 14 ____
\# 21 ____
\# 30 ____

Total ____ / 5 = ____

The Mentor

\# 10 ____
\# 16 ____
\# 18 ____
\# 32 ____

Total ____ / 4 = ____

The Innovator

\# 1 ____
\# 5 ____
\# 17 ____
\# 25 ____

Total ____ / 4 = ____

The Broker

\# 2 ____
\# 20 ____
\# 28 ____
\# 34 ____

Total ____ / 4 = ____

The Producer

\# 3 ____(R)
\# 13 ____
\# 19 ____
\# 29 ____
\# 33 ____

Total ____ / 5 = ____

The Director

\# 4 ____
\# 6 ____
\# 24 ____
\# 31 ____
\# 35 ____

Total ____ / 5 = ____

The Coordinator

\# 7 ____
\# 11 ____
\# 23 ____
\# 26 ____
\# 36 ____

Total ____ / 5 = ____

The Monitor

\# 8 ____
\# 15 ____
\# 22 ____
\# 27 ____

Total ____ / 4 = ____

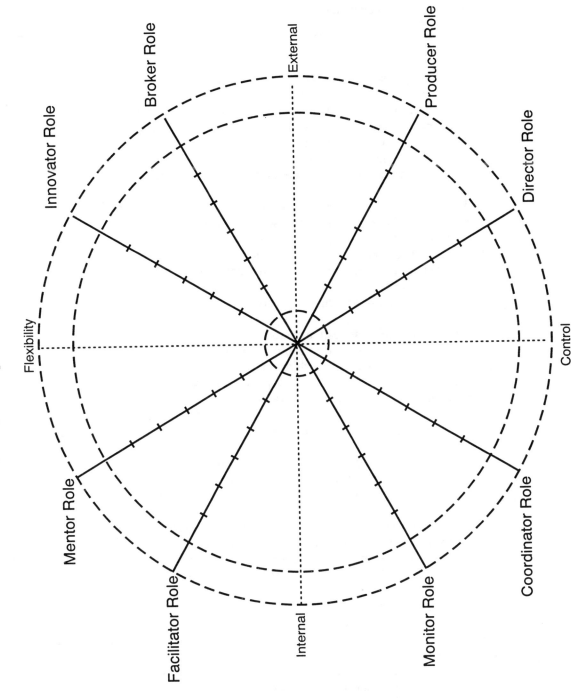

COMPETING VALUES SELF ASSESSMENT: MANAGERIAL SKILLS

Listed below are some statements that describe managerial skills that are essential to each of the eight managerial roles. Indicate your feelings by using the scale below. Please place a number from 1 to 7 in the space beside each question.

Strongly Disagree 1 2 3 4 5 6 7 Strongly Agree

_____ 1. I continually seek feedback on my performance.
_____ 2. I am an intensely motivated person.
_____ 3. I know how to use the basic planning tools in managing projects.
_____ 4. I know how to gather data from potential, as well as current, customers.
_____ 5. I have a clear image of who I am.
_____ 6. I am skilled in team building techniques.
_____ 7. My own personal coping strategies help me to adapt to change.

_____ 8. I know how to build personal power through the involvement of others.
_____ 9. When I have more than one goal, I set clear priorities.
_____ 10. I am skilled at motivating other people.
_____ 11. In organizing, I understand the division of labor principle.
_____ 12. I can diagnose process problems in an organizational unit.
_____ 13. In communicating, I am very sensitive to feelings.
_____ 14. I know when to use participative decision making.

_____ 15. I think of myself as a creative person.
_____ 16. In negotiating, I know how to explore win-win outcomes.
_____ 17. I know how to give people both responsibility and authority.
_____ 18. I always try to begin my day with a personal planning session.
_____ 19. I can explain the concept of a cross-functional team.
_____ 20. I know how to monitor the degree of value provided to the customer.
_____ 21. I am able to coach others effectively.

_____ 22. I know how to create win-win situations in conflicts.
_____ 23. I can accurately assess the forces for and against change in a given situation.
_____ 24. When preparing an oral presentation, I consider the purpose, the audience, and available resources.
_____ 25. I know how to help members of a cross-functional team work together effectively.
_____ 26. I have a passionate commitment to the things I do.
_____ 27. I can divide components of a project so they can be measured in terms of time and cost.
_____ 28. I try to find out how my decisions affect others around me.

_____ 29. I have a clear set of values.
_____ 30. I can turn a collection of individuals into a team.
_____ 31. In dealing with changes that are imposed on the organization, I think about how employees will react to change.
_____ 32. I know how to employ formal authority in an effective way.
_____ 33. I always have a clear set of objectives.
_____ 34. I can create high performance expectations in others.
_____ 35. I know how to consider the organization's environment in creating an organizational design.

_____ 36. I understand the principles of process reengineering.
_____ 37. In conversations, I put people at ease.

_____ 38. I know how to employ participative decision making techniques.
_____ 39. I always try to look at old problems in new ways.
_____ 40. In negotiating, I know how to base the result on an objective standard.
_____ 41. I feel comfortable with the concept of delegation.
_____ 42. I always end the day with the feeling that I have accomplished at least one significant task.

_____ 43. I can design a self-managed work team.
_____ 44. I know how to construct a performance monitoring matrix.
_____ 45. I feel comfortable acting as an advisor to people.
_____ 46. I can manage tensions and get people to relax during a conflict.
_____ 47. I am able to deal effectively with forces of resistance when managing change.
_____ 48. I am an effective public speaker.
_____ 49. I can influence people through rational persuasion.

_____ 50. I am comfortable living with change.
_____ 51. I know how to turn a work group into a smooth functioning team.
_____ 52. I am very honest with myself.
_____ 53. I seek out divergent opinions on how my performance is seen by others.
_____ 54. I can produce a critical path diagram.
_____ 55. I love to feel challenged by the tasks I have to do.
_____ 56. I know how to redesign a job based on consideration of the task and the employee's needs.

_____ 57. Each day I have a well defined plan.
_____ 58. I often inspire people to do more than they are expected to do.
_____ 59. I can design a matrix organization.
_____ 60. I know how to find and eliminate unnecessary activities in a unit.
_____ 61. During a conversation, I am in touch with the other's reactions.
_____ 62. I know which situations are inappropriate for participative decision making.
_____ 63. I know the advantages and disadvantages of job enlargement.

_____ 64. In negotiating, I know how to effectively acknowledge the existence of a conflict.
_____ 65. Delegating work frees up time to do more important things.
_____ 66. I know how to best involve people in designing organizational changes.
_____ 67. I am able to call on different conflict management approaches, depending on the situation.
_____ 68. I am able to mentor people, and to help them grow and develop.
_____ 69. I know how to gain a profound knowledge of customer needs.
_____ 70. I can list the challenges that are faced by cross-functional teams.

_____ 71. I always do the most important parts of my job during the time of day when I perform the best.
_____ 72. I am skilled at delegation.
_____ 73. I know how to use reward to effectively influence others.
_____ 74. I adjust well to changing conditions.
_____ 75. I frequently encourage team members to take on different task and group maintenance roles in order to improve the team's effectiveness.
_____ 76. I recognize and work on my inconsistencies and hypocrisies.
_____ 77. I encourage people to give me negative, as well as positive, feedback on my performance.

_____ 78. I know how to do resource leveling for project management.

_____ 79. I am driven by a need for continuous improvement in what I do.
_____ 80. I know how to create a vision for my organization.
_____ 81. In negotiating, I know how to keep the discussion issue-oriented.
_____ 82. I like to explore new ideas.
_____ 83. I feel comfortable involving people in group decisions.
_____ 84. I am very sensitive to nonverbal messages in a conversation.

_____ 85. I am able to implement a process improvement plan.
_____ 86. I understand the advantages of organizing by divisional form.
_____ 87. I am skilled in getting the best out of people.
_____ 88. I always seek clear feedback about how I am doing.
_____ 89. I understand and know how to apply the principles of effective delegation.
_____ 90. In making an oral presentation, I know how to get people's attention.
_____ 91. I am skilled at facilitating organizational change.

_____ 92. I know how to keep a conflict situation moving towards a productive conclusion.
_____ 93. I am able to advise subordinates on important matters relating to their growth and development.
_____ 94. I know how to monitor trends that will help me anticipate what customers want.
_____ 95. I can list the principles of managing a cross-functional team.
_____ 96. I know how to manage stress.
_____ 97. I can implement the concept of job rotation.
_____ 98. I am an unusually hard worker.

_____ 99. I know how to determine the advantages and disadvantages of different organizational designs.
_____ 100. I have a systematic process for getting honest evaluations on my performance.
_____ 101. I work hard at being honest and sincere.
_____ 102. I know how to run a meeting in which everyone feels involved and influential in the decisions that are made.
_____ 103. I know how to use the organizational culture to help employees adapt to change.
_____ 104. I am able to influence others through persuasion.
_____ 105. I always establish a specific set of challenging goals.

_____ 106. I can get others to excel in their work.
_____ 107. I know how to locate the most crucial issues in a workflow problem.
_____ 108. I effectively use empathy and reflective listening.
_____ 109. I try to treat any new problem as an opportunity.
_____ 110. I am very relaxed when I have to speak to a group of people.
_____ 111. I often come up with useful innovations.
_____ 112. I regularly use stress management techniques.

_____ 113. I know how to analyze the dynamics of an on-going organizational change process.
_____ 114. I can design a job using the concept of job enrichment.
_____ 115. I can produce a Gantt chart.
_____ 116. I know how to stimulate conflict in a meeting in order to ensure that different points of view are heard.
_____ 117. I can specify the advantages of a cross-functional team.

Computational Worksheet for Self-Assessment

The Mentor

Developing Subordinates
- # 21 _____
- # 45 _____
- # 68 _____
- # 93 _____

Total _____ / 4 = _____

Communicating Effectively
- # 13 _____
- # 37 _____
- # 61 _____
- # 84 _____
- # 108 _____

Total _____ / 5 = _____

Understanding Self and Others
- # 5 _____
- # 29 _____
- # 52 _____
- # 76 _____
- # 101 _____

Total _____ / 5 = _____

The Facilitator

Managing Conflict
- # 22 _____
- # 46 _____
- # 67 _____
- # 92 _____
- # 116 _____

Total _____ / 5 = _____

Using Participative Decision Making
- # 14 _____
- # 38 _____
- # 62 _____
- # 83 _____
- # 102 _____

Total _____ / 5 = _____

Building Teams
- # 6 _____
- # 30 _____
- # 51 _____
- # 75 _____

Total _____ / 4 = _____

The Monitor

Monitoring Personal Performance Performance
- # 1 _____
- # 28 _____
- # 53 _____
- # 77 _____
- # 100 _____

Total _____ / 5 = _____

Managing Collective Performance
- # 12 _____
- # 36 _____
- # 60 _____
- # 85 _____
- # 107 _____

Total _____ / 5 = _____

Managing Organizational
- # 4 _____
- # 20 _____
- # 44 _____
- # 69 _____
- # 94 _____

Total _____ / 5 = _____

The Coordinator

Managing Projects
- # 3 _____
- # 27 _____
- # 54 _____
- # 78 _____
- # 115 _____

Total _____ / 5 = _____

Designing Work
- # 43 _____
- # 56 _____
- # 63 _____
- # 97 _____
- # 114 _____

Total _____ / 5 = _____

Managing Across Functions
- # 19 _____
- # 25 _____
- # 70 _____
- # 95 _____
- # 117 _____

Total _____ / 5 = _____

The Director

Delegating Effectively

- # 17 _____
- # 41 _____
- # 65 _____
- # 72 _____
- # 89 _____

Total _____ / 5= _____

Designing and Organizing

- # 11 _____
- # 35 _____
- # 59 _____
- # 86 _____
- # 99 _____

Total _____ / 5= _____

Visioning, Planning and Goal Setting

- #   9 _____
- # 33 _____
- # 57 _____
- # 80 _____
- # 88 _____
- # 105 _____

Total _____ / 6= _____

The Producer

Managing Time and Stress

- # 18 _____
- # 42 _____
- # 71 _____
- # 96 _____
- # 112 _____

Total _____ / 5= _____

Fostering a Productive Work Environment

- # 10 _____
- # 34 _____
- # 58 _____
- # 87 _____
- # 106 _____

Total _____ / 5= _____

Working Productively

- #   2 _____
- # 26 _____
- # 55 _____
- # 79 _____
- # 98 _____

Total _____ / 5= _____

The Broker

Presenting Ideas Effectively

- # 24 _____
- # 48 _____
- # 90 _____
- # 110 _____

Total _____ / 4= _____

Negotiating Agreement and Commitment

- # 16 _____
- # 40 _____
- # 64 _____
- # 81 _____

Total _____ / 4= _____

Building and Maintaining a Power Base

- #   8 _____
- # 32 _____
- # 49 _____
- # 73 _____
- # 104 _____

Total _____ / 5= _____

The Innovator

Creating Change

- # 23 _____
- # 47 _____
- # 66 _____
- # 91 _____
- # 113 _____

Total _____ / 5= _____

Thinking Creatively

- # 15 _____
- # 39 _____
- # 82 _____
- # 109 _____
- # 111 _____

Total _____ / 5= _____

Living with Change

- #   7 _____
- # 31 _____
- # 50 _____
- # 74 _____
- # 103 _____

Total _____ / 5= _____

The Competing Values Skills Assessment Skills Profile

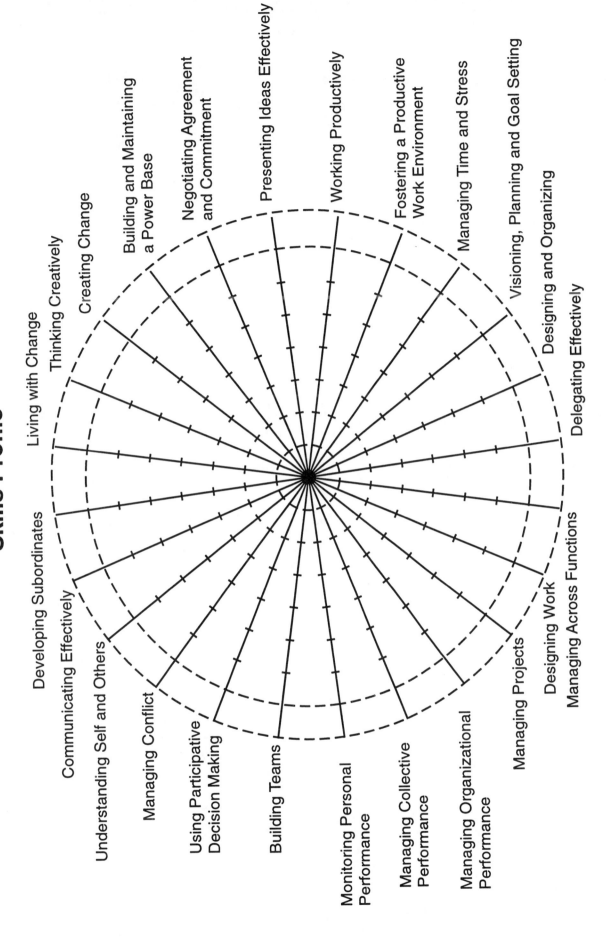

CHAPTER 2 — MENTOR ROLE

The Mentor Role is the first role in the Human Relations Model, and in many ways epitomizes the posture of the Human Relations School. Managers in the Mentor Role provide concern and support for subordinates, develop people and reward performance. In the words of one of the authors, "It is the concerned human role. Note that in Western society, caring and concern are seen as weak; good leaders are seen as powerful and in control. This is a mistake."

Of all the roles, the manager in the mentor role may most directly experience the tensions between the interests of the organization to control individuals, and the interests of individuals in being autonomous. Managers, as mentors, often find themselves in the middle of this tension.

Students tend to relate strongly to the mentor role competencies. The concepts involving self-understanding and communication skills are easily viewed as necessary life competencies, important to individuals regardless of chosen career. As such, these competencies are readily recognized as being immediately applicable to students' personal lives. Frequently, students find themselves enthusiastically subscribing to these competencies; they realize that many problems facing people and organizations alike are basically communication problems. Eagerly embracing these skills, they may believe that the world would be a better place if everyone practiced them. They may perceive how much happier they would be if all of their friends, loved ones, acquaintances, and professors used these skills. They may be quick to recognize where others need to improve these skills, and not so quick to realize their own need to improve.

It is not surprising, then, to find students--or anyone--believing that any problems that organizations have would be solved with the diligent use of the communication and self-understanding competencies associated with this role. And organizations often are quick to identify their problems as being based in communication. While not taking away from the importance of these skills, it may be necessary with some students to raise this issue explicitly, pointing out the need for the rest of the framework in order for organizations to function and function effectively.

While several paradoxes are apparent in the mentor role, one of the more compelling deals with communication skills: the balance between expressing ourselves clearly to others (as in feedback) and actively listening to them. The process is more interactive than it may appear to some. Providing feedback is taking the other person into account and responding to their reflections on what the speaker has said. Receiving feedback involves responsibility to ask for clarification and elaboration when needed and taking the risk of saying: "I'm not sure what you mean. . ."

On the same token, active and reflective listening involves more than being a tape player with the record button pushed, and more than just repeating back to assure surface understanding. Real listening also involves a measure of vulnerability, of feeling with the other person, of letting oneself be affected by the other. Paradoxically, there is strength in vulnerability.

The competencies in the Mentor Role: The three competencies of this role and their corresponding topics in the learning activities are:

Competency 1: Understanding Self and Others
Topics: Values and assumptions
                        Theory X and Theory Y
                Values and understanding yourself

                    Johari Window
                    Values and understanding others
                    Rules for practicing empathy

Competency 2: Communicating Effectively
Topics: A Basic model of interpersonal communication
                    Feedback and noise
                Problems in interpersonal communication
                    Rules for effective communication
                Reflective listening

Competency 3: Developing Employees
Topics: Uses and problems of performance appraisal
                    Two-step process to performance evaluation
                    Guidelines for giving and receiving feedback

Conceptually, these are not the only competencies in this role. Other competencies have been identified as:
                Showing sensitivity and concern
                Counseling and coaching
                Interviewing and active listening
                Career planning and development of subordinates
                Giving performance feedback in effective ways
                Working with problem employees
                Using rewards and incentives

The Mentor Role and current issues: The Mentor Role bears a direct relationship to the issue of managing a culturally diverse work force. The competencies and skills defined by the Mentor Role, including communication and feedback, prepare managers to meet the challenges of the changing composition of the work force. It also bears an obvious relationship to ethics in the work force. Furthermore, the skills acquired in the Mentor Role may be helpful as managers are called upon to deal with international markets and concerns.

Some questions to consider in this chapter are:

      1. While the value of the competencies involved in the Mentor Role are widely acclaimed, what would be the consequences if this role were taken too far? What would it be like, for the organization and for employees, if the managers carried the Mentor Role to extreme?
      2. What types of organizational designs, are more conducive to the qualities in the Mentor Role? Which are less?
      3. Under what circumstances is an emphasis on the Mentor Role more appropriate, and under what circumstances is it less appropriate?
      4. It has been argued that the Mentor Role is more important for managers in volunteer organizations, which lack a financial incentive and depend on people to want to be involved, than for managers in the work place. Do you think this is accurate?

A note from one of the authors: The single most valuable course he ever took was an undergraduate course in reflective listening. He spent the entire semester on this one skill. It has since proved to be his most used and most effective interpersonal skill.

CHAPTER 2	MENTOR ROLE
COMPETENCY 1	UNDERSTANDING SELF AND OTHERS

Assessment: Managerial Orientation Measure
Activity Flow Sheet

PURPOSE: Measure students' attitudes toward managing others, and begin to increase awareness of how attitudes influence employee behavior at work. Scoring will indicate whether students have a general Theory X orientation, or an orientation towards Theory Y.

KEY TOPICS: Theory X and theory Y.

TIME ESTIMATE: 10 minutes for response and scoring; 10-15 for discussion.

FORMAT: Individual activity followed by large group discussion.

SPECIAL NEEDS: None in addition to blackboard to discuss scores.

SEQUENCE:
1. Assign students to complete the scale before reading the learning activity.

2. Have them score their answers and be prepared to report their score for the class discussion.

3. Conduct large group discussion of implications.

4. Summarize.

VARIATION: Steps 1 and 2 can be completed as a homework assignment.

KEY POINTS:
1. Attitudes towards employees and work affect the interaction between manager and employees.

2. Expectations and assumptions influence behavior and outcomes.

3. Awareness of one's own attitudes about values and openness to learning about the values of others are important.

CHAPTER 2	MENTOR ROLE
COMPETENCY 1	UNDERSTANDING SELF AND OTHERS

Assessment: Managerial Orientation Scale
Process Guide

PURPOSE: A first step towards understanding ourselves and others is to determine what assumptions we have about people. This activity helps students to measure their attitudes toward managing others, and to increase their awareness of how attitudes influence employee behavior at work. Scoring will indicate whether students have a general Theory X orientation, or an orientation towards Theory Y.

STEP 1. Assign students to complete the scale at home before reading the learning activity. (If you wish to do this in class, allow approximately 10 minutes). Brief instructions for the completion of this activity are in the text. If you wish to elaborate, you could indicate the following:

> The Managerial Orientation Scale (MOS) measures one's attitude toward management and employee performance. In this activity you will be measuring whether you think more like a "Theory X" or a "Theory Y" manager. Descriptions of Theory X and Theory Y are explained in the learning activity. Before reading that section of the assignment, fill out the MOS by noting the extent to which you agree - or disagree - with each of the items in the scale, on pp. 30-31 of the text.

STEP 2. Instruct them to score their answers and be prepared to report their score for the class discussion. Instructions for scoring at on p. 31 of the text.

STEP 3. Conduct a large group discussion of the activity and its implications. Record comments and scores on the blackboard. Suggestions of questions include:

> A. How many of you scored more like a Theory X manager? Theory Y?
>
> B. How would either of these orientations affect what a manager tends to perceive in terms of employee work behavior?
>
> C. How would either of the orientations affect the manager's behavior? Consider this in terms of "self-fulfilling prophecy"; that is, people often behave according to our expectations of them.
>
> D. If you were employed and had a choice to be supervised by a Theory X-oriented manager or by a Theory Y-oriented manager, which would you choose to be supervised by and why?

E. Question for students with a Theory Y orientation: can you think of situations where a Theory X approach might be more appropriate than a Theory Y? (Reverse the question and pose to Theory X students.) Can you think of situations where the reliance on either orientation to the exclusion of other considerations might be dysfunctional?

F. What organizational designs might be more conducive to the development of the Theory X orientation in its managers? Which types of structures might be less friendly to the display of a Theory X oriented attitudes? (Reverse the question for Theory Y.)

G. If you had the opportunity to develop a theory of your own, what would it be?

STEP 4. Summarize. The following is an interpretation of MOS scores:

Theory X is "shorthand" for the traditional managerial viewpoint (or set of attitudes) emphasizing control and close supervision. The assumption is that workers are lazy and must be told what to do. In fact, the assumption is that workers want to be told because they are too lazy to think for themselves, and must be coerced to work. A "soft" version of Theory X is the notion that people can be gently "prodded" to work. Low MOS scores are linked to Theory X beliefs.

Theory Y refers to a set of assumptions that different from Theory X and at times are opposite of Theory X. Theory Y assumes that workers want (or can easily learn to want) greater responsibility for and control over their own job activities. Workers are assumed to be challenged by rewards. According to Theory Y, people are generally capable to innovation and making real contributions to the organization. High MOS scores are related to Theory Y attitudes.

Notice how Theory X and Theory Y are contradictory, and yet how both are useful.

CHAPTER 2	MENTOR ROLE
COMPETENCY 1	UNDERSTANDING SELF AND OTHERS

Analysis Activity: The Sherwood Holmes Case
Activity Flow Sheet

PURPOSE: Increase awareness of how prejudices, assumptions, and self-concepts influence perceptions and decisions.

KEY TOPICS: Understanding ourselves in order to understand our perceptions.

TIME ESTIMATE: About 60-70 minutes.

FORMAT: Individual, small group work, and large group discussion.

SPECIAL NEEDS: Inference sheet (follows the process guide).

SEQUENCE:
1. Introduce the activity.
2. Give examples of observation/ knowledge/ inference.
3. Have students individually complete the Inference Sheet.
4. Divide students into 4-5 person groups.
5. Discuss as a large group.
6. Summarize.

VARIATIONS:
1. Step 3 may be completed as homework. Then for the next class, after a few initial comments, the process can be completed using steps 4-6.
2. At step 3 students can complete the Inference Sheet in groups of two.
3. At step 4 the small groups can be instructed to produce a composite profile of the CEO.

KEY POINTS:
1. Inference, observation, and knowledge all have value.
2. The key is to be aware of which is which.
3. Our inferences of others usually reveal more about ourselves than about those we are observing.
4. Biases and preconceptions interfere with understanding and communication.

CHAPTER 2	MENTOR ROLE
COMPETENCY 1	UNDERSTANDING SELF AND OTHERS

Analysis Activity: The Sherwood Holmes Case
Process Guide

PURPOSE: The purpose of this activity is to increase students' awareness of how prejudices, assumptions, and self-concepts influence perceptions and decisions. In this analysis, students have the opportunity to distinguish among observation, knowledge, and inference. Students then can proceed to explore the relationships among these three concepts. In addition, the activity is designed to help students become aware of their personal preconceptions and biases.

Step 1. Introduce the activity by referring students to the case on pages 35-37 of the text.

Step 2. Give examples of observation, knowledge, and inference.

Step 3. Have students read the case and complete the Inference Sheet.

Example 1:

Observation	picture of woman and child on desk
Knowledge	people commonly place pictures of spouse and children on desk
Inference	The woman and child are probably the CEO's wife and son; the CEO is probably a man.

Example 2:

Observation	The CEO has a copy of *You Are What You Eat* in the office.
Knowledge	This publication is read by people who are interested in nutrition and health.
Inference	The CEO is probably interested in nutrition and general health.

NOTE: Step 1 may be assigned as homework.

Step 4. Break them into groups and have them compare their responses. Assign a recorder to complete the group's Inference Sheet.

Step 5. Conduct a large group discussion. Suggestions to facilitate that discussion include:

A. Divide the blackboard into three parts, outlining a large Inference Sheet. Using a round-robin approach, ask for one response from each group (the recorder may respond) until the board-sheet is filled. In this way, groups can see the responses of other groups, and also see the variety of inferences.

   1. Ask the class as a whole to discuss the similarities and differences among the groups' responses, and to account for them.

   2. Ask the class for alternative inferences. For instance, one might infer from the picture (example 1) that the CEO has a traditional married life. In fact, he may have been widowed.

An alternative inference in example 2 is the possibility that the CEO is concerned about being overweight.

      3. Other discussion questions can be used. See B below.

B. Additional discussion questions may include:

    1. How do our prejudices, assumptions, and self-concepts affect our observations and decisions?

    2. What are some examples from your experience where personal biases and assumptions affected your perceptions of others' perceptions of you? What did you do in these situations? What would you do differently now?

    3. What sort of impressions do we gain about people we have never met by the nature of their surroundings?

    4. In what ways can people contrive for others to have certain impressions by what they display in their surroundings? Can you give examples? (For instance, if a professor does most of her research and writing outside of the office, could she possibly feel compelled to make sure her office at school has a lot of books? What might students and colleagues possibly assess her performance to be if she has no books at school?)

    5. How do we deal with inconsistencies in our observations of others?

    6. What is the nature of the relationship among observation, knowledge, and inference?

    7. What can we do to increase our accuracy in our perceptions and relationships with others?

    8. What steps can managers take to more accurately view the behaviors of their employees?

    9. In what ways do our inferences increase our knowledge of our own biases and perceptions? How can our inferences help us better to understand ourselves?

Step 6. Summarize by asking students to state the major points of this activity. For instance:

A. Our own biases and preconceptions can influence the inferences we make, based upon our knowledge and observations.

B. We can improve our ability to make inferences by becoming more aware of the relationship between observation and knowledge. For example, although the CEO has an issue of *Ebony* in the office, it is a surmise that the CEO is Afro-American, rather than indicating that the CEO is interested in minority concerns.

C. Inferences can be useful tools in deciphering our environment.

THE SHERWOOD HOLMES CASE INFERENCE SHEET

DIRECTIONS: Read carefully the description of the CEO's office and study the room diagram. Complete this Inference Sheet as follows:

1. In the left-hand column (observation) note data from your reading that you think are important clues about the kind of person who occupies the room.

2. In the middle column (knowledge) note any experiences that you may have had that influence your observation.

3. In the right-hand column (inference) note whatever conclusions you reach as a result of your observations.

OBSERVATION Raw data	**KNOWLEDGE** Experiences that influence your observation	**INFERENCE** Resulting perception

CHAPTER 2	MENTOR ROLE
COMPETENCY 1	UNDERSTANDING SELF AND OTHERS

Practice Activity: The Marvins are Missing, Again
Activity Flow Sheet

PURPOSE: Help students see how the same behavior observed in different employees may call for different responses.

KEY TOPICS: Values and understanding others.

TIME ESTIMATE: 50 minutes

FORMAT: Individual work, then 4-5 person groups followed by large group discussion.

SPECIAL NEEDS: None

SEQUENCE:
1. Have students, individually, read the cases of the Marvins and prepare their responses.

2. Divide students into 4-5 person groups.

3. Conduct a large group discussion.

4. Summarize.

VARIATIONS: Step 1 can be assigned as homework, with the activity resuming with step 2 the next class session. This would cut the time estimate by about 20 minutes.

KEY POINTS:
1. Different people in different circumstances require different responses.

2. Our own values, experiences, and style influence our perceptions of and responses to others.

3. Empathy can be a useful tool for understanding others and can assist the manager and employee in finding a solution to problems at work.

4. This case portrays the classic tension between organizational needs and the needs of individuals. It further illustrates the dilemma of managers who are caught in that conflictual situation.

CHAPTER 2	MENTOR ROLE
COMPETENCY 1	UNDERSTANDING SELF AND OTHERS

Practice Activity: The Marvins are Missing, Again
Process Guide

PURPOSE: "The Marvins are Missing, Again" details the story of three Marvins, each of whom are absent from work. This activity is designed to help students understand how the same behavior observed in different employees may call for different responses. This activity is an opportunity to practice empathy and understanding others.

In order to solve may problems with employees, attention to individual factors is necessary. Only by recognizing that a different approach is needed for each Marvin can the situation be optimized for the manager and the employee.

Step 1. Have students, individually, read the cases of the Marvins and prepare a response for each one. Remind students to try to use the skills discussed in the learning activity. (Allow about 20-25 minutes).

Step 2. Break students into small groups and have them discuss their responses with other group members. (Allow about 15 minutes).

Step 3. Conduct a large group discussion. Several possible discussion questions are listed below:

   A. How did you respond to each of the Marvins?

   B. How did your own managerial style (Theory X or Theory Y) influence your responses?

   C. What were your first impressions of these three Marvins?

   D. Were some people in your group more sympathetic to some Marvins than others? How did this affect your response?

   E. If you were one of the Marvins, how would you need for your manager to handle your situation? What if your manager were inflexible? What effect would this have on your performance and loyalty and morale?

   G. If you decided to be lenient and flexible with the Marvins, how would you handle this with your boss?

Step 4. Summarize, using students' main ideas and the key points on the activity flow sheet.

CHAPTER 2	MENTOR ROLE
COMPETENCY 1	UNDERSTANDING SELF AND OTHERS

Application Activity: Understanding and Changing Relationships
Activity Flow Sheet

PURPOSE: Apply skills in appreciating individual differences, empathy, and use of perception in making inferences.

KEY POINTS: Changing perceptions and the use of empathy.

TIME ESTIMATE 30 minutes.

FORMAT: Individual activity followed by large group discussion.

SPECIAL NEEDS: None.

SEQUENCE:
1. Explain activity and direct its completion.
2. Explain importance of honesty in completing it.
3. Have volunteers share insights.
4. Conduct a large group discussion and summarize.

VARIATIONS: This may be assigned as homework; steps 3 and 4 could begin the next class session.

KEY POINTS:
1. Sometimes we are too busy to reflect upon our perceptions, assumptions, etc. about others.
2. Sometimes we fail to see the changes in them or the inaccuracies of our perceptions.

WATCH FOR: possible student resistance - **not to the activity, but to completing it honestly. They may be more inclined to be candid if you give a personal example, answering the questions of the activity while giving the directions.**

CHAPTER 2	MENTOR ROLE
COMPETENCY 1	UNDERSTANDING SELF AND OTHERS

Application Activity: Understanding and Changing Relationships
Process Guide

PURPOSE: This activity provides a format for students to apply skills in appreciating individual differences, empathy, and the use of perception in making inferences. This activity: examines how perceptions of others have changed over time (or how they have been reinforced); details possible problems in the relationships and ways in which the respondents may have contributed to those problems; increases insight into how personal characteristics influence our relationships; encourages the use of concepts in this section to improve these relationships.

Step 1. Briefly review the questions in the activity and direct students to respond to the questions.

Step 2. Explain the importance of honesty in completing it. Emphasize that their responses are not for anyone else to read or to evaluate. Some students may especially view steps 3 and 4 as risky; however, if it becomes too uncomfortable, they can always choose another person.

The significance of this activity is highlighted by the fact that awareness of perceptions is essential to increasing our understanding of ourselves and others.

Step 3. Ask for volunteers to share insights. If you would like, give an example from your own experience to illustrate how a work relationship changed as a result of your increased awareness of your impressions and perceptions.

Step 4. Conclude by summarizing the main points brought out in the discussion.

CHAPTER 2	MENTOR ROLE
COMPETENCY 2	COMMUNICATING EFFECTIVELY

Assessment: Communication Skills
Activity Flow Sheet

PURPOSE: Most people think they are excellent communicators. This activity helps students to understand that people tend to be self-deceptive about communication skills.

KEY TOPICS: Communication skills.

TIME ESTIMATE: 15 minutes.

FORMAT: Individual activity followed by large group discussion.

SPECIAL NEEDS: None.

SEQUENCE:
1. Introduce the activity by instructing students to identify two relationships: one that is very pleasant and one that is very painful.

2. Emphasize that this activity is not graded, but is for their personal use only.

3. Direct them to complete the questionnaire.

4. Have students respond in writing to the interpretation questions.

5. Conduct large group discussion.

6. Summarize.

VARIATION: Steps 3 and 4 may be completed as homework.

KEY POINTS:
1. When we are in painful relationships, we may tend to see the other person as having communication problems and feel that we do not have problems with communication.

2. We tend to think of ourselves as having good communication skills; it is easy to be self-deceptive in this regard.

3. Since we experience the consequences of a painful, dysfunctional relationship, it is in our interest to consider our role in maintaining its status.

CHAPTER 2	MENTOR ROLE
COMPETENCY 2	COMMUNICATING EFFECTIVELY

Assessment: Communication Skills
Process Guide

PURPOSE: This activity increases student awareness of the need to examine their communication skills. While most people think they are excellent communicators, this activity helps students to realize that they bear the emotional consequences of the perpetuation of painful relationships. Students are asked to respond to a questionnaire, analyzing their communication in two relationships. One relationship is very pleasant and the other is very painful. This activity helps students to identify specific problems in the painful relationship that they need to work on.

Step 1. Instruct students to identify two relationships: one that is very pleasant and one that is very painful. Write the names of these two individuals on a piece of paper.

Step 2. Emphasize that this activity is for their use only, and their written responses will not be evaluated or read by anyone else.

Step 3. Direct them to complete the questionnaire regarding their communication with these two individuals.

Step 4. Reiterate the interpretation questions; have students respond in writing by making notes of their thoughts.

Step 5. Conduct a large group discussion. Additional questions may include:

   A. How do you feel about this activity? Did you find parts of it difficult? If so, which parts, and why were they difficult?

   B. Did you find that your communication behavior varied in these two relationships? How?

   C. Do you consider it important to examine your communication behavior in the painful relationship? Do you think this would be a wise use of your time?

   D. In reflecting on the painful relationship, how much does that person mean to you? Often we find that the hurt in the relationship would diminish considerably if we did not care about the person. The more important a person is to us, the greater the potential for pain.

   E. What consequences to you experience from the maintenance of the painful relationship?

   F. What specific steps could to take to improve your communication skills in the painful relationship?

Step 6. Conclude by summarizing the key points on the activity flow sheet and the main ideas in the discussion. The following may surface:

A. Both individuals identified in the activity may be very important to us - not only the one with whom we enjoy a very pleasant relationship. If the person with whom we have a painful relationship did not mean anything to us, there likely would be less pain.

B. Maintaining the painful nature of the troublesome relationship does not punish the other person, as we often would like to think. We suffer - if we didn't, we would not have identified the relationship as painful.

CHAPTER 2	MENTOR ROLE
COMPETENCY 2	COMMUNICATING EFFECTIVELY

Analysis Activity: One-Way, Two-Way Communication
Activity Flow Sheet

PURPOSE: This activity allows students to focus on the elements of communication and the barriers to effective communication.

KEY TOPICS: Communication and feedback.

TIME ESTIMATE: 45 minutes.

FORMAT: Dyads followed by large group discussion.

SPECIAL NEEDS: Diagram 1, diagram 2, and the One-Way, Two-Way Communication Response Sheet for participants and for observers (all of which follow the process guide).

SEQUENCE:
1. Introduce activity and sheets.

2. Divide students into dyads; designate one as the speaker.

3. Have pairs sit back-to-back. Review directions. Give Diagrams 1 ONLY to speakers.

4. Allow 5 minutes for the drawing.

5. Have pairs sit facing each other. Review directions. Give Diagram 2 ONLY to speakers.

6. Allow 5 minutes.

7. Have students complete the One-Way, Two-Way Communication Response Sheet.

8. Conduct large group discussion.

9. Summarize.

VARIATIONS:
1. Place students into 4-5 person groups, assigning some students to be observers.

2. One constraint with dividing the class into dyads is that it is important for the listeners to hear only their partners. An alternative is to use this as a fishbowl, perhaps using 2 or 3 dyads in different parts of the room.

KEY POINTS: Due to space limitations, they are included on the process guide.

CHAPTER 2	MENTOR ROLE
COMPETENCY 2	COMMUNICATING EFFECTIVELY

Analysis Activity: One-Way Two-Way Communication
Process Guide

PURPOSE: The purpose of this activity is to enable students to focus on the elements of communication and the barriers to effective listening and communication. In this activity students are asked to draw a diagram based on the directions given by the partner. Through this activity they learn the importance of nonverbal signals, hand gestures, etc. that assist in the communication process. They also learn the importance of feedback provided in two-way communication.

STEP 1. Introduce the activity by referring students to the directions on page 43-44 of the text.

STEP 2. Divide students into dyads; designate one as the speaker. Point out that one member of the dyad will act as the speaker, giving instructions verbally, and the other will be the listener. The listener draws the figure on paper according to the information provided by the speaker. Dyad members will remain in their designated roles for both parts of the activity.

> **NOTE:** Dyad members should sit so that they cannot hear the interaction among the other dyads.

STEP 3. Once the students are in place, review the directions. Have pairs sit back-to-back. Give Diagram 1 ONLY to speakers. Note the following instructions on page 44 of the text:

Instruct speakers to:

Sit back to back with the listener and describe the drawing. You are to give drawing instructions without allowing the listener to see you or the figure. Do not answer any questions.

Instruct listeners to:

Sit back-to-back with the speaker and draw the figure as it is described to you. Correct your drawing as you think necessary. Do not look at the speaker; do not ask any questions.

STEP 4. Allow 5 minutes.

STEP 5. Have pairs sit facing each other. Give Diagram 2 ONLY to the speakers. Review the directions, noting the differences between instructions for this part of the exercise and instructions for the former. Note the instructions on page 44 of the text.

STEP 6. Allow 5 minutes.

STEP 7. Have students individually complete the One-Way, Two-Way Communication Response Sheet.

STEP 8. Reassemble students into a large group and discuss their responses to questions 1-5 of the One-Way, Two-Way Communication Response Sheet. The following could be highlighted in the discussion:

    A. Skills needed for effective one and two way communication.

    B. Difficulties encountered in each part of the exercise and their similarities to managerial communication problems.

    C. The feelings that the listeners had about asking questions to the speakers. How would those feelings be different if the speakers were the listeners' bosses?

    D. Advantages of two-way communication over one-way communication.

    E. Examples of instructions we receive which are one-way communications.

STEP 9. Summarize by asking students what they feel are the positive and negative aspects of nonverbal communication and how these aspects can either help or hinder communication for the manager. Note the key points below:

        1. Two-way communication tends to produce more accurate results than one-way communication.

        2. Two-way communication permits speakers' testing of their assumptions of what how their partner is interpreting their instructions.

        3. Difficulties in this activity may parallel difficulties in organizations.

        4. Point out positive and negative aspects of non-verbal communication.

ANALYSIS ACTIVITY: ONE-WAY, TWO-WAY COMMUNICATION

SPEAKER ONLY

DIAGRAM 1: One-Way Communication

DIRECTIONS: Study the series of squares below. With your back to your listener, direct him/her to draw the figures. Begin with the top square and describe each in succession, taking particular note of the relationship to each to the preceding one.

Do not allow your listener to ask any questions.

ANALYSIS ACTIVITY: ONE-WAY, TWO-WAY COMMUNICATION

SPEAKER ONLY

DIAGRAM 2: Two-Way Communication

DIRECTIONS: Study the series of squares below. Face your listener and direct him/her to draw the figures. Begin with the top square and describe each in succession, taking particular note of the relationship of each to the preceding one. Answer all questions and repeat if necessary, but do not show this paper to your listener.

ONE-WAY, TWO-WAY COMMUNICATION RESPONSE SHEET
FOR PARTICIPANTS IN THE DYADS

Respond to the following questions and be prepared to discuss your answers in the large group discussion.

1. What were the differences between seeing and not seeing your partner?

2. What were the effects of not being able to ask questions?

3. Based on the role you played in this exercise, how would you rate your effectiveness as a listener or as a speaker?

4. What did you learn about yourself as a listener or speaker?

5. How does this experience apply to on-the-job situations?

ONE-WAY, TWO-WAY COMMUNICATION RESPONSE SHEET
FOR OBSERVERS OF THE DYADS

Compare the role players in the dyads for both parts of the activity.

1. In which part of the activity was the listener the most confident? Why?

2. In which part of the activity was the listener the most frustrated? Why?

3. In which part of the activity was the speaker the most frustrated? Why?

4. From what you observed, what were the effects of not being able to ask questions?

5. What were the effects of the two people not being able to see each other?

6. What non-verbal communication did you notice in the two-way communication? What were the benefits of it?

CHAPTER 2	MENTOR ROLE
COMPETENCY 2	COMMUNICATING EFFECTIVELY

Practice Activity: Reflecting Feelings and Ideas
Activity Flow Sheet

PURPOSE: This activity allows students to practice reflective listening responses in order to determine the speaker's meaning.

KEY TOPICS: Reflective listening.

TIME ESTIMATE: 45 minutes.

FORMAT: Individual activity followed by large group discussion.

SPECIAL NEEDS: None.

SEQUENCE:
1. Introduce the activity.
2. Have students complete the instrument.
3. Conduct large group discussion.
4. Summarize.

VARIATIONS:
1. After step 2, divide the class into dyads and have them role-play the situations.
2. After step 2, have a demonstration fishbowl role play, give feedback, and discuss as a large group.

KEY POINTS:
1. While there is no right answer, the reflective response can be identified.
2. The reflective response (even if not accurate) can encourage the sender to further clarify the message.
3 Attending skills on the part of the responder are as important as the actual words of the response. Attending skills include: eye contact, leaning towards the speaker, and using an empathetic tone of voice.

CHAPTER 2	MENTOR ROLE
COMPETENCY 2	COMMUNICATING EFFECTIVELY

Practice Activity: Reflecting Feelings and Ideas
Process Guide

PURPOSE: The purpose of this activity is to allow students to practice reflective listening responses in order to clarify the meaning of speaker's comments. This activity also illustrates the differences involved in making objective judgments about feelings and ideas without the help of additional information such as nonverbal cues and past history.

STEP 1. Introduce the activity by reminding students about the tenets of reflective listening.

STEP 2. Have students individually complete the instrument. Allow approximately 15 minutes.

STEP 3. Conduct large group discussion based on their responses. Additional questions include:

A. What difficulties did you have in choosing one answer instead of another? What would have helped you better determine the intended meaning?

B. Would you have responded in a way other than the choices given? If so, what responses do you consider more appropriate?

NOTE: There are no absolute right or wrong answers. Reinforce the difference between a reflective response and the "right answer." There is, in most cases, only one reflective answer given. The others may be acceptable as responses but are not truly reflective. If the students disagree with a suggested answer, ask them to justify their response and discuss it with the class members.

Suggested most reflective answers are: 1. b; 2. a; 3. c; 4.c; 5. a; 6. c; 7. b; 8. b; 9. d; 10. a

STEP 4. Summarize by asking students to share their difficulties with completing this exercise. Ask if it would have helped if they could have seen and heard the speakers and why.

VARIATIONS: This activity can be expanded by adding the following steps:

STEP 5. Divide the class into dyads and have them role-play the situations. Partner A should role-play the initial remarks to the first 5 situations with Partner B responding in his/her own words using a reflective response.

Have students reverse roles for situations 6-10.

In each instance the student making the initial remarks should give the respondent feedback as to the effectiveness of the reflective response. Partners who wish to make up remarks rather than use situations 1-10 can be encouraged to do so provided they role-play and *NOT* just talk about a situation.

STEP 6. Have a demonstration fishbowl role play, give feedback, and discuss as a large group.

CHAPTER 2	MENTOR ROLE
COMPETENCY 2	COMMUNICATING EFFECTIVELY

Application Activity: Active Listening
Activity Flow Sheet

PURPOSE: The purpose of this activity is to allow students to apply active listening skills in their interactions.

KEY TOPICS: Active and reflective listening.

TIME ESTIMATE: 45 minutes.

FORMAT: 3-person groups followed by large group discussion.

SPECIAL NEEDS: The Listening Response Sheet and the Guidelines for Active Listening sheet (both of them follow the process guide).

SEQUENCE:
1. Divide students into groups of 3.

2. Hand out the Guidelines for Active Listening sheet and review briefly.

3. Review the directions on pages 48-49.

4. Time the rounds to 10 minutes per round.

5. Have students complete the Listening Response Sheet.

6. Conduct a large group discussion, using the Listening Response Sheet and the questions supplied at the bottom of page 49.

7. Summarize.

VARIATIONS:
1. This activity can be assigned as homework, with students forming groups with other class members. Then for the next class meeting, the discussion can be initiated by referring to their responses on the Listening Response Sheet. With this variation, you may want to assign the Referee in each round to be the time keeper.

2. More than three students can be placed in a group, increasing the times a student is Referee.

KEY POINTS:
1. Listening is neither easy nor passive, but takes considerable concentrated effort.

2. Focusing on what our responses will be is a hindrance to effective listening.

CHAPTER 2	MENTOR ROLE
COMPETENCY 2	COMMUNICATING EFFECTIVELY

Application Activity: Active Listening
Process Guide

PURPOSE: This activity allows students to apply active listening skills in their interactions. Through this activity students increase their understanding of the difficulties and energy involved in active and reflective listening.

STEP 1. Divide students into groups of 3. Give them the Guidelines for Active Listening Handout.

STEP 2. Briefly review the Guidelines for Active Listening handout. Remind students that reflective and active listening skills involve the following:

   A. Paying close attention to what is said.

   B. Observing nonverbal cues given.

   C. Listening for both feelings and ideas.

   D. Clarifying, restating and paraphrasing statements to test your understanding.

   Indicate to students that in this activity they will apply these skills.

STEP 3. Review the directions on pages 48-49.

STEP 4. Inform students of the beginning and ending times for each round. The total process of speaking and summarizing should take a maximum of 10 minutes per round.

STEP 5. After the rounds, have students complete the Listening Response Sheet.

STEP 6. Conduct a large group discussion on the barriers to effective listening, using the Listening Response Sheet and the questions supplied at the bottom of page 49.

STEP 7. Summarize, focusing on the application of these skills to their personal interactions.

GUIDELINES FOR ACTIVE LISTENING

1. Try to ask only open-ended questions; avoid questions that can be answered by "yes," "no," or "I don't know."

2. Listen patiently to what the other person has to say, even though you may believe it is wrong or irrelevant. Indicate simple acceptance (not necessarily agreement) by nodding or injecting an occasional "um-hm" or "I see."

3. Try to understand the feeling the person is expressing, as well as the intellectual content. Many people have difficulty talking clearly about their feelings, so careful attention is required.

4. Restate the other person's feeling, briefly but accurately. At certain times you should simply serve as a mirror and encourage the other person to continue talking. Occasionally make summary responses such as "you think the director does not understand how this unit operates" or "you feel the manager is playing favorites;" but in doing so, keep your tone neutral and try not to lead the person to your pet conclusions.

5. Avoid direct questions and arguments about facts; refrain from saying "that's just not so," "hold on a minute, let's look at the facts," or "prove it." Allow the other person to express his or her feelings.

6. When the person touches on a point you want to learn more about, use reflective listening techniques, such as repeating or rephrasing his or her statements as a question. For example, if a person remarks " no one can ever talk to the boss around here," you can probe by replying "you say no one can ever talk to the boss around here?" or "are you saying that there is no communication between the workers and the boss?" With this encouragement, the other person will probably expand on their previous point.

7. Listen for what is not said--evasions of pertinent points or perhaps too-ready agreement with common clichés. Such omissions may be clues to a bothersome fact that the person wishes were not true.

8. Limit the expression of your own views, since these may condition or limit what the other person says.

9. Focus on the content of the message; do not try to think about your next statement until the person is finished talking.

Adapted from: Gordon, Judith R. *A Diagnostic Approach to Organizational Behavior*, Boston, MA: Allyn and Bacon, Inc., 1987

LISTENING RESPONSE SHEET

List some of the difficulties you encountered in each of the following roles:

    SPEAKER:

    LISTENER:

    REFEREE:

What barriers to effective listening became evident?

What did you learn about your own communication effectiveness

    AS A SPEAKER?

    AS A LISTENER?

    AS A REFEREE?

How can you apply what you learned about yourself to your personal interactions?

CHAPTER 2	MENTOR ROLE
COMPETENCY 3	DEVELOPING SUBORDINATES

Assessment: Assumptions about Performance Evaluations
Activity Flow Sheet

PURPOSE: This activity points out a contradiction between performance evaluation as an organizational requirement and the managerial posture inherent in the Mentor Role. This activity helps students understand how performance evaluations can be used to develop subordinates.

KEY TOPICS: Performance evaluation.

TIME ESTIMATE: 20 minutes.

FORMAT: Individual activity followed by large group discussion.

SPECIAL NEEDS: None.

SEQUENCE:
1. Direct students to complete the Assumptions about Performance Evaluation Questionnaire on page 50, as well as respond to the interpretation questions.

2. Discuss interpretation question #1.

3. Present interpretation of the questionnaire.

4. Discuss interpretation questions #2 and #3.

5. Summarize.

KEY POINTS:
1. Performance evaluations tend to be threatening times for subordinates.

2. Performance evaluations perform organizational functions of justifying pay increases and promotions.

3. Properly used, performance evaluations can be valuable tools for developing subordinates, as well as giving valuable feedback to managers.

CHAPTER 2	MENTOR ROLE
COMPETENCY 3	DEVELOPING SUBORDINATES

Assessment: Assumptions about Performance Evaluations
Process Guide

PURPOSE: This activity points out a contradiction between the use of an organizational requirement and the managerial posture inherent in the Mentor Role. Performance evaluations typically are formal processes which advance the interests of the organization. However, performance evaluations may also function as useful tools in employee development. This activity helps students understand how performance evaluations can be used to develop subordinates.

STEP 1. Direct students to complete the Assumptions about Performance Evaluation Questionnaire on page 50, as well as respond to the interpretation questions. This should be completed before reading the learning activity.

STEP 2. Discuss interpretation question #1 as a large group. In this discussion, students may identify the intended interpretation of the questionnaire (see Step 3).

STEP 3. Present interpretation of the questionnaire, which is as follows:

The A response in all 8 questions suggests an organization centered, formal process orientation. A responses reflect traditional control values.

The B response suggests a participative, subordinate developmental, employee central orientation. B responses reflect values of involvement, trust, and communication.

Discuss this assessment in terms of A vs. B answers.

Note that in many organizations, the performance evaluation process is for organizational reasons not employee development reasons. This is why the process is so universally detested.

STEP 4. Discuss interpretation question #2 as a large group.

STEP 5. Summarize by discussing interpretation question #3: How would you design an effective process?

Points to note:

The importance of feedback in employee development.

The inherent threatening nature of the process, which demands additional consideration and care for it to be a positive experience.

CHAPTER 2	MENTOR ROLE
COMPETENCY 3	DEVELOPING SUBORDINATES

Analysis Activity: United Chemical Company
Activity Flow Sheet

PURPOSE: This activity allows students to analyze a situation of a conversation between a manager and a subordinate, and reframing the conversation in a way that is consistent with supportive communication skills.

KEY TOPICS: Communication and listening skills.

TIME ESTIMATE: 30 minutes.

FORMAT: An individual exercise, followed by fishbowl role-play and large group discussion.

SPECIAL NEEDS: None.

SEQUENCE:
1. Introduce the activity.

2. Direct students to read the case and write out their responses to the discussion questions.

3. Ask for two students to volunteers to role play Max and Sue.

4. Conduct fishbowl role-play.

5. Discuss the responses as a large group.

6. Summarize.

VARIATION: Students may role-play Max and Sue in small groups with observers, in addition to, or instead of, the fishbowl.

KEY POINTS:
1. Both Max and Sue benefit from using of supportive communication skills.

2. When people feel strongly about issues, it may be more difficult to use reflective listening and feedback skills.

3. Use of reflective listening and feedback enhance one's chances of identifying the real issues, and making them explicit.

CHAPTER 2	MENTOR ROLE
COMPETENCY 3	DEVELOPING SUBORDINATES

Analysis Activity: United Chemical Company
Process Guide

PURPOSE: The purpose of this activity is to allow students to analyze a situation of a conversation between a manager and a subordinate. Using supportive communication skills, they reframe the conversation, allowing them to note the difficulties, as well as the benefits.

STEP 1. Introduce the activity by reminding students of the listening skills learned in Competency 2, along with the guidelines for effective feedback in Competency 3. Note the added complexities of those skills in situations where employees feel that they are being evaluated in some way.

STEP 2. Direct students to read the case and write out their responses to the discussion questions at the end of the case, on page 54.

STEP 3. Ask for two students to volunteers to role play Max and Sue.

STEP 4. Conduct fishbowl role-play. Intervene to note how points are demonstrated. Have other students step in to play Max and Sue. Note especially the emotional component of the conversation.

STEP 5. Discuss the responses as a large group. Additional discussion questions may include:

   A. How did the redesigned conversation between Max and Sue help to clarify the situation?

   B. Without the use of supportive communication skills, what assumptions might Sue have made regarding her value to the company?

STEP 6. Summarize, using students' main points as well as noting:

   A. The emotional and conceptual differences between the original conversation and the redesigned conversation.

   B. How use of supportive communication skills assists in clarifying issues.

CHAPTER 2	MENTOR ROLE
COMPETENCY 3	DEVELOPING SUBORDINATES

Practice: Giving and Receiving Feedback
Activity Flow Sheet

PURPOSE: The purpose of this activity is to allow students to practice giving and receiving feedback, using a role-play situation.

KEY TOPICS: Giving and receiving feedback.

TIME ESTIMATE: 30 minutes.

FORMAT: Dyads followed by large group discussion.

SPECIAL NEEDS: None.

SEQUENCE:
1. Review with students the guidelines on page 52-53.
2. Divide students into dyads.
3. Review the two roles in the activity and assign roles.
4. Conduct a large group discussion.
5. Summarize.

VARIATION: After Step 3, ask for a pair to volunteer to do their role-play in front of the class, in a fishbowl activity.

KEY POINTS:
1. The effective use of feedback is essential in setting a climate of trust.

2. The effective use of feedback also hinders employees from making the wrong assumptions about "what is really being said" about the employee's value.

3. Following the guidelines for effective feedback takes concentrated effort.

CHAPTER 2	MENTOR ROLE
COMPETENCY 3	DEVELOPING SUBORDINATES

Practice: Giving and Receiving Feedback
Process Guide

PURPOSE: This activity allows students to practice giving and receiving feedback, using a role-play situation. Unlike the immediately preceding analysis activity, this activity describes a situation between a manager and subordinate without detailing their conversation. Only their respective viewpoints are described.

STEP 1. Review with students the guidelines on page 52-53.

STEP 2. Divide students into dyads.

STEP 3. Review the two roles in the activity. Assign one student to play the role of Klaus Schultz, and the other to play the role of Martin LeFete. Allow students time to read their respective roles and to "get into them". Time the role play to 10 minutes or so.

As a variation: Conduct fishbowl role-play. Intervene to note how points are demonstrated. Have other students step in to play Klaus and Martin. Note especially the emotional component of the conversation.

STEP 4. Discuss as a large group. Discussion questions may include:

   A. How well was each guideline implemented? Were some easier to implement than others? Why?

   B. What were some of their hindrances to following the guidelines?

   C. What did you learn from the role play?

STEP 5. Summarize by asking students to list some of the barriers to and benefits from using the guidelines for giving and receiving feedback.

CHAPTER 2
COMPETENCY 3

MENTOR ROLE
DEVELOPING SUBORDINATES

Application: The Coach at Work
Activity Flow Sheet

PURPOSE: This activity allows students the opportunity to apply the guidelines to their personal lives, noting when they have been the recipients of feedback the effects of such feedback.

KEY TOPICS: Giving and receiving feedback.

TIME ESTIMATE: 30 minutes.

FORMAT: Individual activity, followed by small group work and large group discussion.

SPECIAL NEEDS: None.

SEQUENCE:
1. Introduce the activity by mentioning the concept of "coach" and its relationship to feedback.

2. Direct students to individually write out responses.

3. Have students meet in groups of 4-6 to make up a composite list.

4. Note the mistakes that might more likely be made by managers.

5. Conduct a large group discussion.

6. Summarize.

VARIATION: Step 2 may be completed as homework, and the other steps completed in class.

KEY POINTS:
1. We have had feedback modeled to us throughout our lives.

2. From this modeling, we have learned how to give feedback, inheriting many of the strengths and weaknesses of our "coaches."

3. Skills that people learn in their personal lives often carries over to their roles as managers in organizations.

4. Some organizational structures are more conducive to giving effective feedback than are others.

CHAPTER 2	MENTOR ROLE
COMPETENCY 3	DEVELOPING SUBORDINATES

Application: The Coach at Work
Process Guide

PURPOSE: This activity allows students the opportunity to apply the guidelines for effective feedback to their personal lives. By noting when they have been the recipients of feedback, they are able to identify the effects of feedback. They do this by identifying someone who has coached them, or given them feedback. Students individually make a list, distinguish the strengths and weaknesses of that feedback. Students then meet in groups to compile a list of common mistakes.

STEP 1. Introduce the activity by mentioning the concept of "coach" as indicating someone who helps us grow by guiding the development of our capabilities. Effective use of feedback is seen as essential to effective coaching.

STEP 2. Direct students to individually write out responses to questions 1, 2, and 3 of the activity.

STEP 3. Have students meet in groups of 4-6 to make up a composite list of the most common coaching mistakes made by people giving feedback.

STEP 4. Note the mistakes that might more likely be made by managers, and why.

STEP 5. In a large group discussion, using the round robin technique, list the common mistakes on the blackboard.

STEP 6. Summarize by asking students what can be done to avoid those mistakes.

CHAPTER 3   FACILITATOR ROLE

The Facilitator Role, together with the Mentor Role, comprises the Human Relations Model of the Competing Values Framework. As such this managerial role is associated with "people skills" and attention to building cohesion and morale among employees. The manager in this role fosters collective effort and manages interpersonal conflict. Using the listening and empathetic skills of the mentor, the efforts of the facilitator are directed to groups of individuals. As such the facilitator relates well to others, builds trust, manages conflict, promotes input from others, emphasizes mutual helping, and designs and chairs meetings.

While at first glance the skills of the facilitator role may seem remote to some students, reflection will assure them that they are probably already using some facilitation skills. As they consider their social situations, for example, they likely can identify instances where they made sure that everyone present knew each other, and that everyone became a part of the conversation. In addition, conflict management is a competency to which people quickly relate, as most individuals would like to manage conflict in their lives. Furthermore, the facilitator role encompasses leadership development skills that students use as leaders of student organizations and groups.

More than any other managerial role, the facilitator role embodies important values of a democratic society. These values affirm each individual, and the importance of everyone's viewpoints and perspectives. While American society espouses these values, people work in organizations where the need for control and structure often mitigates against the advancement of these values within the organizational setting (Weisbord, 1989). It can be argued that when individuals find these fundamental values confirmed by their workplace, any degree of dissonance experienced with their work is likely to decrease. The manager as facilitator not only nurtures these values for the benefit of the individuals, but for the benefit of the organization, as well.

Unless you began the course with the Human Relations Model, you likely have demonstrated facilitation skills to your class before students get to this role. You may wish to point out to students what has transpired in the classroom as you have used facilitation techniques. You have espoused that you value the knowledge, skills, experiences, and ideas of your students. While your job as instructor is clearly to make sure that students understand concepts, you have encouraged them to participate actively in the process. This experience can be tied to organizational life. The idea of employee involvement programs in the workplace is to draw from those who are closest to the jobs. In like manner, your use of facilitation skills, as an instructor, reflects the view that, in essence, you draw from those closest to the learning tasks, involving them in the process, and valuing their input.

While the facilitator role provides managers with skills which empower employees within the organization, paradox clearly characterizes the role. Groups have tasks to do: how do you maintain group morale, while completing the task? When is participative decision making dysfunctional? When is conflict good? These questions and others demonstrate the need for individual discretion and judgment of the manager in this role.

Competency 1: Building Teams
Topics: Work groups and work teams
                             Roles of team members
                             Role clarity and role ambiguity

Task and group maintenance roles vs. self-oriented roles
Team development and team building
Formal approaches to team building
Informal approaches to team building
Barriers to team building

Competency 2: Using Participative Decision Making
Topics:	A Range of decision making strategies
Who should participate - and when
Increasing meeting effectiveness
Groupware--Computer aids to group decision making

Competency 3: Managing Conflict
Topics:	Different perspectives on conflict
Levels, sources, and stages of conflict
Stages of the conflict process
Conflict management strategies
Advantages and disadvantages of conflict management approaches
How to use collaborative approaches to conflict management
How to stimulate conflict and manage agreement

Conceptually the facilitator role is not limited to these competencies. Other competencies have been identified as:
Introducing new work procedures so as to gain employee cooperation
Consensus building
Understanding group process
How to identify and remedy dysfunctional group behavior
Basic teaching and coaching skills
Team supervision
Designing group goals

The Facilitator Role and current issues: The facilitator role advances for managers a posture of openness to feedback and ideas from employees. Increasingly, firms are using task forces in creating new work designs. Such task forces necessitate the use of facilitator role competencies.

Additionally, as we face an increasingly diverse work force, the importance of such feedback from employees is even more pronounced. While the skills of managing group processes, team building, and conflict management are potentially more difficult to apply in a culturally diverse work force, the values underlying these skills are consonant and, in fact, the competencies are appropriate for managing a diverse work force.

Some questions to consider in this chapter are:
1. What would be the consequences if managers took the facilitator role to extreme, neglecting the other roles?
2. In what ways do the competencies of the facilitator role affirm other people as individuals of worth?
3. Why are organizations experiencing an increasing need for managers to demonstrate facilitation skills?

CHAPTER 3	FACILITATOR ROLE
COMPETENCY 1	BUILDING TEAMS

Assessment: Are You a Team Player?
Activity Flow Sheet

PURPOSE: This activity allows students to assess the extent to which they tend to be team players in organizational settings. In doing so, their definition of team membership is likely to become more refined.

KEY TOPICS: Leads into a discussion of the importance of work teams and work groups, and the roles of team members.

TIME ESTIMATE: 5-10 minutes.

FORMAT: Individual activity followed by large group discussion.

SPECIAL NEEDS: None.

SEQUENCE:
1. Introduce the activity.
2. Allow students 5-10 minutes to complete the activity.
3. Conduct a large group discussion.
4. Summarize.

KEY POINTS:
1. Teams are not just for athletic activities, but are important in organizational settings, as well.
2. There are many dimensions to team membership.
3. People can acquire the skills necessary to becoming better team members.

CHAPTER 3	FACILITATOR ROLE
COMPETENCY 1	BUILDING TEAMS

Assessment: Are You a Team Player?
Process Guide

PURPOSE: This activity allows students to assess the extent to which they tend to be team players in organizational settings. In doing so, their definition of team membership is likely to become more refined. Students begin to distinguish between groups and teams.

STEP 1. Introduce the activity by referring students to the questionnaire and directions on page 61-62. Point out that there are no right or wrong answers to these questions. Explain that they should reflect on behaviors and feelings they have experienced in the past, rather than how they feel they *should* respond. Suggest that if they finish before the other class members, to begin considering their responses to the interpretation questions on page 64.

STEP 2. Allow students a 5-10 minutes to complete the activity.

STEP 3. Conduct a large group discussion based on the interpretation questions, to lead into the learning section. Additional discussion questions may include:

   A. What surprised you about this assessment?

   B. Does the instrument reflect your view of what a team is? Explain.

   C. How would you define the characteristics of an effective team player?

   D. Do individual have to relinquish their best interests in order to become effective team players? Explain your position.

   E. How do you distinguish between a group and a team?

   F. How are teams important in organizations and in the workplace? When do teams tend to become very important in the workplace?

   G. Why is team building necessary? Aren't groups enough?

STEP 4. Summarize, using students' main ideas and the key points from the activity flow sheet.

CHAPTER 3	FACILITATOR ROLE
COMPETENCY 1	BUILDING TEAMS

Analysis: Stay Alive Inc.
Activity Flow Sheet

PURPOSE: This activity allows students to work in consulting teams to analyze a dysfunctional work situation and to recommend remedies. In this situation employees seem to exhibit considerable cohesion and strong team membership. This case demonstrates the importance of task maintenance functions.

KEY TOPICS: Roles of team members, team development stages.

TIME ESTIMATE: 50 minutes.

FORMAT: Individual activity, work in 4-5 person groups, followed by large group discussion.

SPECIAL NEEDS: None.

SEQUENCE:
1. Introduce the activity.
2. Divide students into 4-5 person consulting teams.
3. Allow time for consulting team reports and discussion.
4. Conduct a large group discussion and summarize.

VARIATIONS:
1. Step 1 may be completed as a homework assignment.
2. Step 2 may be completed as an out-of-class group assignment, followed by step 3 to being the next class session.
3. The class can omit the small group work and proceed directly from individually analyzing the case to the large group discussion.

KEY POINTS:
1. Emotional closeness to group members does not necessarily constitute an effective team.
2. Teams experience various stages of team development; appropriate task and group maintenance behaviors differ accordingly.
3. Both task maintenance and group maintenance are necessary in order for the team to function effectively.

CHAPTER 3	FACILITATOR ROLE
COMPETENCY 1	BUILDING TEAMS

Analysis: Stay-Alive, Inc.
Process Guide

PURPOSE: This activity allows students to work in consulting teams to analyze a dysfunctional work situation and to recommend remedies. In this situation employees seem to exhibit considerable cohesion and strong team membership. This case demonstrates the importance of task maintenance functions.

STEP 1. Introduce the activity by directing students to the case and instructions on page 76 of the text. Explain that they will be placed into consulting teams to analyze a work situation in terms of team development and task maintenance processes. Direct them to read the case and respond in writing to the questions on page 76. This individual work is important to their group recommendations.

STEP 2. Divide students into 4-5 person consulting teams. Explain that each group is an organization consulting team that has been retained for the purpose of diagnosing the problems at Stay Alive, Inc. and suggesting remedies. Based on their responses to the questions, what suggestions would they present to the agency director and staff?

STEP 3. Allow time for consulting team reports and discussion.

STEP 4. Conduct a large group discussion. Summarize, using students' main ideas and the key points from the activity flow sheet.

CHAPTER 3	FACILITATOR ROLE
COMPETENCY 1	BUILDING TEAMS

Practice: "Students as Customers" Task Force
Activity Flow Sheet

PURPOSE: This activity provides students with the opportunity to practice and observe specific team building skills.

KEY TOPICS: Task maintenance behaviors and group maintenance behaviors.

TIME ESTIMATE: 40 minutes.

FORMAT: Small groups of about 6 persons each.

SPECIAL NEEDS: Team Building Behaviors Observation Guide which follows the process guide.

SEQUENCE:

1. Introduce the activity.

2. Divide students into small groups.

3. Direct the groups to read the memo and respond to the Task Force Meeting agenda on pages 77-78 of the text.

5. After the small group discussions are completed, have each individual respond to the discussion questions on page 78 of the text.

6. Conduct a large group discussion based the reported feelings about the discussion.

7. Summarize.

KEY POINTS:

1. Team building involves a number of group dynamics principles.

2. Use of team building and group facilitating behaviors increases the effectiveness of communication and the bond among group members.

3. Both task and maintenance behaviors are necessary for effective group decision making.

CHAPTER 3	FACILITATOR ROLE
COMPETENCY 1	BUILDING TEAMS

Practice: "Students as Customers" Task Force
Process Guide

PURPOSE: This activity provides students with the opportunity to practice, identify, and observe specific team building skills.

STEP 1. Introduce the activity by explaining that some each group will be a task force, and will meet to accomplish two tasks. Direct students to the case and instructions on page 77-78 of the text.

STEP 2. Divide students into small two groups of no more than 6 people.

STEP 3. After the groups have completed their tasks, have group members respond individually, in writing, to their discussion questions on page 78.

STEP 4. Conduct a large group discussion based on the individual responses to the discussion questions.

STEP 5. Summarize the major points brought out in the discussion.

CAUTION: Make sure that the class does not get caught up in the content or substance of this exercise but instead focuses on the process. For instance, the outcome of meetings do not matter as much as how the groups reached their conclusions.

TEAM BUILDING BEHAVIORS OBSERVATION GUIDE

DIRECTIONS: Record the number and type of behaviors displayed by the persons(s) you observed. You may find it helpful to identify the person who displayed the particular behavior by writing his/her initials next to the description of the behavior.

1. The *Initiator*: gets the group moving; offers new ideas; suggests ways to approach a task or problem; reminds others that there is a task to perform

2. The *Encourager*: supports team members; encourages and raises others' ideas; builds cohesiveness and warmth; asks for contributions from quiet members

3. The *Information Giver*: Clarifies important facts; brings in knowledge from personal experiences; raises issues; supports opinion with fact

4. The *Information Seeker*: encourages others to raise facts; asks others to justify their argument; asks for further information from others

5. The *Harmonizer*: helps members to see past their differences; reduces tension with humor and friendliness; helps members to work together and appreciate divergent viewpoints

6. The *Coordinator*: brings together the activities of others; schedules activities; combines activities

7. The *Gatekeeper*: asks to hear opinions from everyone; maintains an "open gate" to others' participation; ensures that all members have opportunities to share their ideas and feelings; uses statements such as : "Let's hear him/her out."

8. The *Evaluator*: helps group assess quality of its suggestions/solutions; tests to see if the ideas will work in reality; points out consequences of implementation; points out how parties external to the group will view the solution

9. The *Standard Setter*: helps the group set goals; helps group assess the quality of the process; points out procedural matters

10. The *Summarizer*: restates ideas presented to the group; pulls together the range of ideas presented to the group; offers a decision or conclusion for the group to consider

11. The *Follower*: agrees with other members; pursues ideas and suggestions of others

Other observations:

CHAPTER 3
COMPETENCY 1

FACILITATOR ROLE
BUILDING TEAMS

Application: Team Building Action Plan
Activity Flow Sheet

PURPOSE: This activity permits students to apply team building principles to a situation in which they are currently engaged.

KEY TOPICS: Task and group maintenance roles

TIME ESTIMATE: In class set up time: 10 minutes; outside of class: 3 hours; in class follow up discussion: 20 minutes.

FORMAT: Individual activity followed by large group discussion.

SPECIAL NEEDS: None.

SEQUENCE:
1. Introduce the activity. Assist students in choosing a group.

2. Set a date when the 3-5 page report is due.

3. On the due date, ask for volunteers to share their experiences.

4. Conduct a large group discussion and summarize.

KEY POINTS:
1. Team building skills can be developed.

2. The skills of team building are useful in any situation where collaborative problem solving is needed.

3. Team building skills are applicable to a wide variety of situations.

CHAPTER 3	FACILITATOR ROLE
COMPETENCY 1	BUILDING TEAMS

Application: Team Building Action Plan
Process Guide

PURPOSE: This activity permits students to apply team building principles to a situation in which they are currently engaged. Students choose a group in which they are currently participating, and consciously alter their behavior during a group meeting in order to advance the efforts of the group.

STEP 1. Introduce students to the activity by referring them to the instructions on page 78 of the text. Explain that they are to identify a group in which they currently participate, and apply team building strategies to their participation. Assist them in choosing a group, if necessary.

STEP 2. Set a date when the 3-5 page report is due. By necessity, this date may have to be a 3-4 weeks away, due to the varying meeting schedules of the groups. Also, students may wish to use the observation forms for the previous activity as a guide.

STEP 3. On the due date, ask for volunteers to share their experiences.

STEP 4. Conduct a large group discussion and summarize. Additional discussion questions may include:

    A. What surprised you about your experience?

    B. How did other group members respond to your change in behavior?

    C. What were some of your challenges in implementing these changes?

CHAPTER 3	FACILITATOR ROLE
COMPETENCY 2	USING PARTICIPATIVE DECISION MAKING

Assessment: Meeting Evaluation
Activity Flow Sheet

PURPOSE: This activity enables students to begin to define the elements of meeting effectiveness.

KEY TOPICS: Key elements of meeting effectiveness.

TIME ESTIMATE: 20 minutes.

FORMAT: Individual activity followed by large group discussion.

SPECIAL NEEDS: None.

SEQUENCE:
1. Introduce the activity. Have students identify the specific meeting which they will assess.

2. Allow time to respond to the scale as well as to the interpretation questions.

3. Conduct a large group discussion based upon their responses.

4. Summarize students' major points.

VARIATION: After step 2, place students into 4-5 person groups to compare their responses and discuss the interpretation questions. Ask each group to identify the most effective meeting of their group members, and the least effective, and to list the characteristics of each.

KEY POINTS:
1. Meetings can be identified as more or less effective, based on discernible characteristics.

2. Meetings are important activities; considerable time is spent in meetings.

3. Many people value their time and resent time spent in poorly managed meetings.

CHAPTER 3	FACILITATOR ROLE
COMPETENCY 2	USING PARTICIPATIVE DECISION MAKING

Assessment: Meeting Evaluation
Process Guide

PURPOSE: This activity enables students to begin to define the elements of meeting effectiveness. After identifying a meeting in which they have participated, students examine their experience in the meeting, assessing the effectiveness of the meeting.

STEP 1. Introduce the activity by directing students to the instructions and questions on pages 79-80 of the text. Explain that they are to assess a meeting. It may take them a few minutes to settle on which meeting. In order to ensure that they focus on one meeting, it may be helpful to have them write down the date and time of the specific meeting.

STEP 2. Allow time to respond to the scale as well as to the interpretation questions.

STEP 3. Ask for scores results, such as:

Who assessed a meeting that was closest to a 5? Who assessed a meeting that was closest to a 1? Ask for volunteers to describe those meetings.

Who experienced wide discrepancy between the pre-scale assessment score and the scale assessment score? How do you account for the discrepancy? Are there additional factors which, to you, influence the effectiveness of a meeting?

Conduct a large group discussion based upon their responses to the scale and to the interpretation questions on page 79-80. Additional discussion questions may include:

A. Why are meetings important in organizations?

B. How would you define meeting effectiveness?

C. How do you feel when you are in a poorly managed meeting? Do you feel that the chairperson or convener does not hold a high regard for your time? What are some of the consequences of these feelings?

D. It has been observed that by bringing a number of people together to focus on an agenda, meetings have potential to accomplish significant outcomes. Yet often meetings are regarded as a waste of people's times. How do you account for this discrepancy between the potential of meetings and their actual outcomes?

STEP 4. Summarize, using students' main ideas as well as key points from the activity flow sheet.

CHAPTER 3	FACILITATOR ROLE
COMPETENCY 2	USING PARTICIPATIVE DECISION MAKING

Analysis: Decision by the Group
Activity Flow Sheet

PURPOSE: This activity permits students to analyze a situation in terms of the advantages and disadvantages of participative decision making.

KEY TOPICS: Who should participate in decision making, and when.

TIME ESTIMATE: 30 minutes.

FORMAT: Individual activity, work in 4-5 person groups, followed by large discussion.

SPECIAL NEEDS: None.

SEQUENCE:
1. Introduce the activity.

2. Divide the students into 4-5 person groups, asking them to take on the role of Professor Mennon.

3. Conduct a large group discussion.

4. Summarize the major points made by the group.

VARIATION: The small group activity can be omitted by asking each individual to take on the role of Professor Mennon. In step 3, ask for volunteers to share their advice.

KEY POINTS:
1. Participative decision making is not appropriate in all instances.

2. When managers use participative decision making, they must be committed to accept the group's decision.

3. Managers who use participative decision making need to be clear about expectations, limits of authority, and responsibilities.

CHAPTER 3	FACILITATOR ROLE
COMPETENCY 2	USING PARTICIPATIVE DECISION MAKING

Analysis: Decision by the Group
Process Guide

PURPOSE: This activity permits students to analyze a situation in terms of the advantages and disadvantages of participative decision making. This case helps students to understand that participative decision making is appropriate in certain situations, not in all instances.

STEP 1. Introduce the activity by directing students to the instructions and the case on page 91 of the text. Explain that they are to analyze this case in terms of the appropriateness of participative decision making. Ask them to read the case and respond in writing (jot down notes - nothing formal to turn in) to the discussion questions on page 91.

STEP 2. Divide the students into 4-5 person groups. Ask them to take on the role of Professor Mennon. Have them specify the advice that Professor Mennon should have given to John when he called.

STEP 3. Conduct a large group discussion, asking groups for their advice. Some important points include:

   A. Intelligent participative decision making has the potential for increasing the effectiveness of performance. However, participation is not a gimmick for manipulation. John tried a superficial, quick-fix approach and it backfired. In order for group participation to work, the manager and the group need a common goal. The transition to participative decision making needs to be well considered before it is implemented.

   B. John might have been able to avoid this problem by explaining why production standards were too low rather than confining his initial remarks to telling employees that the standards were too low. Further, he should have remained with the group and discussed the production standards. He failed to "communicate," air differences and provide reasons why certain actions could or could not be taken. He should have stayed with the group until he had supplied them with more information, and then asked for their opinions regarding the approaches he outlined. The ensuing discussion would have shaped a suggested course of action to follow, representing the group's opinion as well as John's.

   C. It is poor practice for a manager to abdicate authority as John did in this situation. An important part of a manager's role is to provide effective leadership by offering a plan, giving reasons why, and taking into account suggestions offered by those who will be affected by the plan. Using this approach, the group's wishes and the needs of the organization can be blended into an effective program.

STEP 4. Summarize by asking students to state what they felt to be the main points of this activity.

CHAPTER 3	FACILITATOR ROLE
COMPETENCY 2	USING PARTICIPATIVE DECISION MAKING

Practice: Ethics Task Force
Activity Flow Sheet

PURPOSE: This activity provides students with the opportunity to practice and observe specific participative decision-making skills.

KEY TOPICS: Group decision-making strategies and meeting management

TIME ESTIMATE: 50 minutes.

FORMAT: Small groups of 5-7 persons each.

SPECIAL NEEDS: Post-Discussion Questionnaire for Task Force Members which follows the process guide.

SEQUENCE: 1. Introduce the activity. Explain that each small group will be a task force.

2. Divide students into small groups, with instructions for them to complete the task as per the directions on page 91 of the text.

3. After completing the task, give each task force member a copy of the Post-Discussion Questionnaire for Task Force Members, and give them a few minutes to complete it. Also, ask them individually to reflect on the discussion questions on page 91 of the text.

6. Conduct a large group discussion based on the reported feelings about the discussion.

7. Summarize.

VARIATION: Demonstration of the impact of group size can be made by varying the task force group sizes. A group of 15-20 members, for example, will have quite a different experience than a group of 5, or a group of 3.

KEY POINTS: 1. Meetings involve a number of group dynamics principles.

2. Successful participative decision making in group meetings takes care and planning. It is not spontaneous.

3. Both task and maintenance behaviors are necessary for effective group decision making.

CHAPTER 3	FACILITATOR ROLE
COMPETENCY 2	USING PARTICIPATIVE DECISION MAKING

Practice: Ethics Task Force
Process Guide

PURPOSE: This activity provides students with the opportunity to practice and observe specific participative decision-making skills.

STEP 1. Introduce the activity by explaining that class members will take the role of the ethics task force members. The choice of number of students on each task force is at the discretion of the instructor, but 5-7 persons is ideal. Direct students to the case and instructions on page 91 of the text.

STEP 2. Divide students into small groups, and direct them to complete the task of the task force, on page 91 of the text. This might take 20 minutes.

STEP 3. After the task force discussions are completed, have each group announce its decision. Give each task force member a copy of the Post-Discussion Questionnaire for Task Force Members, and give them a few minutes to complete it.

STEP 4. Allow each individual to respond to the discussion questions in the text on page 91.

STEP 5. Conduct a large group discussion based students' observations and reported feelings about the discussion. Ask for volunteers to share their responses.

Additional discussion questions may include:

A. Use of work time for personal business is a volatile issue for many people. Did you have any difficulty listening to other member's viewpoints?

B. What kinds of task maintenance and group maintenance behaviors did you notice?

C. What is your overall assessment of what happened in your group?

STEP 6. Summarize the major points brought out in the discussion.

CAUTION: Make sure that the class does not get caught up in the content or substance of this exercise but instead focuses on the process. For instance, the outcome of ethics meeting does not matter as much as how the task force reached its conclusion.

POST-DISCUSSION QUESTIONNAIRE FOR TASK FORCE MEMBERS

Indicate how you are now feeling about the group discussion that has just taken place. Draw a circle around the number that best represents your feelings.

1. **The objectives of the discussion were**

    Very clear 1   2   3   4   5   6   7 Not at all clear

2. **The abilities, knowledge, and experience of the persons in the group were used**

    Fully and effectively 1   2   3   4   5   6   7 Poorly and inadequately

3. **The level of involvement of all group members in the discussion was**

    Very low 1   2   3   4   5   6   7 Very high

4. **Control, power, and influence in the discussion were**

    Imposed on group members 1   2   3   4   5   6   7 Shared by all members

5. **Leadership functions were**

    Concentrated in 1 or 2 persons 1   2   3   4   5   6   7 Shared by all

6. **The task, norms, and standards were**

    Too vague 1   2   3   4   5   6   7 Clearly understood by all

7. **The process stimulated**

    Hardening of ideas 1   2   3   4   5   6   7 New ways of looking at issues

8. **In order to evaluate various alternatives, we developed**

    An unorganized approach 1   2   3   4   5   6   7 A logical framework

9. **Taking all things into consideration, how satisfied were you with this discussion?**

    Not at all satisfied 1   2   3   4   5   6   7 Very satisfied

10. **How committed do you feel to the conclusion or decision arrived at by the group?**

    Fully committed 1   2   3   4   5   6   7 Not at all committed

CHAPTER 3	FACILITATOR ROLE
COMPETENCY 2	USING PARTICIPATIVE DECISION MAKING

Application: Meeting Management
Activity Flow Sheet

PURPOSE: This activity allows students to apply the guidelines of effective meeting management to their personal experience.

KEY TOPICS: Participative decision making and increasing meeting effectiveness.

TIME ESTIMATE: In class set up time: 10 minutes: outside of class: 2 hours; in class follow up discussion: 20 minutes.

FORMAT: Individual activity followed by large group discussion.

SPECIAL NEEDS: Students need to attend several meetings.

SEQUENCE:
1. Introduce the activity.
2. Explain that they are to write a report on a meeting.
3. Assist students in the selection of a meeting.
4. Set a date when the paper is due.
5. Conduct a large group discussion and summarize.

VARIATIONS: Students could complete this assignment in pairs, submitting one paper. If this option is chosen, it should be emphasized that the two students in each pair may not agree on everything, and points of disagreement should be noted in the paper.

KEY POINTS:
1. The components of effective meetings are readily observable.

2. Running effective meetings is not a skill that comes naturally to people, but is a learned competency.

3. Effective meetings generally result in higher quality solutions. They also improve morale by avoiding the impression that the conveners are respectful of participants' time.

CHAPTER 3	FACILITATOR ROLE
COMPETENCY 2	USING PARTICIPATIVE DECISION MAKING

Application: Meeting Management
Process Guide

PURPOSE: This activity allows students to apply the guidelines of effective meeting management to their personal experience. Students attend several meetings and write a 3-5 page report on one of them, responding to the set of questions in the text.

STEP 1. Introduce the activity by directing students to the instructions on page 92 of the text.

STEP 2. Explain that they are to observe several meetings and write a report on one of them. Emphasize that this assignment allows them to apply the principles discussed in the learning section to their experience.

STEP 3. If necessary assist students in the selection of meetings to attend. Note that by attending several meetings, they allow themselves options in the subject of their paper. Some meetings may produce richer material than others, for the purposes of the papers.

STEP 4. Set a date when the paper is due. You may need to allow 2-3 weeks.

STEP 5. On the due date of the paper, conduct a large group discussion. Ask for volunteers to share their experience. Summarize the main points of the discussion. Additional discussion questions may include:

   A. Did anything surprise you about the meetings? Explain.

   B. Did you feel that people's time was being respected by the meeting? Why or why not?

   C. Do you think that enough attention was being made to participants' social and emotional needs? Explain.

   D. Did you observe any difficult situations? If so, what were they? How were they handled? How would you have handled them differently?

   E. Did one or two group members try to dominate the discussion? If so, how was this handled? Was it effective? What would you have done differently?

CHAPTER 3	FACILITATOR ROLE
COMPETENCY 3	MANAGING CONFLICT

Assessment: How Do You Handle Conflict?
Activity Flow Sheet

PURPOSE: This activity allows students to consider various behavioral and attitudinal dimensions of handling conflict.

KEY TOPICS: This activity leads into a discussion of Robbins' three views of conflict: traditional, behavioral, and interactionist. In addition, Thomas' five conflict management approaches correspond to the three categories of conflict handling strategies: nonconfrontational (includes avoidance and accommodation), solution-oriented (collaboration and compromise), and control (synonymous with competition).

TIME ESTIMATE: 15 minutes.

FORMAT: Individual activity followed by large group discussion.

SPECIAL NEEDS: None.

SEQUENCE:
1. Introduce the activity.
2. Direct students to respond to the scale in writing.
3. Have students interpret their responses.
4. Conduct a large group discussion and summarize.

VARIATIONS:
1. After step 2, divide students into 4-5 person groups for step 3. Ask groups to report the most important points of their discussions.

2. Assigning as homework, direct students to choose three individuals with whom they have had conflict, and to respond to the scale three times, once for each individual. Write a short paper, noting any patterns of similarities, differences, and what this tells them about their approach to conflict.

KEY POINTS:
1. Conflict is not necessarily bad or something to be avoided at all costs. It can be a source of individual growth as well as organizational effectiveness.

2. Individuals often have different ways of handling conflict with different people in their lives. We might expect to handle conflict differently with our best friend than we would with the manager of a local store with whom we have a dispute.

CHAPTER 3	FACILITATOR ROLE
COMPETENCY 3	MANAGING CONFLICT

Assessment: How Do You Handle Conflict?
Process Guide

PURPOSE: This activity allows students to consider various behavioral and attitudinal dimensions of handling conflict. Students assess their own patterns of handling conflict.

STEP 1. Introduce the activity by having students think of a person with whom they have had disagreements. Students should be encouraged to write down the person's name and recall specific instances of disagreement with this person.

STEP 2. Direct students to read the instructions on page 93 and to respond to the scale in writing. Note that there are no right or wrong answers. Remind them that it is in their interest NOT to look at the scoring and interpretation until after they have responded to the items on the scale.

STEP 3. Have students interpret their responses according to the instructions on pages 93-94 of the text, and to respond to the discussion questions.

> **NOTE ON THE SCORING:** A study conducted by Putnam and Wilson of 360 participants produced the following scores:
>
> Solution-orientation = 3.73
> Control = 2.43
> Nonconfrontational = 2.42

STEP 4. Conduct a large group discussion based on students' reactions to the scale, and on the discussion questions. Summarize their major points.

　A. Did anything in your responses surprise you? If so, explain.

　B. How would your responses have been different with another person instead of the one you chose?

　C. How do you feel about yourself and the relationship when you consistently avoid asserting your point of view?

SPECIAL NOTE: Many people report that in conflictual situations, their objective is not to have their way, but to be understood by the other party, and to be acknowledged as holding a legitimate point of view.

CHAPTER 3	FACILITATOR ROLE
COMPETENCY 3	MANAGING CONFLICT

Analysis: Zack's Electrical Parts
Activity Flow Sheet

PURPOSE: This activity allows students to analyze a case in terms of sources of conflict in the workplace setting.

KEY TOPICS: Levels and sources of conflict, stages of the conflict process, and conflict management strategies.

TIME ESTIMATE: 30 minutes.

FORMAT: 4-5 person groups followed by large group discussion.

SPECIAL NEEDS: None.

SEQUENCE:
1. Introduce the activity.
2. Have students read the case and respond.
3. Place students into 4-5 person groups.
4. Have the groups report to the class and discuss.
5. Summarize.

VARIATIONS:
1. Step 2 can be completed at home; begin the next class meeting with the small group discussions.
2. Omit the small group discussion and proceed directly from the individual responses to a large group discussion.

KEY POINTS:
1. Conflictual situations can be broken down into identifiable stages.
2. Once a conflict is fully developed, collaborative approaches can be used in order to manage the conflict.

CHAPTER 3	FACILITATOR ROLE
COMPETENCY 3	MANAGING CONFLICT

Analysis: Zack's Electrical Parts
Process Guide

PURPOSE: This activity allows students to analyze a case in terms of sources of conflict in a workplace setting. This case demonstrates a highly conflictual situation involving several levels and work units in a firm.

STEP 1. Introduce the activity by directing students to the instructions and the case on page 105-106 of the text.

STEP 2. Have students read the case and respond in writing to the discussion questions on page 106.

STEP 3. Place students into 4-5 person groups each to discuss their responses and to generate a group analysis.

STEP 4. Have the groups report to the class and discuss. Additional discussion questions may include:

   A. What benefits do you think might be gained by the organization from this conflict? In other words, are there any changes within the organization that might be precipitated by this conflict? If so, what?

   B. How might individuals benefit from this conflict?

STEP 5. Summarize, the main ideas generated in the discussion as well as the key points from the activity flow sheet.

CHAPTER 3	FACILITATOR ROLE
COMPETENCY 3	MANAGING CONFLICT

Practice: Win as Much as You Can
Activity Flow Sheet

PURPOSE: This activity allows students to practice the skills of conflict management in a role-play group situation.

KEY TOPICS: Conflict management strategies.

TIME ESTIMATE: 50 minutes

FORMAT: 8-person groups followed by large group discussion.

SPECIAL NEEDS: None

SEQUENCE:
1. Divide the class into 8-person groups as per the directions on page 106 of the text.

2. Direct students to the instructions on page 106 of the text.

3. Give the groups 20-30 minutes to role play.

4. Conduct a large group discussion and summarize.

KEY POINTS:
1. Tendencies towards preferred conflict handling situations vary according to individuals.

2. Conflict management strategies are learned skills and require practice to master them.

3. There are frequently benefits from conflictual situations, which can be reaped if handled properly.

| CHAPTER 3 | FACILITATOR ROLE |
| COMPETENCY 3 | MANAGING CONFLICT |

Practice: Win as Much as You Can
Process Guide

PURPOSE: This activity allows students to practice the skills of conflict management in a role-play group decision making situation. This activity presents students with a problem situation that requires important decisions to be made under difficult circumstances with few options available.

STEP 1. Divide the class into 8-person groups, and subdivide those groups into dyads as per the directions on page 106 of the text. Be certain that the group members are positioned for interaction, and that they can hear one another without being overhead by the other groups.

STEP 2. Direct students to the instructions on page 106 of the text. Explain that each group will role play the same situation, and that group members will be able to practice conflict management strategies. The instructor keeps scores. Answer any questions that the students might have.

STEP 3. Give the groups 20-30 minutes to role play.

STEP 4. Conduct a large group discussion based on the discussion questions on pages 108 of the text and summarize major points.

CHAPTER 3	FACILITATOR ROLE
COMPETENCY 3	MANAGING CONFLICT

Application: Managing Your Own Conflicts
Activity Flow Sheet

PURPOSE: This activity allows students to apply conflict management strategies to a situation which they are currently facing.

KEY TOPICS: Conflict management approaches and how to use collaborative approaches to conflict management.

TIME ESTIMATE: In class set up time: 10 minutes; outside of class: 60-90 minutes; in class follow up discussion: 20 minutes.

FORMAT: Individual activity with assigned 3-5 page paper, followed by large group discussion.

SPECIAL NEEDS: None.

SEQUENCE:

1. Introduce the activity.

2. Direct students to the instructions on page 108 of the text.

3. Assist students in selecting a conflict situation.

4. Review the assigned questions on page 108.

5. Set a due date for the report.

6. On the due date, conduct a large group discussion of their experiences and insights.

KEY POINTS:

1. Conflict management strategies are generic to all kinds of conflict, even to conflict that we experience in our personal relationships.

2. Sometimes we may resist resolving conflict. As much pain as we may receive from it, we may sometimes find ourselves prolonging the conflict in order to justify our view of the other person or of the situation.

3. The skills involved in conflict management strategies are learned, requiring attention and practice.

CHAPTER 3	FACILITATOR ROLE
COMPETENCY 3	MANAGING CONFLICT

Application: Managing Your Own Conflicts
Process Guide

PURPOSE: This activity allows students to apply conflict management strategies to a situation which they are currently facing. After defining the conflictual situation, students examine the array of strategic options available to them, decide on which strategies to use, and plan to implement their decision.

STEP 1. Introduce the activity by explaining that students will be allowed to apply conflict management strategies to a conflict situation which they are currently experiencing. Remind them that the strategies they have studied are valid in interpersonal relationships outside of the organizational setting, as well as in the workplace.

STEP 2. Direct students to the instructions on page 108 of the text.

STEP 3. Assist students in selecting a conflict situation. If they are not currently experiencing conflict, help them recall one that did exist for them in the recent past.

STEP 4. Review the assigned questions on page 108 in detail with the students, and respond to their concerns.

STEP 5. Set a due date for the report. Because of the introspective nature of this assignment, students can reasonably be expected to complete it well within a week.

STEP 6. On the due date, conduct a large group discussion of their experiences and insights. Additional discussion questions may include:

   A. Did anything about this assignment surprise you? If so, explain.

   B. Which strategies did you find successful? Which strategies did you find difficult?

   C. Did you find that you have a tendency to be more comfortable with one strategy than with the others? If so, why?

   D. Did you find yourself resisting actions to resolve the conflict? What barriers to conflict resolution do you think people experience?

   E. Do you think that some people *like* conflict? If so, why?

   F. What was the most valuable thing you learned from this assignment?

CHAPTER 4 — MONITOR ROLE

The Monitor Role, along with the Coordinator Role, comprises the Internal Process Model of the Competing Values Framework. While some organizations epitomize the monitoring process (such as the Internal Revenue Service), monitoring skills are necessary for managers in any organization. In this role, managers pay attention to details, collect, maintain, and disseminate routine information, monitor employee compliance to standards, do statistical and financial analyses, and write procedural material.

While some may not feel comfortable with the paper-intense, detail-focus of this role, the fact is, attention to this detail permits top functioning in the other roles. For instance, only if we know where we are and what we have, can we strengthen our positions as brokers and innovators. Thus, while monitor appears in the framework opposite of broker, the fact is they are complementary. Both roles collect information which is necessary for the organization. Monitor collects data from within with organization, and broker collects data from outside of the organization. It is apparent that effective monitoring is enabling to the proficient functioning of the other roles in the framework.

The competencies in the Monitor Role. The three competencies in this role and their corresponding topics in the learning activities are:

Competency 1: Monitoring Personal Performance

Topics:
    The TRAF System
        Filing
        Taking Good Notes
        External Monitoring
    Are you in data overload?
    Monitoring the mess: building your own information network
    Good Monitoring versus micro-managing
    The facts are friendly: pursuing the truth about your own performance
    Why we don't necessarily learn from experience
    Continuous improvement at the individual level
    Working from the left-hand column: making undiscussable issues
        discussable

Competency 2: Managing Collective Performance

Topics:
    Managing collective performance learning
    We monitor "output"--but what is that?
    Monitoring the value chain: how do we know how we're doing?
    Re-engineering the process
    Keeping the ball in play: some principles of process re-engineering
        Combine multiple jobs into one where possible
        Workers make decisions
        The steps in the process are performed in a natural order

Processes have multiple versions
Checks and controls are reduced
What we watch and why?
The next revolution: service-sector activity
Boiling eggs: look for the limiting step and design around it
Monitoring variation: the enemy of quality

Competency 3: Managing Organizational Performance

Topics:	Quality: beyond performance to internal standards
Customer management data is a more powerful predictor than financial data
See the future first: anticipating what customers want before they ask for it

Conceptually, these are not the only competencies in this role. Other competencies have been identified as:

Monitoring the effectiveness of the work unit
Simple roads to quantitative analysis
The essentials of financial analysis
Keeping detailed records
Tracking and evaluating routine information
Monitoring employee performance
Receiving and analyzing routine information
Reducing information overload
Analyzing information with critical thinking
Presenting information: writing effectively

The Monitor Role and current issues: The monitor role is related to issues surrounding globalization due to the increasing need to address an international audience as well as to collect information from an international audience. With regard to managing a culturally diverse work force, what cultural differences affect monitoring employee and organizational performance?

Some questions to consider in this chapter are:

1. Do bureaucracies demand the competencies of the monitor role more than, for instance, the innovator role? What is it about the structure that might lead managers to define "good management" more in terms of monitor skills than in terms of innovator skills?

2. Managers in the monitor role track employee performance and compliance with the control systems of the organization. How do the competencies of the mentor role provide balance, and enable the manager to do a better job of managing?

3. How is "output" defined differently in different types of organizations: private firms, public agencies, and not-for-profit organizations?

CHAPTER 4	MONITOR ROLE
COMPETENCY 1	MONITORING PERSONAL PERFORMANCE

Assessment: Data Overload and Information Gaps
Activity Flow Sheet

PURPOSE: This activity is designed to help students assess how much information they are being exposed to, and how they are sorting, ignoring, or using that information.

KEY TOPICS: Many people feel deluged by it information; TRAF

TIME ESTIMATE: 15-20 minutes to respond to the questions and discuss.

FORMAT: Individual activity followed by a large group discussion in class.

SPECIAL NEEDS: None.

SEQUENCE:
1. Introduce the activity and have students individually complete the questions.

2. Conduct large group discussion.

3. Summarize. As a lead into the learning activity, TRAF can be presented as a proven strategy.

VARIATION: The questionnaire may be completed as homework, with the large group discussion beginning at the next class session.

KEY POINTS:
1. The amount of information to which we are exposed will likely increase instead of lessen.

2. Information overload is a problem common to many people, managers and students alike.

3. There are systems and techniques which can handle information.

CHAPTER 4	MONITOR ROLE
COMPETENCY 1	MONITORING PERSONAL PERFORMANCE

Assessment: Data Overload and Information Gaps
Process Guide

PURPOSE: This activity is designed to help students assess how much information they are being exposed to, and how they are sorting, ignoring, or using that information. While the focus in this activity is on paper information, the principles in this chapter also help students to manage information they receive from non-paper sources: conversations over the telephone, information disseminated in meetings, and the vast array of verbal information. Students are asked to consider how they deal with incoming information, and what they do when they feel overwhelmed with information.

STEP 1. Introduce the activity on page 116 and have students individually complete the questions in writing.

STEP 2. Conduct large group discussion based on their responses, focusing on what strategies students presently use to handle information, barriers to using strategies, and the extent to which these strategies are useful. Additional discussion questions may include:

    A. How do you know if you are experiencing information overload?

    B. As you look to your future, do you expect the amount of information to which you are exposed to automatically increase or decease without any action on your part? Why?

    C. What causes the overload and how do you recover from it?

    D. What problems do you now have in handling information?

    E. What techniques and skills have you found helpful in handling routine information?

STEP 3. Summarize the major problems that students voiced in handling information. Note any skills that they may have found helpful in handling information. This discussion leads into the learning activity where TRAF can be presented as a proven strategy.

A NOTE FROM ONE OF THE AUTHORS: This section on dealing with information overload can be very stimulating and helpful to the class, or it can be deadly - depending upon how it is introduced and handled. For background information, I would suggest two books: *Information Anxiety* (see references) By Richard Saul

Wurman, and *Organized To Be The Best* by Susan Silver (Adams Hall, 1989). Wurman's book is a provocative and creative discussion about the blessing and curse information is in our lives, and how we can cope with it. I've loaned my copy to many people, and they have been grateful for the help Wurman offers. I use Wurman when I teach sections on writing. He has great things to say about displaying and presenting information.

Silver's book is a fundamental, hands-on, how-to book on channeling and sorting mountains of paper. Both books are very practical and help students immensely.

I have found that there are always three or four "structure freaks" (I use the term with affection) in the class who are great resources on handling routine information. Recruit them to help teach the others. Have some students give presentations on filing and record keeping systems; on setting up files on their personal computers, or tricks and strategies for handling the information a college student often gets buried under.

The main point I make when I teach this stuff is that we have to find a match between our personality type and the organizing methods we use. A highly structured, compulsively organized person will do this stuff almost reflexively; others, like, me, will never be able to tolerate a system that requires too much maintenance and too much attention to detail. We must be realistic. I like some ambiguity and a little confusion in my life, but I don't like waking up in Pittsburg when I'm supposed to be in Chicago, or missing meetings, or forgetting my son's birthday.

CHAPTER 4	MONITOR ROLE
COMPETENCY 1	MONITORING PERSONAL PERFORMANCE

Analysis A: Why was Allan So Effective?
Activity Flow Sheet

PURPOSE: This activity allows students to apply what they have learned in the learning activity, analyzing how someone handles giving difficult feedback

KEY TOPICS: The necessity of receiving feedback on performance, coupled with the painful difficulty at times in providing it, disscussable and undiscussable issues.

TIME ESTIMATE: 30 minutes.

FORMAT: Individual activity followed by large group discussion.

SPECIAL NEEDS: None.

SEQUENCE:
1. Introduce the activity.
2. Remind students of salient points.
3. Give assignment.
4. Conduct large group discussion.

VARIATIONS:
1. Form class members into groups of 4-5 students each to discuss the questions in the text and to present in a large group discussion their responses.
2. Ask for student volunteers to present a role-play of the situation.

KEY POINTS:
1. This activity represents a delicate situation whereby someone very much needed honest feedback, and yet it was difficult to provide it.
2. Allen Cox was effective because he knew the man, Cox's motives were genuine, and the feedback was accurate. In order to be effective, as was Allan Cox, we need to pay the price of knowing the person well and appreciating the person.

CHAPTER 4	MONITOR ROLE
COMPETENCY 1	MONITORING PERSONAL PERFORMANCE

Analysis A: Why was Allan So Effective?
Process Guide

PURPOSE: This activity allows students to apply what they have learned in the learning activity, analyzing how someone handles giving difficult feedback.

STEP 1. Introduce the activity by referring students to the activity and instructions on page 131 of the text.

STEP 2. Remind students that at times individuals need honest feedback, yet it may be a very delicate and difficult matter to provide it.

STEP 3. Direct students to read the Allan Cox example on pages 127-128, and to jot down their responses to the questions in the activity on page 132.

STEP 4. Conduct a large group discussion. Additional points to be made in the discussion may include:

   A. What are the common difficulties portrayed by this situation?

   B. Reflect on times when you have been in a similar situation--what was difficult for you and why?

   C. In what ways can the receiver of feedback facilitate matters for the giver of feedback?

   D. What is the role of trust in this situation? How do we go about fostering trust in the workplace? What barriers are there to the development of trust?

CHAPTER 4	MONITOR ROLE
COMPETENCY 1	MONITORING PERSONAL PERFORMANCE

Analysis B: Monitoring Your Own Behavior
Activity Flow Sheet

PURPOSE: This activity allows students to apply what they have learned in the learning activity, tracking their own target behaviors for a period of time

KEY TOPICS: Monitoring one's own performance

TIME ESTIMATE: 10 minutes in class, followed by work outside of class, followed by large group discussion in class of about 20 minutes

FORMAT: Individual activity followed by large group discussion.

SPECIAL NEEDS: Target Behaviors Tracking Sheet, which follows the process guide

SEQUENCE:
1. Introduce the activity.
2. Remind students of salient points.
3. Give assignment.
4. Conduct large group discussion.

VARIATIONS:
1. Form class members into dyads to discuss this experience.
2. Ask for student volunteers to share their experience to the entire class.
3. The time-frame may vary, but 3 days would be considered the minimum

KEY POINTS:
1. Identifying target behaviors to work on is a valuable self-monitoring experience.
2. Tracking those behaviors can give us great insights to our behaviors, and the ability to change them.

CHAPTER 4	MONITOR ROLE
COMPETENCY 1	MONITORING PERSONAL PERFORMANCE

Analysis B: Monitoring Your Own Behavior
Process Guide

PURPOSE: This activity allows students to apply what they have learned in the learning activity, tracking their own target behaviors for a period of time.

STEP 1. Introduce the activity by referring students to the activity and instructions on page 132 of the text.

STEP 2. Remind students that one of the first steps to changing undesirable behaviors is to track them, to ascertain any triggers and results.

STEP 3. Give each student a copy of the Target Behaviors Tracking Chart (next page) and walk them through it.

STEP 4. After the designated time period, conduct a large group discussion on this experience. Additional points to be made in the discussion may include:

   A. What are some situations where tracking one's behavior is recommended? (examples include time management and weight loss efforts)

   B. What was difficult about this assignment, and why?

   C. What do people learn from engaging in a tracking activity of this sort?

Target Behaviors Tracking Chart
for: Name _____

Date: _____

Target Traits and Behaviors	Date	Event	Evaluation

CHAPTER 4	MONITOR ROLE
COMPETENCY 1	MONITORING PERSONAL PERFORMANCE

Practice: Monitoring Your Performance by Inviting Feedback
Activity Flow Sheet

PURPOSE: With this activity students practice inviting feedback from someone regarding as aspect of their performance.

KEY TOPICS: Feedback, monitoring one's own performance.

TIME ESTIMATE: 20 minutes.

FORMAT: Individual activity and large group discussion at a later date.

SPECIAL NEEDS: None.

SEQUENCE:
1. Introduce the activity.

2. Direct students to read the assignment on page 133.

3. After the specified time period, when students have submitted their written memo to you, conduct a large group discussion and summarize.

VARIATION: Before sending students out to do the assignment, put them into dyads to discuss this with each other, and to help each other decide who to approach. Their partner is a source of support.

KEY POINTS:
1. The information gathered is available and needs to be interpreted in a meaningful manner.

2. The skill of asking for feedback is a difficult skill to master for many people.

CHAPTER 4	MONITOR ROLE
COMPETENCY 1	MONITORING PERSONAL PERFORMANCE

Practice: Monitoring Your Performance by Inviting Feedback
Process Guide

PURPOSE: With this activity students practice inviting feedback from someone regarding an aspect of their performance

STEP 1. Introduce the activity by referring students to the directions on page 133 of the text.

STEP 2. Direct students to complete this activity by a designated date, and to respond in writing by submitting a memo to you, as per the directions.

STEP 3. After they have submitted the assignment, and after you have read the memos, conduct a large group discussion on this experience. While their memos will prompt points that need to be made in the large group discussion, additional questions for discussion might include:

A. How did you decide whom to choose for giving you feedback? What are the characteristics of this person and your relationship with the individual?

B. What was difficult about this assignment and why?

C. What was the most fulfilling aspect of this assignment and why?

D. What specifically can you do to facilitate the efforts of someone who might need to ask you for feedback?

CHAPTER 4	MONITOR ROLE
COMPETENCY 1	MONITORING PERSONAL PERFORMANCE

Application: Working In the Left-hand Column: Stacy Brock and Terry Lord
Activity Flow Sheet

PURPOSE: The purpose of this activity is to allow students to apply some of the concepts from the learning section. Specifically, in this activity, they are to apply discussing the undiscussable.

KEY TOPICS: Discussable and undiscussable issues.

TIME ESTIMATE: 40 minutes.

FORMAT: A dyad activity followed by large group discussion.

SPECIAL NEEDS: None.

SEQUENCE:
1. Direct students to the instructions and case on pages 133-135 of the text.

2. Divide students into dyads and have them role-play the characters of Stacy and Terry.

3. Conduct a large group discussion.

VARIATION: Instead of the dyads, ask for two volunteers to role-play Stacy and Terry, in a fishbowl activity.

KEY POINTS:
1. Situations like this one are painful, but not uncommon.

2. Managing relationships to minimize these situations is very important.

3. Surfacing undiscussable issues is a critical skill to develop.

CHAPTER 4	MONITOR ROLE
COMPETENCY 1	MONITORING PERSONAL PERFORMANCE

Application: Working In the Left-hand Column: Stacy Brock and Terry Lord
Activity Flow Sheet

PURPOSE: The purpose of this activity is to allow students to apply some of the concepts from the learning section. Specifically, in this activity, they are to apply discussing the undiscussable.

STEP 1. Direct students to the instructions and the case on pages 132-135 of the text.

STEP 2. Divide the students into dyads (if necessary, use one 3-person group) and have them role-pay the characters of Stacy and Terry.

STEP 3. Conduct a large group discussion on the results of the exercise. Additional discussion questions may include:

A. What specific issues were not discussable? Why?

B. What strategies did you use for surfacing these issues?

C. What was the most part of fulfilling your role in this assignment?

CHAPTER 4	MONITOR ROLE
COMPETENCY 2	MANAGING COLLECTIVE PERFORMANCE

Assessment: What Went Wrong?
Activity Flow Sheet

PURPOSE: The purpose of this activity is to allow students to identify a situation that did not go well, and to discern some possible reasons for the outcome.

KEY TOPICS: The importance of monitoring collective performance

TIME ESTIMATE: 20-30 minutes.

FORMAT: A small group activity followed by large group discussion

SPECIAL NEEDS: None.

SEQUENCE:
1. Divide students into small groups.
2. Direct them to follow the directions on page 135-136
3. Conduct a large group discussion.

KEY POINTS:
1. A number of different types of things can go wrong in organizations, causing undesired outcomes.

2. Sometimes organizational members know that a procedure or action is flawed, but will not tell others of their fears and assessment.

3. The things that go wrong might be technical, but if people know about it and refuse to take remedial action, then other dynamics are involved.

CHAPTER 4	MONITOR ROLE
COMPETENCY 2	MANAGING COLLECTIVE PERFORMANCE

Assessment: What Went Wrong?
Process Guide

PURPOSE: The purpose of this activity is to allow students to identify a situation that did not go well, and to discern some possible reasons for the outcome.

STEP 1. Divide students into small groups, of no more than 6 people each.

STEP 2. Have them read the directions on page 135 of the text. Ask them to identify several incidents of things that went wrong in organizations, and to choose one to explore more carefully.

STEP 3. Have each group choose one example to examine in detail, and to list some possible root causes of the problem.

STEP 3. Conduct a large group discussion, drawing on their observations. Respond to the questions on page 135-136. Additional discussion points include:

　A. What are the possible categories of things that went wrong in the examples they identified?

　B. Why it is difficult to bring problems to the attention of those at higher levels in organizations?

CHAPTER 4	MONITOR ROLE
COMPETENCY 2	MANAGING COLLECTIVE PERFORMANCE

Analysis: Can This Process Be Improved?
Activity Flow Sheet

PURPOSE: This activity allows students to analyze a case and make a determination as to how a process might be improved.

KEY TOPICS: Productivity, process re-engineering

TIME ESTIMATE: 45 minutes.

FORMAT: 2-3 person groups, followed by large group discussion.

SPECIAL NEEDS: None.

SEQUENCE:
1. Place class members into 2-3 person groups.

2. Instruct students to read the activity and respond to the questions on page 150.

3. Conduct a large group discussion and summarize.

KEY POINTS:
1. The system is not designed to allow improvement; in order for there to be improvement, the system must be redesigned.

2. Limiting factors are critical--since it takes 60 seconds to do step 3 in the activity, then there is no possible way for more than 60 applicants to be processed in an hour without redesigning the system. If two clerks do that task, then the limiting factor becomes the 40-second eye test.

3. Organizations and managers often face considerable resistance when faced with making system changes.

CHAPTER 4	MONITOR ROLE
COMPETENCY 2	MANAGING COLLECTIVE PERFORMANCE

Analysis: Can This Process Be Improved?
Process Guide

PURPOSE: This activity allows students to analyze a case and make a determination as to how a process might be improved.

STEP 1. Place students into 2-3 person groups.

STEP 2. Have them respond in writing to the questions on page 150.

STEP 3. Conduct a large group discussion, having each group report their solution. Additional questions might include:

1. What is the output of the Department of Motor Vehicles?

2. Break down the activities according to the following 4 categories: Unit of competitive advantage, value-added support work, essential support work, and nonessential work. How do the activities of the Department of Motor Vehicles apply to these categories?

3. What is the limiting factor in this case? (NOTE: according to the chart on the top of page 150 in the text, the limiting factor is step #3: Check file for violations and restrictions. With this being a 60-second process, then no more than 60 applications per hour can be processed. If two clerks are doing this task, then the limiting factor becomes the eye test, at 40 seconds, which means that 90 applications per hour could be processed.)

CHAPTER 4	MONITOR ROLE
COMPETENCY 2	MANAGING COLLECTIVE PERFORMANCE

Practice: A Better Way to Handle Loan Applications
Activity Flow Sheet

PURPOSE: This activity allows students to practice system redesign.

KEY TOPICS: Process re-engineering and redesign

TIME ESTIMATE: 30 minutes.

FORMAT: Small groups of 3 students followed by large group discussion. The memo may be assigned as homework, if desired

SPECIAL NEEDS: None.

SEQUENCE:
1. Divide the class members into groups of 3.

2. Direct each group to complete the task on pages 151-154.

3. Conduct a large group discussion by summarizing the findings of the groups.

KEY POINTS:
1. Redesigning systems takes creative effort.

2. Redesigning the system is critical to meeting the goal of improved customer service.

CHAPTER 4	MONITOR ROLE
COMPETENCY 2	MANAGING COLLECTIVE PERFORMANCE

Practice: A Better Way to Handle Loan Applications
Process Guide

PURPOSE: This activity allows students to practice system redesign.

STEP 1. Divide the class members into groups of 3. Give them the instructions that they comprise a special Customer Service Team for a bank, and it is their task to redesign the manner of handling loan applications.

STEP 2. Direct them to the activity on pages 151-154 of the text. Allow teams 20 minutes to analyze the situation and redesign the process before presenting their solutions to the rest of the class.

STEP 3. Conduct a large group discussion by summarizing the observations of the teams. Additional questions might include:

1. What is the output of the bank with regards to this activity?

2. Break down the activities according to the following 4 categories: Unit of competitive advantage, value-added support work, essential support work, and nonessential work. How do the activities of the bank's loan process apply to these categories?

3. What are the limiting factors in this case?

CHAPTER 4	MONITOR ROLE
COMPETENCY 2	MANAGING COLLECTIVE PERFORMANCE

Application: Mapping and Improving a Process Yourself
Activity Flow Sheet

PURPOSE: This activity allows students to apply mapping and redesign skills to an organizational situation.

TIME ESTIMATE: In class: 10 minutes to set up; over a week period outside of class: approximately 3 hours; in class follow up discussion: 15-20 minutes.

FORMAT: A small group activity followed by large group discussion.

SPECIAL NEEDS: None.

SEQUENCE:
1. Divide the class into groups of 4-5 people.

2. Direct students to the instructions on page 154.

2. Conduct a clarifying discussion regarding their choice of activity.

3. Remind them of the due date.

4. On the due date, conduct a large group discussion.

KEY POINT: Notice the creativity involved in this process of mapping and redesign.

CHAPTER 4	MONITOR ROLE
COMPETENCY 2	MANAGING COLLECTIVE PERFORMANCE

Application: Mapping and Improving a Process Yourself
Process Guide

PURPOSE: This activity allows students to apply critical mapping and design skills to an organizational situation.

STEP 1. Direct students to the instructions on page 154.

STEP 2. Conduct a clarifying discussion regarding what type of organization they may wish to choose for this activity.

STEP 3. Walk through the questions with them.

STEP 4. Remind them of the due date for their written map and response.

STEP 5. On the due date, conduct a large group discussion regarding their experience in completing the assignment. Summarize their responses to the questions of the assignment. Make the key points.

CHAPTER 4	MONITOR ROLE
COMPETENCY 3	MANAGING ORGANIZATIONAL PERFORMANCE

Assessment: Take the Role of the Customer
Activity Flow Sheet

PURPOSE: This activity allows students to assess their ability to take a customer perspective in evaluating performance.

KEY TOPICS: Criteria for evaluation.

TIME ESTIMATE: 50 minutes.

FORMAT: 6-person groups, followed by large group discussion.

SPECIAL NEEDS: None.

SEQUENCE:
1. Introduce the activity by walking students through the instructions on page 154-155.

2. Place students into 6-person groups to accomplish the task.

3. Have students report their findings to the class.

4. Conduct a large group discussion, summarizing their revisions.

KEY POINTS:
1. Surface the notion of different criteria and values.

2. Note the different ideas of product value.

CHAPTER 4	MONITOR ROLE
COMPETENCY 3	MANAGING ORGANIZATIONAL PERFORMANCE

Assessment: Take the Role of the Customer
Process Guide

PURPOSE: This activity allows students to assess their ability to take a customer perspective in evaluating performance.

STEP 1. Introduce the activity by walking students through the instructions on page 154-155. You will likely need to be very specific and detailed in order for them to understand the factors and the weights.

STEP 2. Place students into 6-person groups. Be prepared to assist groups in choosing a facilitator. You may wish to remind them of the skills they have already covered in the facilitator role.

STEP 3. Direct students to perform the task.

STEP 4. After the groups are finished, have each group report their findings to the entire class.

STEP 5. Conduct a large group discussion, addressing the questions on page 155 and summarizing their points.

CHAPTER 4	MONITOR ROLE
COMPETENCY 3	MANAGING ORGANIZATIONAL PERFORMANCE

Analysis: Conducting a Real Customer Value Profile
Activity Flow Sheet

PURPOSE: This activity provides students with an opportunity to build a customer value profile with people in a real organization.

KEY TOPICS: Quality, value, customer expectations

TIME ESTIMATE: 15 minutes to introduce the activity, several weeks for students to complete it, and 30 minutes for large group discussion afterwards..

FORMAT: 2-3 person groups followed by large group discussion.

SPECIAL NEEDS: Factor Table for each group (follows process guide).

SEQUENCE:
1. Introduce the activity; form class into groups.
2. Walk students through the activity.
3. Have the groups complete the task.
4. In 2-3 weeks, have groups report back to the class.
5. Summarize.

NOTE: This is an organizational development activity, and it also can be seen as building on the assessment activity at the beginning of this competency.

KEY POINTS:
1. Attention to customer satisfaction is critical to managing organizational performance.

2. Customer satisfaction assessment involves a good look at those who buy from the competition.

CHAPTER 4	MONITOR ROLE
COMPETENCY 3	MANAGING ORGANIZATIONAL PERFORMANCE

Analysis: Conducting a Real Customer Value Profile
Process Guide

PURPOSE: This activity provides students with an opportunity to work with people in a real organization, and build a customer value profile for them.

STEP 1. Introduce the activity by referring to the instructions on page 162-164, and form class into 2-3 person groups.

STEP 2. Walk students through the activity, referring them back to what they learned in the assessment activity.

> It may be necessary to help students identify what sorts of organizations they might wish to work with and how to approach these organizations. Its likely that some students, through their local contacts, will be able to offer suggestions and help to other groups.

STEP 3. Be sure to set a time schedule and a date when the task is to be completed.

STEP 4. At the end of the time period, have each group report on their experiences to the class. Discuss as a large group. Some things to look for include:

   A. The reactions of the group they worked with, and how that process evolved.
   B. The role of looking closely at the competition.
   C. Ideas about the dynamics of quality and value.

STEP 5. Summarize by eliciting students' feelings regarding the experience.

FACTOR TABLE

Factors	Weights per factor	Our product's score (X weight)	Competitor #1's score (X weight)	Competitor #2's score (X weight)
TOTAL				

CHAPTER 4	MONITOR ROLE
COMPETENCY 3	MANAGING ORGANIZATIONAL PERFORMANCE

Practice: A Role Play for Challenging Customer Service Situations
Activity Flow Sheet

PURPOSE: This activity allows students to identify and role-play a challenging customer service situation.

KEY TOPICS: Quality, value, customer expectations

TIME ESTIMATE: 45 minutes.

FORMAT: 3-person groups followed by large group discussion.

SEQUENCE:
1. Introduce the activity.

2. Place students into 3-person groups.

3. Have students share their role play with the entire class.

4. Conduct large group discussion and summarize.

KEY POINTS:
1. Challenging customer service situations are handled with interaction skills.

2. Challenging customer service situations can advance into a more difficult situation if they are not handled properly.

CHAPTER 4	MONITOR ROLE
COMPETENCY 3	MANAGING ORGANIZATIONAL PERFORMANCE

Practice: A Role Play for Challenging Customer Service Situations
Process Guide

PURPOSE: This activity allows students to identify and role-play a challenging customer service situation.

STEP 1. Introduce the activity by referring students to the directions on page 164.

STEP 2. Place students into 3-person groups for this activity.

STEP 3. Given students 15 minutes to complete the task.

STEP 4. Have each group share its situation with the entire class.

STEP 5. Conduct a large group discussion, allowing students to present their situations and responses. Summarize their major points.

CHAPTER 4	MONITOR ROLE
COMPETENCY 3	MANAGING ORGANIZATIONAL PERFORMANCE

Application A: Creating Customer Value Profile with Real Customers
Activity Flow Sheet

PURPOSE: This activity provides students with an opportunity to build a customer profile with real customers.

KEY POINTS: Value, quality, customer expectations.

TIME ESTIMATE: 20 minutes to introduce, followed by 2-3 weeks for completion, following by large group discussion.

FORMAT: 2-4 person groups followed by large group discussion.

SEQUENCE:
1. Introduce students to the activity and form class into groups.
2. Walk students through the activity.
3. Have the groups complete the task.
4. In 2-3 weeks, have groups report back to the class.
5. Summarize.

NOTE: This is an organizational development activity, building on the analysis activity.

KEY POINTS:
1. Attention to customer satisfaction is critical to managing organizational performance.
2. Asking the right questions is critical to the data obtained.

CHAPTER 4	MONITOR ROLE
COMPETENCY 3	MANAGING ORGANIZATIONAL PERFORMANCE

Application A: Creating Customer Value Profile with Real Customers
Process Guide

PURPOSE: This activity provides students with an opportunity to build a customer profile with real customers.

STEP 1. Introduce students to the activity by directing their attention to the directions on pages 165 of the text. Form class into 2-4 person groups.

STEP 2. Walk students through the activity, referring them back to what they learned in the assessment and analysis activities.

> Again, it may be necessary to help students identify what customers of what organizations they might wish to work with, and how to approach these customers. Its likely that some students, through their local contacts, will be able to offer suggestions and help to other groups.

STEP 3. Be sure to set a time schedule and a date when the task is to be completed.

STEP 4. At the end of the time period, have each group report on their experiences to the class. Discuss as a large group. Some things to look for include:

- A. The reactions of the customers they worked with, and how that process evolved.

- B. Comparing the ratings of employees with those of external customers

- C. Ideas about the dynamics of quality and value.

STEP 5. Summarize by eliciting students' feelings regarding the experience.

CHAPTER 4	MONITOR ROLE
COMPETENCY 3	MANAGING ORGANIZATIONAL PERFORMANCE

Application B: Analyzing Customer Service
Activity Flow Sheet

PURPOSE: This activity allows students to apply concepts from this chapter by observing customer service transactions first-hand.

KEY POINTS: Quality, value, customer expectations

TIME ESTIMATE: Time to plan plus 60 minutes for the transactions.

FORMAT: Individual activity followed by large group discussion.

SEQUENCE:
1. Introduce students to the activity.
2. Instruct students to complete the task within the week.
3. Conduct a large group discussion.
4. Summarize.

KEY POINTS:
1. Challenging customer service situations are handled with interaction skills.
2. Challenging customer service situations can advance into a more difficult situation if they are not handled properly.

CHAPTER 4	MONITOR ROLE
COMPETENCY 3	MANAGING ORGANIZATIONAL PERFORMANCE

Application B: Analyzing Customer Service
Process Guide

PURPOSE: This activity allows students to apply concepts from this chapter by observing customer service transactions first-hand.

STEP 1. Introduce students to the activity by directing their attention to the assignment on page 166 of the text.

STEP 2. Walk students through the activity to help them be clean on what they are to do. Set a time frame and assign a written report, if desired.

STEP 3. After the time for the assignment is completed, conduct a large group discussion based on student reports of their experiences. Respond to the questions on page 166 and summarize their major concerns. Additional discussion questions include:

A. If any transaction was handled poorly, what can you say about the differences between the issues that prompted the transaction with the customers, and the issues which developed through the interaction with the customers? What does this say to you about the importance of lower-level participants in organizations who interact with customers?

B. What was the most difficult part of this assignment?

C. If you had more time and this were a work project, what additional information would you have wanted to include?

CHAPTER 5 — COORDINATOR ROLE

The Coordinator Role, along with the Monitor Role, comprises the Internal Process Model of the Competing Values Framework. As such this managerial role is often associated with the organization as a closed system, with attention to detail and documentation, and with tracking activity and performance. The manager as coordinator is responsible for operational planning, organizing and maintaining the work flow, trouble shooting, controlling resources, providing procedural advice, advancing rule observance, and enforcing compliance to standards.

While the coordinator role competencies may appear rather ordinary and unexciting to some, they have formed the basis for the concept of management for decades. These competencies may not be the current focus of most trade books and magazines, but they are essential to organizational and managerial functioning. In the words of one of the authors, "Central to the coordinator role is the need to make sure that the right people are in the right place at the right time to do the right work."

The competencies of the coordinator role are also important in our personal lives. Most people realize that budgeting and controlling their financial resources, planning their futures, and organizing their homes provide for a level of predictability in life which enhances personal freedom. Failure to apply these competencies may lead to unpleasant surprises, such as returned checks from the bank.

While paradox is reflected to some extent in each of the competencies, the competency of control raises a basic paradox. On the one hand organization need control systems; they need to control the behaviors of individuals within those organizations. On the other hand, individuals need some autonomy and to experience a measure of control in their lives. To add to this mixture, some controls are deemed necessary for human freedom. Paradoxically, anarchy is not characteristic of a society where individual freedom is maximized.

It is important for students to understand the human side of control. The basic dilemma here is between the organization's need for some measures of control and employees' or human needs for some measure of autonomy and control over their own situations. Students need to understand both sides of this argument and to find solutions that address both sets of concerns.

The competencies of the Coordinator Role: The three competencies in this role and their corresponding topics in the learning activities are:

Competency 1: Managing Projects
Topics:
- Projects and project management: a definition
- Planning tools
- Statement of work
- Work breakdown structure
- Program evaluation and review technique and critical path method
- Resource leveling
- Gantt charts
- Human resource matrix
- Cost/schedule integration

The human side of project management

Competency 2: Designing Work
Topics:
    A brief history of job design in the 1900s
    Job design (redesign): motivational criteria
    Job design strategies
        Job enlargement
        Job rotation
        Job enrichment
    Self-managed work teams
    Choosing between job and team approaches

Competency 3: Managing Across Functions
Topics:
    Cross-functional teams within traditional work structures
    The story of Hewlett-Packard's Deskjet printer
    Key guidelines for managing cross-functionally

Conceptually the coordinator role is not limited to these competencies. Other competencies have been identified as:

    Coordinating work group activities
    Keys to rule enforcement
    Buffering your core technology
    When to conform, when to question
    Scheduling job rotations for employees
    Making physical arrangements for meetings
    Overseeing maintenance of buildings, structures, and/or equipment
    Planning
    Organizing
    Controlling

The Coordinator Role and current issues: It has been pointed out that technology and management are related. Certain abilities to manage systems are determined by new computer technologies. Certainly management information systems are technology driven.

Some questions to consider in this chapter are:

    1. How do organizations manage for change? How do organizations maintain stability while meeting rapidly changing demands and conditions?

    2. What are the dilemmas of self-managed teams?

    3. What are sources of individual resistance to organizational control?

    4. What is the relationship between controls and productivity? Is this relationship different among diverse organizations (e.g. business firms, public agencies, charitable organizations, religious organizations, etc.)?

CHAPTER 5	COORDINATOR ROLE
COMPETENCY 1	MANAGING PROJECTS

Assessment: Project Planning
Activity Flow Sheet

PURPOSE: This activity gives students the opportunity to surface some of the steps and skills involved in planning projects.

KEY TOPICS: Different levels of planning, coordination, and time lines.

TIME ESTIMATE: 45 minutes.

FORMAT: Individual activity followed by large group discussion.

SPECIAL NEEDS: None.

SEQUENCE:
1. Introduce the activity.
2. Allow students 20 minutes to complete the activity.
3. Ask for 5-7 volunteers to present their plans to the class.
4. Conduct a large group discussion and summarize.

VARIATION: This activity can be completed as homework, with the next class beginning with a discussion.

KEY POINTS:
1. Often tasks which appear to be simple need to be broken down into task components, planned, and coordinated.
2. Operational planning involves translation of a big idea into detailed plans.
3. It is easy to neglect some simple details.

CHAPTER 5	COORDINATOR ROLE
COMPETENCY 1	MANAGING PROJECTS

Assessment: Project Planning
Process Guide

PURPOSE: This activity gives students the opportunity to surface some of the steps and skills involved in planning projects. This activity demonstrates the need to plan complex tasks, and the tendency to neglect details.

STEP 1. Introduce the activity by telling students that this activity will help them begin to focus on coordination by giving them an opportunity to consider a project which they had planned or managed. Explain that tasks and projects often appear easy to coordinate and complete, particularly if we do not closely analyze all of the needed components.

STEP 2. Allow students 20 minutes to complete the activity individually.

STEP 3. Ask for 5-7 volunteers to record their plans on the board and present to the class.

STEP 4. Conduct a large group discussion and summarize. While the questions in the text on page 170 may form the basis of this discussion, additional questions could include:

    A. What about this activity surprised you?

    B. Why do people tend to overlook some necessary details?

    C. What were the first three things you did in planning this project?

    D. Was your approach similar to or different from the way you usually approach tasks?

    E. To what extent did you consider the resources you would need to complete this project?

    F. Did you use any kind of schedule or time line? Why or why not?

    G. Did you determine how to check your progress? Explain?

    H. What are some of the differences associated with planning for events involving many people vs. events involving a small number of people?

CHAPTER 5	COORDINATOR ROLE
COMPETENCY 1	MANAGING PROJECTS

Analysis: Project Planning
Activity Flow Sheet

PURPOSE: This activity permits students to analyze a situation of a manager who is responsible for a project and who turns to the tools and concepts in the learning section for help.

KEY TOPICS: Task relationship diagrams; Gantt charts; PERT/CPM.

TIME ESTIMATE: 50 minutes.

FORMAT: Individual activity, small group discussion, followed by large group discussion.

SPECIAL NEEDS: Pert Procedure handout, PERT Chart Table and Critical path diagram (follow Process Guide).

SEQUENCE:
1. Introduce the activity.
2. Students individually read the case and respond to the questions.
3. Place students into 4-5 person groups.
4. Conduct a large group discussion and summarize.

VARIATIONS:
1. Step 2 could be completed as a homework assignment.
2. Eliminate step 3, proceeding directly from the individual activity to the large group discussion.

KEY POINTS:
1. Planning requires care and attention to detail.
2. Neglecting planning can result in major difficulties as far as the project is concerned, as well as a degree of undue stress and psychological distress.
3. The longer we let something go without attention to planning, the more difficult the situation often becomes. In order to get things back on track, we sometimes have to go back to the beginning.

CHAPTER 5	COORDINATOR ROLE
COMPETENCY 1	MANAGING PROJECTS

Analysis: Project Planning
Process Guide

PURPOSE: This activity permits students to analyze a situation of a manager who is responsible for a project and who turns to the tools and concepts in the learning section for help.

STEP 1. Introduce the activity by referring students to the case and questions on pages 184-185. Tell them that they will be analyzing a situation where the manager is responsible for a project and needs to use planning tools. Give each student a copy of the Pert Procedures handout.

There are several points to note here:

1) the Steering Committee (activity 1,4) and the Advisory Committee (activities 4,9; 10,12; 11,13;12,14;13,14) are the same entity.

2) There is another activity that was inadvertantly left out of the list: activity 3,11 needs to be included as a dummy activity.

STEP 2. Allow students 20 minutes to read the case and respond in writing to the questions on page 185.

STEP 3. Place students into 4-5 person groups, if desired, and allow the groups to discuss their solutions.

STEP 4. Conduct a large group discussion based on the group reports and the questions on page 185. Summarize major points. Additional questions may include:

A. What are some psychological consequences of lack of planning skills?

B. Which planning tools did you find to be the most useful and why?

C. What were some of cultural assumptions that could lead to neglect of planning skills? Note that unlike some other societies, in our society we do not tend to focus on the detailed preparation of an event; we tend only to celebrate the event, or the finished product. As an example of our preoccupation with the finished product and neglect of the process, some societies celebrate pregnancy, while American society tends to celebrate birth. Attention to the process, then, requires conscious effort.

PERT Procedure Handout

1. List activities in sequence with time estimate for each. Note activities which proceed in parallel from the same preceding activity.

2. Calculate earliest start time (EST) and earliest finish time (EFT) for each activity. EST for the first activity(ies) to be performed = 0.
   EFT for each activity = EST + Est. Time
   EST for each activity = EFT for preceding activity

3. Identify activity sequence which consumes the longest time. This is the Critical Path (CP).

4. Calculate latest start time (LST) and latest finish time (LFT) for each activity. For CP activities, LST = EST and LFT = EFT (by definition). For non-CP activities, LFT = EST for the next succeeding activity, and LST = LFT - Est. Time.

5. Float for CP activities = 0 (by definition). Float for non-CP activities = LST - EST.

PERT Chart Data

Activity	Earliest Finish Time	Latest Finish Time	Earliest Start Time	Latest Start Time	Time Est.	Float
1,2	4	19	0	15	4	15
1,4	1	18	0	17	1	17
1,5	2	2	0	0	2	0
2,3	5	22	4	21	1	17
2,10	4	19	4	19	0	15
3,11	5	22	5	22	0	17
4,9	2	18	1	17	1	16
5,6	6	6	2	2	4	0
5,7	4	6	2	4	2	2
5,8	4	6	2	4	2	2
6,9	9	9	6	6	3	0
7,9	6	9	4	7	2	3
8,9	6	9	4	7	2	3
9,10	19	19	9	9	10	0
10,11	22	22	19	19	3	0
10,12	21	23	19	21	2	2
11,13	24	24	22	22	2	0
12,14	23	25	21	23	2	2
13,14	25	25	24	24	1	0
14,15	29	29	25	25	4	0

PERT Diagram (Project Planning -- Analysis)

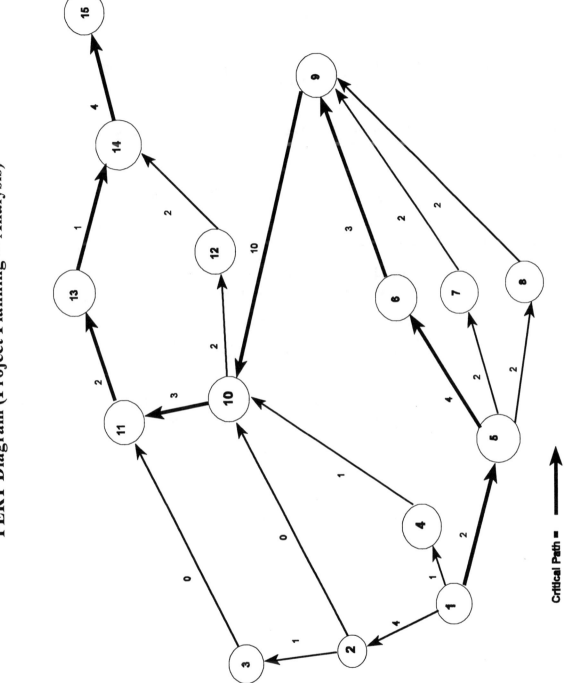

Critical Path = ⟶

CHAPTER 5	COORDINATOR ROLE
COMPETENCY 1	MANAGING PROJECTS

Practice: The Job Fair
Activity Flow Sheet

PURPOSE: This activity allows students to practice the planning concepts involved in the learning section, considering planning tools at their disposal and how they can use those tools.

KEY TOPICS: Task relationship diagrams; Gantt charts; PERT/CPM

TIME ESTIMATE: 40 minutes.

FORMAT: Small group activity followed by large group discussion.

SEQUENCE:
1. Introduce the activity.

2. Divide students into 4-5 person groups, or work teams. Walk them through the directions on page 186.

3. Ask for volunteers to share their conclusions.

4. Conduct a large group discussion and summarize.

KEY POINTS:
1. This competency incorporates a number of skills generic to many situations: social, job, project, and personal.

2. Careful planning has the effect of changing our perceptions of a task from overwhelming to manageable.

3. Life is easier when we plan, break down the task into component parts, and pay attention to the details.

CHAPTER 5	COORDINATOR ROLE
COMPETENCY 1	MANAGING PROJECTS

Practice: The Job Fair
Process Guide

PURPOSE: This activity allows students to practice the planning concepts involved in the learning section, considering planning tools at their disposal and how they can use those tools.

STEP 1. Introduce the activity by directing students to the instructions on page 186. Have them refer to their written response to the assessment activity (Project Planning) at the beginning of this competency. This is their chance to identify and put planning tools to work.

STEP 2. Place students into 4-5 person groups. Direct students to complete the activity and draw up the written work.

STEP 3. After their written work is completed, ask for volunteers to share their findings and conclusions. They may wish to write them on the chalkboard, or if possible, write them on blank transparencies for use with an overhead projector. Another alternative - especially if the discussion takes place on the next class day - is to have the volunteers type their conclusions and photocopy them for class members.

STEP 4. Conduct a large group discussion comparing the findings and conclusions, and summarize. Use students' main ideas as well as the key points from the activity flow sheet. Additional discussion questions may include:

   A. Did anything surprise you about completing this activity? Many students report that at first glance it seemed difficult and overwhelming, but once they got into it, it was easier than expected. A point here is that this response is not unusual with regards to planning.

   B. What applications do you see for these skills in the future?

   C. What are sources of individual resistance to planning?

CHAPTER 5	COORDINATOR ROLE
COMPETENCY 1	MANAGING PROJECTS

Application: Managing Your Own Project
Activity Flow Sheet

PURPOSE: This activity gives students the opportunity to apply planning principles to a project with which they are involved.

KEY TOPICS: Statement of work; WBS; Gantt Chart; PERT/CPM.

TIME ESTIMATE: 45 minutes.

FORMAT: Individual activity followed by large group discussion.

SPECIAL NEEDS: None.

SEQUENCE:
1. Introduce the activity.

2. Discuss with the class what their choice of an activity might be.

3. Set a due date for the project.

4. Conduct a large group discussion and summarize.

VARIATION: Divide the class into 4-5 person teams. Instruct them to plan a project for completion by the end of the term. The project might entail some service to the community or to the campus.

KEY POINTS:
1. Planning tools are not unique to management in organizations. They are generic to many aspects of life and assist in implementing a wide array of projects or activities.

2. Project management is a valuable competency that applies to many aspects of life, and not only to a managerical career.

CHAPTER 5	COORDINATOR ROLE
COMPETENCY 1	MANAGING PROJECTS

Application: Managing Your Own Project
Process Guide

PURPOSE: This activity gives students the opportunity to apply planning principles to a project with which they are involved. This activity demonstrates to students the applicability of project management tools to their activities, and the value of such tools for the effective implementation of those activities.

STEP 1. Introduce the activity by directing students to the instructions on pages 186-187. Note that this activity represents a summation of the competency, essentially involving students in applying the key points of the learning section to improve their effectiveness on a personal project.

STEP 2. Discuss with the class what their choice of projects might be. Encourage them to select a project which is currently facing them.

STEP 3. Indicate that they are require to submit a final report of 3-5 pages, and set a date that the report is due.

STEP 4. On the day the final report is due, conduct a large group discussion and summarize. Discussion questions might include:

   A. What surprised you about this activity?

   B. How did applying planning tools to your project affect your attitude towards that project?

   C. What would you surmise to be the relationship between the use of planning tools and one's tendency to procrastinate?

   D. Someone has said that the act of starting a project takes 50% of the effort to complete it. While this statement may not have scientific validity, do you think it has some merit? How does the use of the planning competency apply to this statement?

   E. What do you feel are the advantages of consistent, efficient planning?

CHAPTER 5	COORDINATOR ROLE
COMPETENCY 2	**DESIGNING WORK**

Assessment: Your Ideal Work Situation
Activity Flow Sheet

PURPOSE: In this introspective activity, students think about what they consider to be their ideal work situation.

KEY TOPICS: Designing work, motivation.

TIME ESTIMATE: 30 minutes.

FORMAT: Individual activity followed by large group discussion.

SPECIAL NEEDS: None.

SEQUENCE:
1. Introduce the activity.
2. Have students complete the activity individually.
3. Ask for volunteers to share their responses.
4. Conduct a large group discussion and summarize.

VARIATIONS:
1. Step 2 may be completed as homework, with the next class session beginning with step 3.
2. After step 2, students may be placed in 4-5 person groups to discuss their responses with one another.

KEY POINTS:
1. Job design has many critical elements and considerations.
2. One's notion of the ideal job requires considerable self-knowledge and reflection.

CHAPTER 5	COORDINATOR ROLE
COMPETENCY 2	DESIGNING WORK

Assessment: Your Ideal Work Situation
Process Guide

PURPOSE: In this introspective activity, students think about what they consider to be their ideal work situation.

STEP 1. Introduce the activity. Encourage students to give serious thought to this, as their response can be very helpful to them regarding their motivations, dreams, and goals. Such information is very useful.

STEP 2. Have students complete the activity individually. Direct them to respond in writing to the interpretation questions on page 187.

STEP 3. Ask for volunteers to share their responses.

STEP 4. Conduct a large group discussion based on responses to the questions on page 187, as well as the responses of the volunteers. Summarize, using the key points from the activity flow sheet, as well as students' main ideas. Note that there may be considerable variation among the responses from students and expect a lively discussion as a result! You may need to remind them that there are no right or wrong answers here, but that the responses reflect different individual needs, goals, and desires.

CHAPTER 5	COORDINATOR ROLE
COMPETENCY 2	DESIGNING WORK

Analysis: What's My Job Design?
Activity Flow Sheet

PURPOSE: In this activity students analyze their own situation in terms of the principles of job design.

KEY TOPICS: Job design

TIME ESTIMATE: 30 minutes.

FORMAT: Individual activity followed by large group discussion.

SEQUENCE:
1. Introduce the activity.
2. Direct students to work individually on the questions.
3. Ask for volunteers to share their responses.
4. Conduct large group discussion and summarize.

VARIATION: Step 2 may be assigned as homework, using step 3 to begin the next class session.

KEY POINTS:
1. Note the relevance of job design concepts when applied to our personal situations.
2. Note how coordination is provided through structure.
3. The value of employee input to effective job redesign has not traditionally been acknowledged.

CHAPTER 5	COORDINATOR ROLE
COMPETENCY 2	DESIGNING WORK

Analysis: What's My Job Design?
Process Guide

PURPOSE: In this activity students analyze their own situation in terms of the principles of job design. This allows students to utilize task analysis techniques and apply these skills to their own situation.

STEP 1. Introduce the activity by explaining the purpose.

STEP 2. Direct students to work individually on the questions.

STEP 3. Ask for volunteers to share their responses.

STEP 4. Conduct large group discussion and summarize. Highlight the importance of applying what they have learned. Summarize the major points which they made in the discussion.

CHAPTER 5	COORDINATOR ROLE
COMPETENCY 2	DESIGNING WORK

Practice: Redesigning Work
Activity Flow Sheet

PURPOSE: In this activity students work with a partner to redesign a job.

KEY TOPICS: Matching people to jobs; job redesign

TIME ESTIMATE: 30 minutes.

FORMAT: Dyads followed by large group discussion.

SPECIAL NEEDS: Individual responses from the previous activity: "Analysis: What's My Job Design?" on page 198 of the text.

SEQUENCE:
1. Introduce the activity.

2. Divide class members into dyads. If the class is not even numbered, make a 3-person group.

3. Direct the groups to complete the activity on page 198 of the text.

4. Ask for volunteers to report their responses to the class.

5. Conduct a large group discussion and summarize.

VARIATIONS:
1. Step 3 may be completed as homework, with the next class session beginning with step 4.

2. Require a 2-3 page written report from the groups, detailing their responses to the activity.

KEY POINTS:
1. People and jobs can be successfully matched.

2. Matching people and jobs, taking into account their abilities and growth/development needs is a win-win situation for employees and the organization.

CHAPTER 5	COORDINATOR ROLE
COMPETENCY 2	DESIGNING WORK

Practice: Redesigning Jobs
Process Guide

PURPOSE: In this activity students work with a partner to redesign a job. This is an empowering activity, as many times people think of themselves as having to "fit into" a job. This activity demonstrates that jobs can be redesigned for the benefit of employee and organization alike.

STEP 1. Introduce the activity. Direct students to the instructions on page 198 of the text. Explain that this activity permits them to build on the previous activity, and allows them to think about decisions involved in job redesign.

STEP 2. Divide class members into dyads. If the class is not even numbered, make a 3-person group. As a reminder: if possible, pair students who chose being a student as their job with students who chose a job in a work organization.

STEP 3. Direct the groups to complete the activity on page 198 of the text.

STEP 4. Ask for volunteers to report their responses to the class.

STEP 5. Conduct a large group discussion based on the groups' reports and on the questions posed in the activity. Summarize students' major points. Additional questions may include:

    A. On what basis did you decide which job to redesign?

    B. How did you feel about redesigning this job? Was it easier or harder than you anticipated?

    3. What are some organizational sources of resistance to redesigning jobs?

    4. What are some advantages to the organization of redesigning jobs? Advantages to employees?

    5. Who should be involved in job redesign?

CHAPTER 5	COORDINATOR ROLE
COMPETENCY 2	DESIGNING WORK

Application: Designing the Work Team
Activity Flow Sheet

PURPOSE: This activity permits students to explore some of the dynamics of an organization which uses work teams to accomplish some of its key tasks. It also provides students with a valuable opportunity to make contact with organizations.

KEY TOPICS: Self-managed work teams; organizational design; lines of authority; technology and organizations.

TIME ESTIMATE: In class set up time: 10 minutes; outside of class: 3 hours; in class follow up discussion: 20 minutes.

FORMAT: Individual activity followed by large group discussion.

SPECIAL NEEDS: Access to one organization.

SEQUENCE:
1. Introduce the activity.

2. Direct students to choose one organization to contact.

3. Assign a written report of their efforts, along with a deadline.

4. Conduct a large group discussion on the day their reports are due.

VARIATION: Permit them to work as 3-4 person teams.

KEY POINTS:
1. Organizations which emphasize work teams have somewhat different dynamics and procedures than more traditionally-structured organizations.

2. Organizational structure is not set but may be changed to adapt to a changing environment.

3. Sometimes the mission of the organization affects the structure.

CHAPTER 5	COORDINATOR ROLE
COMPETENCY 2	DESIGNING WORK

Application: Designing the Work Team
Process Guide

PURPOSE: This activity permits students to explore some of the dynamics of an organization which uses work teams to accomplish some of its key tasks. It also provides students with a valuable opportunity to make contact with organizations.

STEP 1. Introduce the activity by directing students to the instructions on page 199 of the text. Explain that in exploring organizational designs, they become able to appreciate the effect that structure has on the every-day operations of the organization.

STEP 2. Direct students to choose one team-based organization to contact. Discuss with the class various organizations locally that they may contact. Students may choose between a business firm, a state or local government agency, or a non-profit organization.

STEP 3. Assign a 3-5 page written report of their efforts, along with a deadline.

STEP 4. Conduct a large group discussion on the day their reports are due. Additional questions may include:

  A. What were the purposes and missions of your organization?

  B. In what ways did the work team design affirm the value and autonomy of each individual within those teams?

  C. Did anything about this assignment surprise you? If so, what?

CHAPTER 5	COORDINATOR ROLE
COMPETENCY 3	MANAGING ACROSS FUNCTIONS

Assessment: Student Orientation
Activity Flow Sheet

PURPOSE: This activity permits students to identify issues related to managing across functions, and how they would handle such a responsibility

KEY TOPICS: Task-related issues and people-related issues, internal and external integration.

TIME ESTIMATE: 30 minutes.

FORMAT: Individual activity followed by large group discussion.

SPECIAL NEEDS: None.

SEQUENCE:
1. Introduce the activity.
2. Instruct students to write their responses.
3. Record responses on the chalkboard.
4. Conduct a large group discussion.
5. Summarize, leading into a discussion of the learning activity.

VARIATIONS:
1. Assign step 2 to be completed entirely as homework.
2. In between steps 2 and 3, break the class into 4-5 person groups to discuss their lists and their responses to the questions.

KEY POINTS:
1. There are special challenges to managing cross-functional teams within traditional organizational structure.
2. Issues of tasks versus people are highlighted in this activity.
3. Control of individual effort must be considered in different ways when managing across functions.

CHAPTER 5	COORDINATOR ROLE
COMPETENCY 3	MANAGING ACROSS FUNCTIONS

Assessment: Student Orientation
Process Guide

PURPOSE: This activity permits students to identify issues related to managing across functions, and how they would handle such a responsibility

STEP 1. Introduce the activity by directing students to the instructions on page 199-200 of the text. Explain that this activity gives them an opportunity to explore the dynamics of managing cross-functional teams within traditional structures.

STEP 2. Instruct students to write out their responses to the questions in the activity.

STEP 3. Place their responses on the chalkboard

STEP 4. Conduct a large group discussion based on the questions in the activity.

STEP 5. Summarize, leading into a discussion of the learning activity. Additional discussion questions may include:

    A. What difficult issues are raised with cross-functional teams in traditional organizations?

    B. What issues regarding control in organizations are raised by this activity?

    C. What possible sources of tension could there be in these situations?

    D. What evaluation issues arise with regards to cross-functional teams?

CHAPTER 5	COORDINATOR ROLE
COMPETENCY 3	MANAGING ACROSS FUNCTIONS

Analysis: Errors in the Design?
Activity Flow Sheet

PURPOSE: In this activity students analyze a case involving real situation of managing across functional areas.

KEY TOPICS: Cross functional teams in traditional structures.

TIME ESTIMATE: 20 minutes.

FORMAT: Individual activity, followed by large group discussion.

SPECIAL NEEDS: Optional: blank transparencies and overhead projector.

SEQUENCE:
1. Introduce the activity.

2. Ask for volunteers to share their responses to the questions on page 209 with the class.

3. Compare the responses and discuss.

4. Conduct a large group discussion based on responses to the discussion questions on page 209.

5. Summarize students' major points.

VARIATION: Assign the activity as homework. The next class session, place students into 4-5 person groups to discuss their responses to the questions and to generate their responses to the questions.

KEY POINT: In managing cross functional teams, the potential for error is great.

CHAPTER 5	COORDINATOR ROLE
COMPETENCY 3	MANAGING ACROSS FUNCTIONS

Analysis: Errors in the Design?
Process Guide

PURPOSE: In this activity students analyze a case involving real situation of managing across functional areas. This activity demonstrates real issues which surface in managing across functions.

STEP 1. Introduce the activity by directing students to the instructions on page 209 of the text. Explain that they will be reading a case involving errors made in managing across functions. Note that at the end of the case, they will be required to write their analysis in responding to the questions on page 209.

STEP 2. After completion of the activity, ask for volunteers to share their analysis with the class. These may be written on blank transparencies and used with an overhead projector.

STEP 3. Compare their findings and analysis.

STEP 4. Conduct a large group discussion based on their findings and conclusions.

STEP 5. Summarize students' major points. Additional discussion questions may include:

   A. How can you apply the key guidelines for managing cross-functionally (pages 206-208) to this case?

   B. Why are the real issues underlying the errors?

   C. What task versus people issues were involved?

CHAPTER 5   **COORDINATOR ROLE**
COMPETENCY 3   **MANAGING ACROSS FUNCTIONS**

Practice: Student Orientation Revisited
Activity Flow Sheet

PURPOSE: This activity builds on the assessment activity and gives students an opportunity to role-play a team meeting.

KEY TOPICS: Work-teams, managing across functions

TIME ESTIMATE: 45 minutes.

FORMAT: 5-10 person groups, each playing the role of a team planning the student orientation

SPECIAL NEEDS: Students may be assisted in this activity by their responses to the assessment activity.

SEQUENCE:
1. Introduce the activity.

2. Place students into 5-10 person groups.

3. Allow students 20 minutes to conduct the meeting.

4. Allow groups to present the results of their team meetings, and conduct a large group discussion.

5. Summarize students' major points.

KEY POINTS:
1. There are special challenges to managing cross-functional teams within traditional organizational structure.

2. Issues of tasks versus people are highlighted in this activity.

3. Control of individual effort must be considered in different ways when managing across functions.

CHAPTER 5	COORDINATOR ROLE
COMPETENCY 3	MANAGING ACROSS FUNCTIONS

Practice: Student Orientation Revisited
Process Guide

PURPOSE: This activity builds on the assessment activity and gives students an opportunity to role-play a team meeting.

STEP 1. Introduce the activity by directing students to the instructions on page 209-210 of the text. Explain that they will draw on their responses to the assessment activity (pages 199-200 of the text) and role-play the teams.

STEP 2. Place students into 5-10 person groups.

STEP 3. Allow students 20 minutes to meet as a team and address critical issues, completing the task.

STEP 4. Allow groups to present their conclusions, and conduct a large group discussion.

STEP 5. Summarize, using students' main ideas as well as the key points from the activity flow sheet. Additional questions might include:

1. How did you instill in your team a sense of common purpose?

2. How was the process managed?

3. How were team members encouraged to step out of their roles?

CHAPTER 5	COORDINATOR ROLE
COMPETENCY 3	MANAGING ACROSS FUNCTIONS

Application: Examining a Cross-Functional Team
Activity Flow Sheet

PURPOSE: This activity permits students to apply what they have learned regarding managing cross-functional teams to a real situation.

KEY TOPICS: Managing across functions

TIME ESTIMATE: In class set up time: 10 minutes; outside of class: 3 hours; in class follow up discussion: 20 minutes.

FORMAT: Individual activity followed by large group discussion.

SPECIAL NEEDS: Exposure to an organization.

SEQUENCE:
1. Introduce the activity.
2. If necessary, review the guideline for managing across functions.
3. Set a date when the written report is due.
4. Ask for volunteers to share their experience with the class.
5. Conduct a large group discussion.
6. Summarize.

VARIATION: Students may be assigned to work in teams to complete the activity, submitting a team report.

KEY POINT: Attention to process is critical for managing cross-functional teams.

CHAPTER 5	COORDINATOR ROLE
COMPETENCY 3	MANAGING ACROSS FUNCTIONS

Application: Examining a Cross-Functional Team
Process Guide

PURPOSE: This activity permits students to apply what they have learned regarding managing cross-functional teams to a real situation.

STEP 1. Introduce the activity by directing students to the instructions on page 209-210 of the text. Explain that they will apply what they have learned to an organization. It may be necessary to assist them in choosing an organization.

STEP 2. If necessary, review with them the guidelines for managing across functions.

STEP 3. Set a date when the written report is due.

STEP 4. On the day that the assignment is due, ask for volunteers to share their experience with the class.

STEP 5. Drawing on the major points made my students, conduct a large group discussion. Additional questions might include:

    1. What were the successful elements in the situation you observed?

    2. What dynamics account for that success?

    3. What were the dysfunctional aspects of the situation you observed?

    4. What dynamics account for those dysfunctions?

    5. How can the dysfunctions be remedied?

    6. Which aspects of this chapter would you recommend to the persons involved in the situation you observed?

STEP 6. Summarize, using students' main ideas.

CHAPTER 6   DIRECTOR ROLE

The Director Role is the first role in the Rational Goal Model, and in many ways epitomizes the traditional posture of "manager as boss." The manager in the Director Role, clarifies goals and objectives, provides direction and instruction, delegates, and makes final decisions. In the words of one of the authors:

The whole notion of director is the old traditional role of "I'm the boss and I know best." That is in direct conflict with the biggest change in the work force: the push for high involvement management. This new management manifests itself in self-directed work teams brought upon by the increasing educational and technological sophistication of the work force. It is less frequently the case now that the boss knows more than the employees. The dilemma is this: organizations still have a need for the Director Role. How do you provide that in a work force that does not want to be directed? How do you solve this dilemma?

Perhaps the solution to this dilemma is balance, and in the realization that the issue is: *how* to provide direction to a work force that no longer wishes to be directed. The mentor role, located directly opposite the director role, can help provide this needed balance and skill.

Examination of the director role competencies reveals that they enjoy wide applicability, and are acknowledged as critical to personal achievement. Students often recognize the necessity of applying the competencies of the director role in their personal lives. Regardless of their situation in life, they often see themselves as needing to take initiative and set goals. Furthermore, most people find themselves having to ask others to do things, sometimes with mixed results. Improving one's ability to delegate is also seen as a life skill.

The competencies in the Director Role: The three competencies in this role and their corresponding topics in the learning activities are:

Competency 1: Visioning, Planning and Goal Setting
Topics:
- Vision, visionary leaders, and visionary organizations
- Vision, planning, and goal setting
- Goal setting--the basic building block
- Lessons learned from goal setting research and practice
- Using objectives as a management tool: MBO-type approaches

Competency 2: Designing and Organizing
Topics:
- Evolution towards the lateral organization
- The lateral organization
- Designing and organizing: core concepts and principles
- Efficiency as an organizing principle
- Designing organizations through departmentalization
- Lines of authority
- Differentiation and integration

Competency 3: Delegating Effectively
Topics:
- To delegate or not to delegate
  - Reasons for not delegating and counter-arguments
  - Keys to effective delegation
- Potential pitfalls of delegation

Conceptually, these are not the only competencies in this role. Other competencies have been identified as:

    Logical problem solving
    Effective uses of authority
    The art of giving clear directions
    Developing a vision
    Setting priorities
    Defining roles and expectations
    Developing decision making skills

The Director Role and current issues: As was noted earlier, the dilemma of the Director Role is how to direct a work force that does not want to be directed. A related point regards managing a culturally diverse work force. Directing will have to be seen as "individual-specific"; more than ever, it is clear that skills of judgment and discernment are necessary in directing different workers from varying backgrounds.

Some questions to consider in this chapter are:

1. Obviously the competencies in the Director Role are needed and necessary. It is important to consider, however, the possible consequences if the competencies are taken too far. What would it be like for the organization and for employees if managers carried the competencies of the Director Role to the extreme?

2. What organizational designs may rely less on the Director Role? Are there organizations that may need a more subtle emphasis than others? If so, what would be their characteristics?

A note from one of the authors:

"I see the Director Role as what many people typically think of as 'leadership'. It involves two additional competencies that are not well developed in the text. The first is "developing a vision" -- this is more than taking initiative; it is recognizing how to be a leader of followers. The second is "defining roles and expectations." Perhaps this is associated with delegating, but I see it as more - as setting policies and procedures. Again, these are somewhat associated with taking charge, but more concretely than in the case of creating a vision."

CHAPTER 6	DIRECTOR ROLE
COMPETENCY 1	VISIONING, PLANNING AND GOAL SETTING

Assessment I: Understanding the Big Picture
Activity Flow Sheet

PURPOSE: This introspective activity helps students identify their vision for their own lives.

KEY TOPICS: Vision, core values.

TIME ESTIMATE: 30 minutes.

FORMAT: Individual activity followed by large group discussion.

SPECIAL NEEDS: None.

SEQUENCE:
1. Direct students to complete the activity, as per the instructions on page 217.

2. Remind them to consider the specific questions under "HINT."

3. Conduct a large group discussion.

4. Summarize.

VARIATION: After step 2, place students into dyads to share their experience with a partner.

KEY POINTS:
1. Behaviors reflect our vision of ourselves and our values.

2. At the same time, clarity of vision and values provide motivation for action.

2. Coming to terms with the link between our actions and the way our lives turn out, is a critical task. Paraphrasing Yogi Berra's famous quote, People who don't know where they're going, might not like where they end up.

CHAPTER 6	DIRECTOR ROLE
COMPETENCY 1	VISIONING, PLANNING AND GOAL SETTING

Assessment I: Understanding the Big Picture
Process Guide

PURPOSE: This introspective activity helps students identify their vision for their own lives.

STEP 1. Direct students to complete the activity, as per the instructions on page 217.

STEP 2. Acknowledge with them that although they may not have thought in these terms before, this activity is invaluable for the purpose of clarifying their values and what means the most to them in life.

STEP 3. Have them record their responses--simply thinking about these issues is not enough. If you evaluate their responses, make it clear that you will not be evaluating their specific content--only the thoroughness with which they considered these issues.

STEP 4. Conduct a large group discussion. Some discussion questions may include:

    A. What was the most difficult aspect of this activity for you?

    B. What surprised you about your findings?

    C. What did you learn about yourself from this activity?

    D. In your experience, how would you say that vision relates to motivation?

STEP 5. Summarize, using students' main ideas as well as the key points on the activity flow sheet.

CHAPTER 6	DIRECTOR ROLE
COMPETENCY 1	VISIONING, PLANNING AND GOAL SETTING

Assessment II: Personal and Organizational Goal Setting
Activity Flow Sheet

PURPOSE: This activity helps students identify how they focus on goal setting in their personal and professional lives.

KEY TOPICS: Goal setting behaviors.

TIME ESTIMATE: 30 minutes.

FORMAT: Individual activity followed by large group discussion.

SPECIAL NEEDS: While this is a "stand alone" activity, its impact is enriched if it follows completion of Assessment I.

SEQUENCE:
1. Direct students to complete the activity, as per the instructions on page 217-218.

2. Have them reflect on the Interpretation section on page 218, and assess the meaning of the interpretation in their lives.

3. Conduct a large group discussion.

4. Summarize.

VARIATION: After step 2, place students into dyads to share their experience with a partner.

KEY POINTS:
1. Goal setting is not only an important skill for managers in organizations, but for people in their personal lives, as well.

2. Failure to set goals can lead to undesirable consequences.

3. There are organizational sources of resistance to goal setting, just as there are individual sources of resistance to goal setting.

CHAPTER 6	DIRECTOR ROLE
COMPETENCY 1	VISIONING, PLANNING AND GOAL SETTING

Assessment II: Personal and Organizational Goal Setting
Process Guide

PURPOSE: This activity helps students identify how they focus on goal setting in their personal and professional lives.

STEP 1. Direct students to complete the activity, as per the instructions on page 217-218.

STEP 2. Have them write out their response to the Interpretation Section on page 218. Simply thinking about these issues is not enough.

STEP 3. Conduct a large group discussion. Some discussion questions may include:

    A. What was the most difficult aspect of this activity for you?

    B. What surprised you about your findings?

    C. What did you learn about yourself from this activity?

    D. Why do some people resist goal setting? What are they afraid of?

STEP 4. Summarize, using students' main ideas as well as the key points on the activity flow sheet.

CHAPTER 6	DIRECTOR ROLE
COMPETENCY 1	VISIONING, PLANNING AND GOAL SETTING

Analysis: MBO Is Not For Me
Activity Flow Sheet

PURPOSE: This activity allows students to analyze a work situation where S.M.A.R.T. objectives, planning, and MBO could be developed more effectively.

KEY TOPICS: MBO, S.M.A.R.T. objectives.

TIME ESTIMATE: 45 minutes.

FORMAT: Individual activity, work in 4-5 person groups, followed by large group discussion.

SPECIAL NEEDS: None.

SEQUENCE:
1. Introduce the activity.
2. Divide students into groups to discuss the questions.
3. Have students report back to the large group.
4. Conduct a large group discussion and summarize.

VARIATION: Step 1 may be completed as homework.

KEY POINTS:
1. MBO is applicable to many aspects of work.
2. MBO is a valuable tool when used appropriately.
3. S.M.A.R.T. objectives are central to MBO.
4. Performance-based planning and evaluation are valuable tools.

CHAPTER 6	DIRECTOR ROLE
COMPETENCY 1	VISIONING, PLANNING, AND GOAL SETTING

Analysis: MBO Is Not For Me
Process Guide

PURPOSE: MBO is often used by top level management. As a result, many lower-level managers feel that MBO does not apply to them. This activity allows students to analyze a work situation where S.M.A.R.T. objectives, planning, and MBO could be developed more effectively.

STEP 1. Introduce the activity by directing students to read the case individually and respond in writing to the questions on page 229.

STEP 2. Divide students get into 4-5 person groups to discuss their responses to the questions. Someone should be designated as a reporter for the group.

STEP 3. Have the groups report back to the class what they discussed.

STEP 4. Conduct a large group discussion. Summarize, using the main points of the groups and the key points on the activity flow sheet. Some additional discussion questions may include:

   A. What do you think of Don's objectives?

   B. Is an MBO program applicable to Don's position? Why or why not?

   C. How might Don start an MBO program in his work unit?

   D. How might Don benefit from using S.M.A.R.T.?

CHAPTER 6	DIRECTOR ROLE
COMPETENCY 1	VISIONING, PLANNING, AND GOAL SETTING

Practice: Write Your Own MBO
Activity Flow Sheet

PURPOSE: This activity permits students to practice writing MBO's that may be relevant and meaningful in their own lives.

KEY TOPICS: Writing an MBO.

TIME ESTIMATE: 20-30 minutes.

FORMAT: Individual activity followed by large group discussion.

SPECIAL NEEDS: None.

SEQUENCE:
1. Review with students the steps to writing an MBO.
2. Direct them to read the instructions for the activity.
3. Walk them through the first goal of becoming a better manager.
4. Allow 15-20 minutes for them to complete the activity.
5. Discuss and summarize.

VARIATION: If students seem fairly comfortable with writing MBO's, then this activity can proceed as an individual in class or homework activity. However, if you sense that some of them may need some assistance, the could be placed into small groups for Step 3, and report back to the class.

KEY POINTS:
1. MBO is a managerial technique which is applicable to many aspects of life.

2. Notice that the way in which the goals are stated can be psychologically frustrating. We may want to be a more supportive friend, and may berate ourselves for not being more supportive, but unless we are able to articulate *how* to become more supportive, we can be doomed to a cycle of negative feelings about ourselves.

3. Positive benefits that accrue from using MBO are numerous, and include analyzing a situation, breaking it down into manageable components, and feeling a sense of improvement.

4. It is important to recognize personal sources of resistance to MBO's in order to deal with those issues and to defuse that resistance.

CHAPTER 6	DIRECTOR ROLE
COMPETENCY 1	VISIONING, PLANNING, AND GOAL SETTING

Practice: Write Your Own MBO
Process Guide

PURPOSE: This activity permits students to practice writing MBO's that may be relevant and meaningful in their own lives. Such practice in personal life increases the probability that MBO's will be utilized as managerial competency.

STEP 1. Review with students the steps to writing an MBO. Refer them to sections on page 40 of the text which they may find helpful.

STEP 2. Direct them to read the instructions for the activity on page 229.

STEP 3. Walk them through the first goal to be a better manager. Note that being "a better manager" is way too vague. Take S.M.A.R.T. and apply:

1. Be more **SPECIFIC**. Determine to be better at given managerial roles (Director, Innovator, etc.) rather than a better manager.

2. **MEASURE**. How would you make this measurable? One possibility is to use a peer feedback process. Ask three people you work with to tell you how you're doing in each of the roles.

3. **ASSIGNABLE** is next but this goal cannot be assigned because this is a personal improvement goal.

4. Use **REALISTIC** by selecting one competency from each role to improve on.

5. Use **TIME** to set a specific number of months to expect improvement.

STEP 4. Allow 15-20 minutes for them to complete the activity.

STEP 5. Discuss as a large group and summarize. You may want to ask for volunteers to share one of their MBO's, and allow the class to respond. Possible discussion questions include:

   A. Compare your feelings about your likelihood of achieving each goal, without the MBO and with the MBO. Is there a difference? How and why?

   B. Describe any resistance to writing your MBO's which you may have experienced.

   C. What other aspects of your life might you find MBO's helpful?

CHAPTER 6	DIRECTOR ROLE
COMPETENCY 1	VISIONING, PLANNING AND GOAL SETTING

Application: Setting Your Goals
Activity Flow Sheet

PURPOSE: This activity affords students the opportunity to apply the competency of goal setting using specific action plans.

KEY TOPICS: Goal setting; S.M.A.R.T.

TIME ESTIMATE: 30 minutes.

FORMAT: This is an individual homework activity followed by large group discussion.

SPECIAL NEEDS: The Implementation Plan Worksheet (follows process guide).

SEQUENCE:
1. Ask students to select an important goal.
2. Hand out the worksheets; instruct students to read the directions.
3. Ask for volunteers to share their action plans.
4. Conduct a large group discussion.
5. Summarize.

VARIATION: This activity may be completed in class.

KEY POINTS:
1. Goal setting and planning are critical to implementation plans.
2. Using S.M.A.R.T. helps make goals seem more attainable.

CHAPTER 6	DIRECTOR ROLE
COMPETENCY 1	VISIONING, PLANNING, AND GOAL SETTING

Application: Setting Your Goals
Process Guide

PURPOSE: This activity affords students the opportunity to examine an important goal, applying the competency of goal setting. They are directed to translate their goals into specific action plans.

STEP 1. Introduce the activity by asking students to choose an important goal which they consider to be troublesome, overwhelming, and/or difficult. This should be a goal which they have experienced difficulty in handling.

STEP 2. Hand out the worksheets and have students read the directions on page 230 of the text. Ask students if they have any questions about this activity.

STEP 3. Ask for volunteers to share their action plans. Encourage them to share their feelings about the process, and how they were able to overcome any resistance to completing the assignment.

STEP 4. After completion, discuss as a large group. Ask students how they feel about their plans. In what ways does their goal seem more attainable now?

STEP 5. Summarize, using their major points, as well as the key points on the activity flow sheet.

IMPLEMENTATION PLAN WORKSHEET

Choose a goal from your schoolwork, job, or personal life that you consider complex, difficult, troublesome, or overwhelming. Develop an Implementation Plan. Include the following:

Today's date: _____

My goal is: _____

I. S.M.A.R.T. Objectives:

II. Outside factors which might affect the objective:

III. Steps to Achieve Goal: By When?

1.

2.

3.

4.

5.

6.

7.

8.

9.

IV. Criteria for Evaluating Results:

    1. A **GOOD** result would be:

    2. A **SATISFACTORY** result would be:

    3. A **POOR** result would be:

V. Other comments about your plan:

CHAPTER 6	DIRECTOR ROLE
COMPETENCY 2	DESIGNING AND ORGANIZING

Assessment: Redesign for Customer Satisfaction
Activity Flow Sheet

PURPOSE: This activity introduces the learning section by helping students to consider the design of an organizational process with which they are familiar.

KEY TOPICS: Organizational design.

TIME ESTIMATE: 15-20 minutes.

FORMAT: An individual activity, this assessment can be conducted in class, as an introduction to the learning activity, or as homework; followed by large group discussion.

SPECIAL NEEDS: None.

SEQUENCE:
1. Introduce the activity by having students read the directions.
2. Direct students to complete the assignment.
3. Conduct a large group discussion and summarize.

VARIATION: After individually completing the questionnaire, class members can be placed into 4-5 person groups to discuss their interpretations.

KEY POINTS:
1. Organizational design features are directly related to customer/client satisfaction.
2. Organizational design features can be changed.

CHAPTER 6	DIRECTOR ROLE
COMPETENCY 2	DESIGNING AND ORGANIZING

Assessment: Redesign for Customer Satisfaction
Process Guide

PURPOSE: This activity introduces the learning section by helping students to consider the design of an organizational process with which they are familiar.

STEP 1. Introduce the activity by having students read the directions on page 213 of the text.

STEP 2. After completing the activity, conduct a large group discussion as a lead into the discussion of the learning section. Some suggested discussion questions are:.

      A. What aspects of the organization most needed to be changed, in your view?

      B. Why were these aspects so critical?

      C. How does organizational design affect the emotions and perceptions of customers and clients?

CHAPTER 6	DIRECTOR ROLE
COMPETENCY 2	DESIGNING AND ORGANIZING

Analysis: Understanding the Impact of Organizational design on Effectiveness
Activity Flow Sheet

PURPOSE: This activity allows students to analyze the design of an organization and to consider how design elements might be changed in order for the organization to function more efficiency.

KEY TOPICS: Efficiency as an organizing principle.

TIME ESTIMATE: 45 minutes.

FORMAT: Individual activity followed by large group discussion.

SPECIAL NEEDS: Results from the assessment activity, page 230 of the text.

SEQUENCE:
1. Introduce the activity.

2. Have students revisit the assessment activity and direct them to complete the assignment on page 239 of the text.

3. Conduct a large group discussion and summarize.

VARIATION: After completing step 2, divide them into small groups to discuss their analysis. Be sure and have group members working on the same organization (post office or Department of Motor Vehicles).

KEY POINTS:
1. Note the role of specialization, authority, and division of labor in efficiency.

2. Increasing organizational efficiency can be achieved in a variety of ways.

CHAPTER 6	DIRECTOR ROLE
COMPETENCY 2	DESIGNING AND ORGANIZING

Analysis: Understanding the Impact of Organizational design on Effectiveness
Activity Flow Sheet

PURPOSE: This activity allows students to analyze the design of an organization and to consider how design elements might be changed in order for the organization to function more effectively.

STEP 1. Introduce the activity by directing students to read the directions on page 239 and respond in writing to the questions.

STEP 2. Conduct a large group discussion focusing on their responses to the questions on page 239. Summarize, using the main points presented by the students and the key points on the activity flow sheet.

CHAPTER 6	DIRECTOR ROLE
COMPETENCY 2	DESIGNING AND ORGANIZING

Practice: Redesigning Organizations
Activity Flow Sheet

PURPOSE: This activity allows students to explore the process of redesigning another organization and to consider how design elements might be changed in order for the organization to function more efficiency.

KEY TOPICS: Organizational Redesign, efficiency, lateral vs. horizontal design.

TIME ESTIMATE: 40 minutes.

FORMAT: Dyad activity followed by large group discussion.

SPECIAL NEEDS: Student responses to the assessment activity (p. 230 of text) and the analysis activity (page 239 of text).

SEQUENCE:
1. Review with students their previous assessment and practice activities.
2. Divide the students into dyads.
3. Direct them to read the instructions for the activity.
4. Allow 15-20 minutes for each interview.
5. Discuss and summarize.

KEY POINTS:
1. The structural components of organizations can be changed in order to increase efficiency.

2. Organizations can have very similar problems and solutions. Note the two organizations being considered here: the Post Office and the Department of Motor Vehicles.

CHAPTER 6	DIRECTOR ROLE
COMPETENCY 2	DESIGNING AND ORGANIZING

Practice: Redesigning Organizations
Process Guide

PURPOSE: This activity allows students to explore the process of redesigning another organization and to consider how design elements might be changed in order for the organization to function more efficiency.

STEP 1. Review with students their insights from their previous assessment and practice activities.

STEP 2. Divide the students into dyads. Note that one person who had examined the postal service and one person who had examined the department of motor vehicles should be in each dyad.

STEP 3. Walk them through the steps of the activity on page 240 of the text.

STEP 4. Allow 15-20 minutes for them to complete each interview. There are two interviews in each dyad.

STEP 5. Discuss as a large group and summarize.

CHAPTER 6	DIRECTOR ROLE
COMPETENCY 2	DESIGNING AND ORGANIZING

Application: Understanding the design and Organization of Your Company
Activity Flow Sheet

PURPOSE: This activity affords students the opportunity to apply the concepts regarding organizational design to a real organization.

KEY TOPICS: Organizational structure and redesign processes.

TIME ESTIMATE: 15 minutes to introduce, 4 hours to complete, 30 minutes large group discussion.

FORMAT: This is an individual homework activity followed by large group discussion.

SEQUENCE:
1. Introduce the activity.

2. Direct students to the activity on page 240-241.

3. Walk them through the activity and offer suggestions on choice of organization and person to interview.

4. Set a due date and format for their reporting to you their results (orally or written).

5. Conduct a large group discussion.

KEY POINTS:
1. While organizations vary considerably in their structural designs, they do tend to have many similarities.

2. Each of the structural components have consequences in terms of efficiency.

CHAPTER 6	DIRECTOR ROLE
COMPETENCY 2	DESIGNING AND ORGANIZING

Application: Understanding the design and Organization of Your Company
Process Guide

PURPOSE: This activity affords students the opportunity to apply the concepts regarding organizational design to a real organization.

STEP 1. Introduce the activity by reminding students of the concepts they've learned in this competency.

STEP 2. Direct students to the directions on pages 240-241 of the text. Ask students if they have any questions about this activity.

STEP 3. Walk them through the activity and offer suggestions on choice of organization, choice of person to interview, and how to go about conducting the interview.

STEP 4. Be sure to specify a format for reporting the results to you (a 3-5 page paper, or an oral presentation) and a due date.

STEP 5. After the due date, conduct a large group discussion drawing on their experiences. Summarize, using their major points, as well as the key points on the activity flow sheet.

CHAPTER 6	DIRECTOR ROLE
COMPETENCY 3	DELEGATING EFFECTIVELY

Assessment: To Delegate or Not To Delegate
Activity Flow Sheet

PURPOSE: This activity provides students with the opportunity to assess their beliefs and assumptions about delegation.

KEY POINTS: Reasons for not delegating and counter-arguments.

TIME ESTIMATE: 20 minutes.

FORMAT: Individual activity followed by large group discussion.

SPECIAL NEEDS: None.

SEQUENCE:
1. Introduce the activity.
2. Have students complete the assessment.
3. Conduct a large group discussion.
4. Summarize.

VARIATION: Step #2 may be assigned as homework.

KEY POINTS:
1. There are major "myths" regarding delegation. These myths include:
   - Delegation takes too much time
   - Delegation lessens a manager's control
   - Delegation produces inferior work

2. Delegation is related to goal setting.

3. Regarding delegation, there are parallels between the manager-employee relationship and the teacher-student relationship..

CHAPTER 6	DIRECTOR ROLE
COMPETENCY 3	DELEGATING EFFECTIVELY

Assessment: To Delegate or Not To Delegate
Process Guide

PURPOSE: This activity provides students with the opportunity to assess their beliefs and assumptions about delegation, and provides a lead into a discussion of the reasons for not delegating and the counter-arguments.

STEP 1. Introduce the activity by referring students to page 241 of the text.

> **NOTE:** Students should be reminded that there are no right or wrong answers to the assessment; it functions to provide a basis for discussing assumptions regarding delegation.

STEP 2. Have students complete the activity.

STEP 3. Conduct a large group discussion based on responses to the activity. Address the major myths of delegation:

- Delegation takes too much time
- Delegation lessens a manager's control
- Delegation produces inferior work

Additional discussion questions may include:

A. What experiences have you had in delegating?

B. What skills do you think are important to delegating effectively?

C. Recall instances when you have been delegated **to**. In your experience, what factors made the difference between a successful delegation and an unsuccessful delegation?

D. What problems have you faced in trying to delegate?

E. What are characteristics on individuals whom you consider to be successful delegators?

STEP 4. Summarize, using students' main points as well as they key points on the activity flow sheet.

CHAPTER 6	DIRECTOR ROLE
COMPETENCY 3	DELEGATING EFFECTIVELY

Analysis: The Storm Window Assignment
Activity Flow Sheet

PURPOSE: This activity allows students to analyze a work situation in terms of the eight keys to effective delegation.

KEY TOPICS: Eight keys of effective delegation.

TIME ESTIMATE: 20 minutes.

FORMAT: Individual activity followed by large group discussion.

SPECIAL NEEDS: None.

SEQUENCE:
1. Instruct students to read the case.
2. Direct them to respond in writing to the discussion questions.
3. Conduct a large group discussion.
4. Summarize.

VARIATIONS:
1. Steps #1 and #2 can be completed as homework.
2. This activity can be conducted with small groups by having students compare their responses with one another in between .steps 2 and 3. Keep in mind, however, that this case forms the basis for the practice activity, which is conducted in small groups.

KEY POINTS:
1. This case illustrates delegation which was unsuccessful.
2. Fairness was an issue, which George could have used to change the rules.
3. Jack had understandable reasons for not wanting to admit that the irritating remarks of his co-workers had gotten the best of him.
4. The situation escalated into a power play on George's part.

SPECIAL NOTE: This activity forms the basis of the practice activity which follows, entitled: "Improvising a Delegation Problem."

CHAPTER 6	DIRECTOR ROLE
COMPETENCY 3	DELEGATING EFFECTIVELY

Analysis: The Storm Window Assignment
Process Guide

PURPOSE: This activity allows students to analyze a work situation in terms of the eight keys to effective delegation. This case is a classic example of unsuccessful delegation which escalates into a power play on the part of the boss. Students have the opportunity to analyze the situation and determine how the boss could have handled things differently.

STEP 1. Have students read the case beginning on page 245. Refer them to the eight keys to effective delegation on page 244. Remind them to put themselves in the role of George Brown as they are reading the case.

STEP 2. Direct them to respond in writing to the discussion questions on page 248.

STEP 3. Conduct a large group discussion by asking students to share their responses to the discussion questions. Additional questions might include:

    A. What are possible reasons Jack may have had for not wanting to do the windows again?

    B. At what point did George's handling of the situation become a power play?

    C. How could George have used fairness as an issue to resolve the situation?

STEP 4. Summarize, using the major points made by students, as well as the key points on the activity flow sheet.

CHAPTER 6	DIRECTOR ROLE
COMPETENCY 3	DELEGATING EFFECTIVELY

Practice: Improvising a Delegation Problem
Activity Flow Sheet

PURPOSE: This activity permits students to explore the delegation style of George Brown in the previous activity and arrive at a different outcome.

KEY TOPICS: Effective delegation.

TIME ESTIMATE: 30 minutes.

FORMAT: 4-5 person groups followed by large groups discussion.

SPECIAL NEEDS: Students need their responses to the previous analysis activity, "The Storm Window Assignment".

SEQUENCE:
1. Introduce the activity.
2. Divide the class into 4-5 person groups.
3. Assign roles.
4. Have players brainstorm how they would carry out their roles.
5. Conduct a large group discussion and summarize.

VARIATION: If desired, one group could be selected to play their roles in a fishbowl format.

KEY POINTS:
1. Minor changes in George's handling of the conversation could eventuate in a happy outcome.

2. Special efforts to recognize the importance of the assignment could also change the outcome.

3. Students are likely to feel differently towards George as they play him handling this situation fairly.

CHAPTER 6	DIRECTOR ROLE
COMPETENCY 3	DELEGATING EFFECTIVELY

Practice: Improvising a Delegation Problem
Process Guide

PURPOSE: This activity permits students to explore the delegation style of George Brown in the previous analysis case entitled "The Storm Window Assignment." The objective is to arrive at a different outcome than in the case, using the eight keys to effective delegation.

> **NOTE:** Students need their responses to the previous analysis activity, "The Storm Window Assignment".

STEP 1. Introduce the activity by referring to the instructions on page 248, and by reminding students of the conclusions from their discussion of the analysis activity.

STEP 2. Divide the class into groups of 4-5.

STEP 3. Assign 1-2 students in each group to play the role of Jack, and the others to play the role of George. [NOTE: female students may wish to change the names from George to Georgia, and from Jack to Jackie.]

STEP 4. Have each subset of players brainstorm how they would carry out their respective roles.

STEP 5. After the role plays, conduct a large group discussion to summarize. Possible additional questions include:

   A. What minor changes in George's handling of the conversation could eventuate in a happy outcome?

   B. What could have been done to elevate the status of the assignment? Would this be desirable? Why or why not?

   C. Do you feel differently towards George now, that you have played him handling this situation in a positive manner? What accounts for any change in feelings which you might be experiencing?

CHAPTER 6	DIRECTOR ROLE
COMPETENCY 3	DELEGATING EFFECTIVELY

Application: Interviewing a Delegator
Activity Flow Sheet

PURPOSE: This activity allows students to explore the delegator competency by conducting an interview of someone who delegates.

KEY TOPICS: Effective delegation.

TIME ESTIMATE: In class set up time: 10 minutes; outside of class: 45 minutes for the interview; follow-up discussion in class: 20 minutes.

FORMAT: Individual activity followed by large group discussion.

SPECIAL NEEDS: A delegator to interview.

SEQUENCE:
1. Direct students to read the instructions.
2. Have them identify an individual to interview.
3. Instruct students to write out an interview schedule.
4. Ask students to report their findings to the class.
5. Summarize.

VARIATION: Students may be divided into groups for comparing their findings, prior to the large group discussion.

KEY POINTS:
1. Everyone delegates to some extent.

2. This interview encourages the interviewee to delegate and places the student in the position of assisting in the planning of the delegation.

3. The eight keys to delegation have wide applicability.

CHAPTER 6	DIRECTOR ROLE
COMPETENCY 3	DELEGATING EFFECTIVELY

Application: Interviewing a Delegator
Process Guide

PURPOSE: This activity allows students to explore the delegator competency by conducting an interview of someone who delegates. Students in the interview are in the position of encouraging the interviewee to delegate and assist in the planning.

STEP 1. Introduce the activity by directing students to read the instructions on page 249 of the text.

STEP 2. Have them identify someone to interview. Note that people in all sorts of roles delegate. Effective delegation can be regarded as a life skill. You may need to help them identify someone to interview. Indicate that the interview must be conducted by a certain date.

STEP 3. Instruct students to write out an interview schedule, as per the instructions in the book.

STEP 4. Conduct a discussion in class where students share what they have learned from the interviews, and summarize. Addition questions might include:

   A. Did you notice any resistance to delegation on the part of the person you interviewed? If so, what were the sources of the resistance and how did you handle it?

   B. What are your feelings about delegation now, as compared with when you took the assessment? To what do you attribute any change?

| CHAPTER 7 | PRODUCER ROLE |

The Producer Role is the second role in the Rational Goal Model. The manager in this role is described as hard working, personally productive, goes beyond what is expected, meets commitments, stimulates productivity from others, and expects hard work.

The competencies involved in this role are readily recognized by students as being significant in their lives. Many students wrestle with personal motivation, as well as time and stress management issues. As such they will find the material in this chapter to be immediately helpful as well as revealing.

The importance of human motivation is a clear emphasis in this role. The dilemma for the manager is balancing the needs of the organization with the needs of the individual. This role is clear, however, in the belief that employee motivation is a first step toward increasing productivity, and that successful organizational reward systems seek to assess the needs of individuals and to meet them.

The competencies in the Producer Role: The three competencies in this role and their corresponding topics in the learning activities are:

Competency 1: Working Productively
Topics: Personal Peak Performance
  Commitment
  Challenge
  Purpose
  Control
  Transcendence
  Balance
 Workscape
 Empowerment--a key to working productively

Competency 2: Fostering a Productive Work Environment
Topics: Applying motivation theory
  Guide for applying Expectancy Theory
   Tie effort to performance
   Link performance to outcomes
   Understand valences for desired employee outcomes
  Be a positive Pygmalion
  The role of coaching in fostering a productive work environment

Competency 3: Time and Stress Management
Topics: Managing time and stress
  Stress in organizations
  Sources of stress
  Strategies for managing stress
   Clarify your values
   Pay attention to your physical health
   Try using a relaxation technique

          Create a personal support system
          Take energy breaks to help you restore your energy
    Time management
          Clarity your values
          Plan and prioritize on a regular basis
          Maintain your workspace so that you can work most effectively
          Regularly review how you are spending your time

Conceptually, these are not the only competencies in this role. Other competencies have been identified as:
          Personal goal clarification
          Empowering others
         Project/program management
         Personal career planning
         Coping with mistakes, failure, and other personal crises
         Doing the tasks you would rather avoid
         Handling conflicting expectations

The Producer Role and current issues: The Producer Role seems to epitomize "life in the fast lane" for corporate America. Yet due to the increasing numbers of women in the workplace, there is an increasing tendency for firms to recognize and accommodate to family issues. If parents are worried about proper day-care for their children, or the care of an elderly family member, how productive can they be at work? Furthermore, there is an increasing interest in the health and fitness levels of employees. Some firms offer aerobics programs and wellness centers at work, providing opportunities for employees to take "fitness breaks" from their desks. There seems to be a growing recognition that corporate attention to employee stress and health has payoffs in lower absenteeism and turnover rates.

Some questions to consider in this chapter are:

    1. Obviously the competencies in the Producer Role are necessary. It is important to consider, however, the possible consequences for the organization if the competencies are not balanced. What would it be like for the organization and for employees if managers carried the competencies of the Producer Role to the extreme?

    2. How are organizational reward systems related to employee motivation?

A note from one of the authors:

    "There is a paradox between time and stress management. Time management is often presented as how to fit more into a day, which is quite the opposite of the focus of stress management. There is a need to focus on the balance between doing more, achieving peak performance, and knowing how/when to relax."

CHAPTER 7	PRODUCER ROLE
COMPETENCY 1	WORKING PRODUCTIVELY

Assessment: When Are You the Most Productive?
Activity Flow Sheet

PURPOSE: This activity asks students to reflect on a personal experience, identifying their underlying motivators.

KEY TOPICS: Personal peak performance.

TIME ESTIMATE: 15-20 minutes.

FORMAT: Individual activity followed by large group discussion.

SPECIAL NEEDS: None.

SEQUENCE:
1. Introduce the activity.
2. Instruct them to write the paragraph and list their contributing factors..
3. Conduct a large group discussion.
4. Summarize.

VARIATION:
1. Step 2 can be completed as homework.
2. In step 4 nominal group technique could be used to elicit one point from each class member in turn, allowing everyone to participate.

KEY POINTS:
1. Contributing factors may be under one's personal and direct control, or they may be related to external factors.
2. It is important to determine what we can control and what we cannot control.
3. While we may not be able to control external factors, we do control our response to those factors.
4. Making the choice to have a positive perception of external factors may be a source of empowerment in our motivation and productivity level.

SPECIAL NOTE: The results of this activity are required in order to complete the analysis activity which follows.

CHAPTER 7	PRODUCER ROLE
COMPETENCY 1	WORKING PRODUCTIVELY

Assessment: When Are You the Most Productive?
Process Guide

PURPOSE: This activity asks students to reflect on a personal experience. In their reflection they are able to identify factors which were under their direct and personal control, and factors which were external and beyond their control. As they separate the two types of factors, they have the opportunity to identify and dissect their underlying motivators and sources of personal empowerment.

STEP 1. Introduce the activity by directing students to read the instructions on page 253. Remind them that for best results, write the paragraph before reading the interpretation in the assignment.

STEP 2. After they have finished with the paragraph, instruct them to list their contributing factors and compare them with those discussed in the learning section.

STEP 3. Conduct a large group discussion. Ask students to share with the class insights they gained from the assessment, perhaps listing factors which were found to enhance their motivation levels. Additional discussion questions may include:

　　A. What examples can you given from personal experience or from the book of the conscious choice to control the interpretation of an external - or uncontrollable - factors?

　　B. Which of the identified conditions that stimulate personal peak performance enhance a positive interpretation of external events?

　　C. What can organizations and firms do to create a favorable climate for the developing of these conditions which stimulate personal peak performance?

STEP 4. Summarize the major points of the discussion.

CHAPTER 7	PRODUCER ROLE
COMPETENCY 1	WORKING PRODUCTIVELY

Analysis: When Are You the Most Productive and Motivated?
Activity Flow Sheet

PURPOSE: Like the assessment, this activity allows students to reflect on a personal experience and identify their underlying motivators. In addition students are permitted to work in small groups and comparing their contributing motivating factors with each other.

KEY TOPICS: Personal peak performance.

TIME ESTIMATE: 15-20 minutes.

FORMAT: 4-5 person groups followed by large group discussion.

SPECIAL NEEDS: Students need their responses to the previous assessment activity.

SEQUENCE:
1. Instruct class members to form 4-5 person groups.
2. Direct them to answer the 3 questions in the instructions.
3. Have each group share its findings with the class.
4. Conduct a large group discussion and summarize.

KEY POINTS: Mirroring those in the assessment activity, the key points include:

1. Contributing factors may be under one's personal and direct control, or they may be related to external factors.

2. It is important to determine what we can control and what we cannot control.

3. While we may not be able to control external factors, we do control our response to those factors.

4. Making the choice to have a positive perception of external factors may be a source of empowerment in our motivation and productivity level.

CHAPTER 7	PRODUCER ROLE
COMPETENCY 1	WORKING PRODUCTIVELY

Analysis: When Are You the Most Productive and Motivated?
Process Guide

PURPOSE: Like the assessment, this activity asks students to participate in action inquiry by allowing them to look back on a personal experience and identify their underlying motivators. In addition students are permitted to work in small groups and comparing their contributing motivating factors with each other.

STEP 1. Instruct class members to form small groups of 4-5 individuals each.

STEP 2. Using their written work from the assessment activity, direct them to answer the five questions in the instructions on page 256-257.

STEP 3. In the large group, ask each group to share its findings with the class. Two suggestions for this include:

   A. Give each group five minutes to report to the class.

   B. Allow each group could present one point in turn, in an effort to insure that each group has an equal chance of participating.

   As the responses are given, press the class to identify which one are under the direct control of the individuals.

STEP 4. Conduct a large group discussion and summarize, using students' main points.

CHAPTER 7	PRODUCER ROLE
COMPETENCY 1	WORKING PRODUCTIVELY

Practice: "Feeling Dead Ended"
Activity Flow Sheet

PURPOSE: This activity permits students to practice analyzing motivational levels in a work situation, applying techniques to managing the situation, and identifying preventative measures that might have been taken.

KEY TOPICS: Personal peak performance.

TIME ESTIMATE: 30 minutes.

FORMAT: 4-5 person groups followed by large group discussion.

SPECIAL NEEDS: None.

SEQUENCE:
1. Introduce the activity.
2. Divide the class into groups of 4-5 students each.
3. A spokesperson should be chosen from each group.
4. Conduct a large group discussion.
5. Ask individuals to share their answers to question 7.
6. Summarize.

VARIATION: The individual work in step one may be assigned as homework.

KEY POINTS:
1. In order to suggest ways to boost employees' motivation and enthusiasm, one must understand their situation from their point of view.

2. Understanding the situation in this case is assisted by isolating issues and reconnecting them in a meaningful manner.

CHAPTER 7	PRODUCER ROLE
COMPETENCY 1	WORKING PRODUCTIVELY

Practice: "Feeling Dead Ended"
Process Guide

PURPOSE: This activity permits students to practice analyzing motivational levels in a work situation, applying techniques to managing the situation, and identifying preventative measures that might have been taken. They have the opportunity to describe an employee's motivational level and how she got to this point, and practice the skills necessary to help the employee.

STEP 1. Introduce the activity by referring to the instructions on page 257 of the text. Direct them to read the case and respond to the questions on the bottom of page 258 and the top of page 259. This should be done individually.

STEP 2. Divide the class into small groups of 4-5 with the instructions that they compare their individual answers with each other.

STEP 3. A spokesperson should be chosen to report to the class their group's collective response to questions 2, 4, and 6.

STEP 4. Conduct a large group discussion based on the response of the groups to questions 2, 4, and 6. Process answers to questions 4 and 6 in as much detail as possible.

STEP 5. Ask individuals to share their answers to question 7. Noting that this is a public sector example, you may wish to discuss similarities in business firms, public agencies, and other hierarchical organizations (churches, etc.) as structured systems. The universality of the dynamics involved in this case can be acknowledged.

STEP 6. Summarize the discussion using students' main points as well as the key points on the activity flow sheet.

CHAPTER 7	PRODUCER ROLE
COMPETENCY 1	WORKING PRODUCTIVELY

Application: Creating Your Own Strategy for Increasing Personal Motivation and Productivity
Activity Flow Sheet

PURPOSE: This activity permits students to create their own strategy, or action plan, for increasing personal motivation. The activity, building upon the previous activities, encourages students to assume increased control over their motivation level by taking specific steps.

KEY TOPICS: Personal motivation and peak performance.

TIME ESTIMATE: 45 minutes.

FORMAT: Individual activity, work in 4-5 person groups, followed by large group discussion.

SPECIAL NEEDS: None.

SEQUENCE:
1. Introduce the activity; have students write their responses to each question.

2. Point out the introspective nature of this activity.

3. Divide the class into 4-5 person groups.

4. Conduct a large group discussion.

5. Summarize.

VARIATION: Students' individual written responses to the questions may be assigned as homework.

KEY POINTS:
1. This activity allows students to plan for their short-range future, based on what they have determined about their personal motivation.

2. Discussion key points in groups helps to affirm individual efforts and to establish that many blocks and hindrances are shared.

3. Mastering the skill of creating such action plans has the potential for long-term benefit.

CHAPTER 7	PRODUCER ROLE
COMPETENCY 1	WORKING PRODUCTIVELY

Application: Creating Your Own Strategy for Increasing Personal Motivation and Productivity
Process Guide

PURPOSE: This activity permits students to create their own strategy, or action plan, for increasing personal motivation. The activity, building upon the previous activities, encourages students to assume increased control over their motivation level by taking specific steps. Students are able to determine their motivation level in such a way as to increase their personal effectiveness.

STEP 1. Direct students to the activity on page 259, with the instruction to complete each question in writing. Allow 20 minutes for this, if done in class.

STEP 2. Point out the introspective nature of this activity, and that their honest reflections will benefit their emergent strategy.

STEP 3. Divide the class into groups, asking them to discuss their responses to the questions.

STEP 4. Conduct a large group discussion, asking for volunteers to share their action plans.

STEP 5. Summarize. Point out that such action planning is a valuable life skill, and that the key to making this work is for them to analyze their motivation level on a periodic basis, and adjust their plans based on their needs and wants.

CHAPTER 7	PRODUCER ROLE
COMPETENCY 2	FOSTERING A PRODUCTIVE WORK ENVIRONMENT

Assessment: Fostering a Productive Work Environment--Your Motivating Potential
Activity Flow Sheet

PURPOSE: This activity illustrates the issue of motivation within organizational settings; students are allowed to wrestle with the role of the manager in motivating others.

KEY TOPICS: Motivating others in organizational settings.

TIME ESTIMATE: 30 minutes.

FORMAT: Individual activity, work in 4-5 person groups, followed by large group discussion.

SPECIAL NEEDS: None.

SEQUENCE:
1. Introduce the activity.

2. Have students complete the scale.

3. Place class members 4-5 person groups.

4. Conduct a large group discussion and summarize.

VARIATION: Step #2 may be completed as homework.

KEY POINTS:
1. Wide differences between importance of employee needs and opportunities to fill them is a formula for low employee motivation.

2. Organizational effectiveness and efficiency are enhanced when employees are motivated to perform.

3. Organizational design may sometimes counter appropriate sensitivity to employee needs.

4. Managers may find themselves in the position of balancing the needs of the organization with the needs of the employees.

5. Organizations and employees stand to benefit when attention is given to meeting the needs of employees.

CHAPTER 7	PRODUCER ROLE
COMPETENCY 2 FOSTERING A PRODUCTIVE WORK ENVIRONMENT	

Assessment: Fostering a Productive Work Environment--Your Motivating Potential Process Guide

PURPOSE: This activity illustrates the issue of motivation within organizational settings by noting the differences between the importance of identified needs, and the opportunity of individuals to pursue those needs. In completing this assessment, students wrestle with the role of the manager in motivating others. If a need is very important and yet there is little opportunity to fill that need, what can a manager do to reduce the difference?

STEP 1. Introduce this activity by asking students to draw on any work experiences in organizations, or other organizational experiences, to assess the needs of employees.

STEP 2. Have students complete the scale, as per the instructions on page 259-260.

STEP 3. Place class members in groups of 4-5 students each, with the charge of accounting for the differences in importance and opportunity and what they, as managers, would do to minimize that difference. Refer to questions on page 260.

STEP 4. Conduct a large group discussion and summarize. Additional discussion questions may include:

    A. Recall a time when you were in an organization as an employee or as an individual with little power. Did you experience conflict when your needs were not being met? What were your feelings at the time?

    B. In times of such conflict, individuals may feel initially that something is wrong with them rather than with the organization's policies, procedures, etc. How can managers affirm individual employees without operating in a counterproductive fashion within the organization?

CHAPTER 7	PRODUCER ROLE
COMPETENCY 2	FOSTERING A PRODUCTIVE WORK ENVIRONMENT

Analysis: The Case of Michael Simpson
Activity Flow Sheet

PURPOSE: The purpose of this activity is to allow students to analyze a relatively common motivational dilemma in terms of expectancy theory.

KEY TOPICS: Expectancy theory.

TIME ESTIMATE: 40 minutes.

FORMAT: Individual activity, work in 4-5 person groups, followed by large group discussion.

SPECIAL NEEDS: None.

SEQUENCE:
1. Direct students to read the case and respond to the questions
2. Place class members into 4-5 person groups.
3. Conduct a large group discussion.
4. Summarize.

VARIATIONS: Step #1 can be completed as homework.

KEY POINTS:
1. Michael Simpson is confronted with this dilemma: after discovering that he is receiving $2000 less in salary than a newly hired MBA student, does he take a different job in a different company for more money? Or does he stay because every other aspect of his job is exactly the way he wants it, namely opportunity for challenge, responsibility, receiving the toughest assignments, and having a relatively fast career track?

2. An expectancy theory perspective would provide valuable assistance to Simpson in making an informed decision.

3. Simpson needs to consider the multiple outcomes that he gets from his job and the relative importance (i.e. valences) that are attached.

4. Recognize the emotion and put it aside and consider what is important among the tradeoffs.

CHAPTER 7	PRODUCER ROLE
COMPETENCY 2	FOSTERING A PRODUCTIVE WORK ENVIRONMENT

Analysis: The Case of Michael Simpson
Process Guide

PURPOSE: The purpose of this activity is to allow students to analyze a relatively common motivational dilemma in terms of expectancy theory. Students should conclude that without an expectancy theory perspective, it is impossible for Simpson to make an informed decision.

STEP 1. Direct students to read the case of Michael Simpson and respond in writing to the three questions on page 268. Allow approximately 20 minutes for this.

STEP 2. Place class members into small groups of 4-5 students each, to discuss their responses to the three questions and to develop a group response to each question.

STEP 3. Conduct a large group discussion, asking each group to report the key points of their discussions. Additional discussion questions might include:

   A. Expectancy theory suggests that Michael Simpson put aside the emotional components of his situation, allowing him to focus on the rational benefits from his job. How realistic is this suggestion?

   B. In what ways does Michael Simpson feel downgraded in his position, in terms of his value and worth to the company?

   C. How can a manager effectively respond to the emotional component of Michael Simpson's situation?

STEP 4. Summarize, using students main ideas as well as the key points on the activity flow sheet.

CHAPTER 7	PRODUCER ROLE
COMPETENCY 2	FOSTERING A PRODUCTIVE WORK ENVIRONMENT

Practice: The Same Old Job
Activity Flow Sheet

PURPOSE: This activity allows students to practice skills in determining motivation needs and identifying conflict sources that interfere with motivation.

KEY TOPICS: Applying expectancy theory.

TIME ESTIMATE: 25 minutes.

FORMAT: 4-5 person group work followed by large group discussion.

SPECIAL NEEDS: None.

SEQUENCE:
1. Direct students to read the case and answer the questions.

2. Place class members into small groups of 4-5 students each.

3. Conduct a large group discussion.

4. Summarize.

VARIATIONS:
1. Step #1 may be completed as homework.

2. In order to shorten the process, you may assign each group to discuss one of the questions rather than all 6.

KEY POINTS:
1. Turning to the list of needs in the assessment activity, Helen Ames seems to be experiencing a high opportunity for the fulfillment of some of those needs, but low opportunity for the fulfillment of others.

2. Sometimes the syndrome that Helen Ames is experiencing is temporary and may be related to other factors, such as a situation in her personal life. Perhaps it was even triggered by a thoughtless remark from a co-worker. However, it may also be indicative of a more lasting assessment of her job satisfaction.

CHAPTER 7	PRODUCER ROLE
COMPETENCY 2	FOSTERING A PRODUCTIVE WORK ENVIRONMENT

Practice: The Same Old Job
Process Guide

PURPOSE: This activity allows students to practice skills in determining motivation needs, draw out factors that motivate and/or detract from motivation, and identify conflict sources that interfere with motivation.

STEP 1. Direct students to individually read the case on page 268-269, and to respond in writing to the questions on page 269.

STEP 2. Place class members into small groups of 4-5 students each, to discuss their responses to the questions and to develop a group response to each question.

STEP 3. Conduct a large group discussion with each group reporting to the class. Due to the large number of questions, assign the first group to report their findings on question #1. Permit the class to react. Then the second group take question #2 and so forth.

Additional discussion questions may include:

A. As you review the assessment scale on pages 259-260, which of Helen's needs do you think are being met and which are not?

B. What alternative explanations can you think of for her feelings at this time?

C. How might the reward systems of Helen Ames' workplace be redesigned to prevent such feelings as Helen is experiencing?

STEP 4. Summarize by using students' main ideas and the key points from the activity flow sheet.

CHAPTER 7	PRODUCER ROLE
COMPETENCY 2	FOSTERING A PRODUCTIVE WORK ENVIRONMENT

Application: Understanding Organizational Reward Systems
Activity Flow Sheet

PURPOSE: This activity permits students to apply what they have learned about individual motivation to organizational reward systems. Hopefully as they pursue their own career goals, this skill will enable them to better assess the fit between the organization they may consider working for, and their own motivational needs.

KEY TOPICS: Expectancy theory and organizational reward systems.

TIME ESTIMATE: In class set up time: 10 minutes; outside of class: 2 hours for the interviews; in class follow up discussion: 20 minutes.

FORMAT: Individual activity followed by large group discussion.

SPECIAL NEEDS: Three potential employers to interview.

SEQUENCE:
1. Introduce the activity.

2. Refer students to the directions on pages 269-270.

3. Have students select three employers to interview.

4. After the interviews are completed, allow time for students to discuss briefly their interviews in class.

5. Conduct a large group discussion and summarize.

KEY POINTS:
1. Expectancy theory and one's own motivational profile can be used to determine which organizations would pose the best fit for a potential employee.

2. Organizational reward systems vary widely, often reflecting different constraints as well as different assumptions about employee motivation.

CHAPTER 7	PRODUCER ROLE
COMPETENCY 2	FOSTERING A PRODUCTIVE WORK ENVIRONMENT

Application: Understanding Organizational Reward Systems
Process Guide

PURPOSE: This activity permits students to apply what they have learned about individual motivation to organizational reward systems. Hopefully as they pursue their own career goals, this skill will enable them to better assess the fit between the organization they may consider working for, and their own motivational needs. Like the other interview activities, this one functions to assist students in practicing interviewing skills as well as making contacts with the business community.

STEP 1. Introduce students to this assignment by noting the role of organizational reward systems in meeting the motivational needs of employees.

STEP 2. Refer students to the directions on pages 269-270. Note that the interview schedule is provided. If they do not have potential employers yet, just suggest that they interview three employers.

STEP 3. Have students select three employers to interview. You may need to assist them in this task. Clarify that the interviews must be conducted by a certain date.

STEP 4. After their interviews are completed, permit them to briefly discuss their interviews in class.

STEP 5. Conduct a large group discussion and summarize, using students' major points from their experiences.

CHAPTER 7	PRODUCER ROLE
COMPETENCY 3	MANAGING TIME AND STRESS

Assessment: Stress in Your Organization
Activity Flow Sheet

PURPOSE: This activity permits students to assess the (very approximate) stress levels in their lives by responding to an instrument in stress management research.

KEY TOPICS: Stress management, control, and coping.

TIME ESTIMATE: 20 minutes.

FORMAT: Individual activity followed by small group work and large group discussion.

SPECIAL NEEDS: None.

SEQUENCE:
1. Introduce the activity by having students read the directions on page 270-271.

2. Direct students to record their scores and to respond in writing to the interpretation questions on page 271.

3. Place students into 4-5 person groups. Ask them to discuss the items, share their responses, and to add any items, if necessary.

4. Conduct a large group discussion and summarize.

VARIATIONS:
1. This scale may be completed as homework, with steps 3 and 4 being completed during the next class.

2. Students can complete this scale for different years and different jobs, and each of the past five calendar years, and compare their scores.

KEY POINTS:
1. Organizational factors contribute heavily to feelings of stress.

2. Sometimes we tend to think of stress levels as related to our inability to manage time or to lack of psychological strength. It is important to note that organizational factors may trigger stress.

3. While we cannot often control some of the organizational factors that happen to us, we can take action to mitigate any consequent negative effects.

CHAPTER 7	PRODUCER ROLE
COMPETENCY 3	MANAGING TIME AND STRESS

Assessment: Stress in Your Organization
Process Guide

PURPOSE: This activity permits students to assess the (very approximate) stress levels in their lives by responding to an instrument in stress management research. Not only does this personalize the discussion regarding stress, but it helps students to understand that organizational sources of stress.

STEP 1. Introduce the activity by having students read the directions on page 270-271.

STEP 2. Direct students to add any items they wish, record their scores, and respond in writing to the interpretation questions on page 271. As a variation, ask them to also complete the scale for any previous year at a previous job and to compare their scores.

STEP 3. Place students into 4-5 person groups to discuss the scale and share possible items to include.

STEP 4. Conduct a large group discussion, asking students to volunteer their observations regarding the instrument and their responses to the issues it raises.

Additional questions may include:

A. What items did you add to the scale?

B. What patterns can you distinguish regarding items over which you have the least control?

C. What methods of coping are most productive for you? What dysfunctional methods of coping do people sometimes use?

STEP 5. Summarize the discussion, using the key points from the activity flow sheet, and the main ideas which students generate.

CHAPTER 7	PRODUCER ROLE
COMPETENCY 3	MANAGING TIME AND STRESS

Analysis: Wasting Time
Activity Flow Sheet

PURPOSE: The purpose of this activity is to allow students to practice identifying time wasters on the job, and determine strategies for controlling them.

KEY TOPICS: Time management strategies

TIME ESTIMATE: 45 minutes.

FORMAT: Individual activity and small group discussion, followed by large group discussion.

SPECIAL NEEDS: None.

SEQUENCE:
1. Direct students to read the case and instructions on page 285-286 of the text.

2. Divide class members 4-5 person groups.

3. Conduct a large group discussion.

4. Summarize.

VARIATION: Step 1 may be completed as homework, followed by group discussion the next class session.

KEY POINTS:
1. No one is a perfect user of time.

2. Sometimes assertive communication skills are necessary in order to minimize time waste.

3. In order to manage one's time, one must determine one's willingness to handle time wasters, and not merely to use them as excuses.

CHAPTER 7	PRODUCER ROLE
COMPETENCY 3	MANAGING TIME AND STRESS

Analysis: Wasting Time
Process Guide

PURPOSE: The purpose of this activity is to allow students to practice identifying time wasters on the job, and determine strategies for controlling them.

STEP 1. Direct students to read the case of Frank Fernandez on page 285-286 of the text, and to respond in writing to the questions on page 286.

STEP 2. Divide class members into small groups of 4-5 students each. Ask group members to discuss the questions and be prepared to present a composite list of responses to the three questions on page 286.

STEP 3. Conduct a large group discussion based on the responses of the small groups. Additional discussion questions may include:

    A. Most of us can improve our time management techniques. Did any student see themselves in Frank Fernandez? If so, in what way? Explain.

    B. What positive function do time wasters serve, in terms of providing us with excuses for procrastination?

    C. What are some strategies that can reduce the number of interruptions?

STEP 4. Summarize, using students' main ideas and the key points from the activity flow sheet.

CHAPTER 7	PRODUCER ROLE
COMPETENCY 3	MANAGING TIME AND STRESS

Practice: Clarify Your Values
Activity Flow Sheet

PURPOSE: The purpose of this activity is to allow students to practice clarifying their governing values.

KEY TOPICS: Values, time, and stress.

TIME ESTIMATE: 20 minutes.

FORMAT: Individual activity, followed by dyads.

SPECIAL NEEDS: None.

SEQUENCE:
1. Direct students to read the instructions on pages 287 of the text.
2. Divide class members into 2-person groups.
3. Summarize.

VARIATION: Step 1 may be completed as homework, followed by group discussion the next class session.

KEY POINTS:
1. No one is a perfect user of time.
2. Our experience of time pressure and stress is related to how we are doing with regards to our governing values.

CHAPTER 7	PRODUCER ROLE
COMPETENCY 3	MANAGING TIME AND STRESS

Practice: Clarify Your Values
Process Guide

PURPOSE: The purpose of this activity is to allow students to practice clarifying their governing values.

STEP 1. Direct students to read the instructions on pages 287 of the text, and to respond in writing to the questions on page 287. You may wish to read the questions aloud to them, giving examples from your own life, if you feel comfortable with that. Give them plenty of time to reflect and respond honestly. Suggest that they may wish to adjust their responses from time to time, as they reflect on the issues raised by these questions.

STEP 2. Divide class members into dyads. Ask students to share some of their thoughts with their partners, and to perhaps obtain some assistance from them.

STEP 3. Conduct a large group discussion based on the issues raised in the questions and the readings. Additional discussion questions may include:

   A. Do you find this activity useful? If so, in what way? Explain.

   B. Has anyone ever engaged in a similar exercise before? What is the purpose of clarifying one's values?

   C. How do our values--whether or not they are explicitly acknowledged--affect our stress levels and time pressures?

STEP 4. Summarize, using students' main ideas and the key points from the activity flow sheet.

| CHAPTER 7 | PRODUCER ROLE |
| COMPETENCY 3 | MANAGING TIME AND STRESS |

**Application: Improving Your Stress and Time Management
Activity Flow Sheet**

PURPOSE: This activity allows students to apply stress and time management techniques in order to develop their own personal time and stress reduction program.

TIME ESTIMATE: 45 minutes initially.

FORMAT: Individual activity over time followed by small group work and large group discussion.

SPECIAL NEEDS: None.

SEQUENCE:
1. Direct students to read and complete the assignment.

2. Note that this activity is a valuable life skill.

3. Place class members into 4-5 person groups, to share strategies and methods of implementation.

4. Conduct a large group discussion and summarize.

VARIATION: All questions may be completed as homework, followed by small group discussion the next class session.

KEY POINTS:
1. Developing strategies for stress and time management inherently reduces our stress level - even before the strategies are implemented.

2. Its commonplace to need encouragement from others in order to implement strategies.

3. Note that some strategies may require more effective communication skills. See chapter 2, the Mentor Role.

CHAPTER 7	PRODUCER ROLE
COMPETENCY 3	MANAGING TIME AND STRESS

Application: Improving Your Time and Stress Management
Process Guide

PURPOSE: This activity allows students to apply stress and time management techniques in order to develop their own personal time and stress reduction program.

STEP 1. Direct students to read the assignment on page 287, and to respond to all questions in writing.

STEP 2. Note that this activity is a valuable life skill. Encourage students to practice it periodically.

STEP 3. Place class members into small groups of 4-5 students each in order to discuss their responses to the questions. Encourage students to ask their group members for assistance in developing solutions and strategies.

STEP 4. Conduct a large group discussion. Summarize, using students' main ideas and the key points from the activity flow sheet.

CHAPTER 8	BROKER ROLE

The Broker Role, together with the Innovator Role, comprises the Open Systems Model of the Competing Values Framework. On the organizational level the competencies of the Broker Role are closely associated with growth, expansion, and resource acquisition. As such the competencies of this role are often associated with organizational survival. On a more micro level the broker role encompasses some very interesting issues regarding authority, power, and influence in organizations. Again, the competencies of this role are often associated with individual survival within the organizational setting.

Managers in the broker role represent the organization to those outside the organization. Typical activities include: making speeches at public meetings, meeting with reporters, attending business lunches, conferences, and ceremonial events. The broker also engages in interunit and inter-organizational coordination by meeting with directors of other units and may also be involved in contract negotiations.

While this role may be perceived as primarily associated with executive functions, the fact is that the competencies of the broker role involve some very important life skills. All of us build and maintain a power base, both within the organizational setting or in our personal relationships. We also negotiate agreement and commitment; we may sometimes feel that success in our interpersonal relationships requires considerable negotiating skills! Furthermore, everyone presents ideas to others - whether informally or formally.

While several paradoxes are evident in the broker role competencies, perhaps one of the more intriguing relates to the acquisition and use of power. Power is something that most of us want and feel that we need. A measure of personal power affirms a sense that we have some control over our lives. On the other hand, we are likely to respond negatively when someone exercises power over us in a coercive, arbitrary, intimidating, or otherwise explicit manner. Since power is the *potential* to influence, it has been noted-- somewhat paradoxically--that the exercise of power depletes it. To *use* one's resources reduces one's resources, i.e., lessens one's power.

Furthermore, within the organizational setting, it is argued that one gains power through empowering others. I am reminded of a story about a woman who was president of a regional coalition of local community organizations. While the woman possessed acknowledged expert, information and position power, she chose not to assert it. Instead, as she visited the local groups, she actively worked to empower the leaders of those groups to their constituents, pointing out the strengths of those leaders and the value of what they were doing. As was intended, this made the local leaders more effective in their endeavors as they sought cooperation from their constituents. Paradoxically, this also increased her power--her potential to influence. This is an illustration of how power is gained when it is given away.

The competencies of the Broker Role: The three competencies in this role and their corresponding topics in the learning activities are:

Competency 1: Building and Maintaining a Power Base
Topics: Power and dependency
                    Misconceptions about power
                Power at the individual level

>   The myth of the solitary entrepreneur
>   Good power, bad power and no power
>   Five sources of power
>   Influence strategies
>   Influence versus manipulation
>   Increasing influence with superiors, peers, and subordinates

Competency 2: Negotiating Agreement and Commitment
Topics: Reading your organization's culture
            Four principles of Getting to Yes
                Separate the people from the problem
                Focus on interests, not positions
                Generate other possibilities
                Insist on using objective criteria
            The freedom scale: negotiating expectations up and down

Competency 3: Presenting Ideas Effectively
Topics: Presenting ideas
            Switzler's framework for effective communication
                Set
                Sequence
                Support
                Access
                Polish
            The Importance of SSSAP

Conceptually, the broker role is not limited by these competencies. Other competencies have been identified as:

>   Effective confrontation
>   Building coalitions and networks
>   Managing symbols and culture
>   Coordinating interunit relations
>   Representing your organization: effective first encounters
>   Dealing with dissatisfied clients/customers/constituents
>   Contract negotiations and grievance discussions

The Broker Role and current issues: The competencies included in the broker role are rich in implications for current issues in U. S. firms. The connections between broker and globalization are obvious: globalization requires the nurturing of strong relationships with organizations, governments, and cultures in the external environment. Furthermore, salient ethical issues surrounding the use of power and authority in organizations emerge in considering this role.

The broker role, perhaps more than any other role, represents the interacting nature of the organization with the external environment. This role represents the intensifying blurring of boundaries between organizations and their environmental components. For example, many U.S. firms are taking a more active role in educating the work force; they are often called upon to enforce the law; and they are responding to calls for increasing social and environmental responsibility.

In addition, the broker role competencies relate to managing a culturally diverse work force. The manager of the 21st century will certainly have to utilize brokering and mentoring skills in order to create an organizational climate which is welcoming to the voices of culturally diverse employees.

Some questions to consider in this chapter are:

1. How is the use of power within organizations related to the culture of the organization? How is the use of power related to the structure of the organization?

2. What is the distinction between power and authority? Why do people follow authority?

3. What are some ways in which one can increase one's personal power by empowering others? Under what conditions can managers empower subordinates in organizations? To what extent is it desirable to do so?

4. What are the most common patterns in the abuse of power?

5. How can a failure to develop a power base create problems for managers and the people in their work units?

A note from one of the authors:

I realize that it is difficult to take the time to allow students practice with oral presentations but it is very important. But for many students, this course may be one of their only opportunities to give some presentations and to receive supportive feedback. I encourage you to allow time and opportunity for students to improve their skills.

I feel very strongly about this because many students (MBA, MPA, and graduate accounting students) have told me that the course in Oral Communications is the most worthwhile class in our program. In seems that in degree programs, we teach students a lot of cognitive information. But in oral communication class, they have to structure and present information. Its the only place they receive real feedback.

Management is a social enterprise as much as a cognitive enterprise. Yet the degrees in management degree programs are largely cognitive. Allowing students to practice giving oral presentations gives them a rare opportunity to receive feedback on how they present themselves, and how to integrate and focus on problems and present solutions.

CHAPTER 8	BROKER ROLE
COMPETENCY 1	BUILDING AND MAINTAINING A POWER BASE

Assessment: A Power/Dependency Analysis of Your Position
Activity Flow Sheet

PURPOSE: This activity allows students to examine the ideas of power from the perspective of the interdependence of most relationships and the use of power within those relationships.

KEY POINTS: This activity leads to discussion of interdependency, of stakeholders in organizations who influence the performance of the organization, its access to resources, and the socio-political legitimacy of the organization. From this point it's logical to move to building and maintaining a power base, beginning with misconceptions about power.

TIME ESTIMATE: 30 minutes.

FORMAT: Individual activity followed by large group discussion.

SPECIAL NEEDS: None.

SEQUENCE:
1. Introduce the activity.
2. Have students complete the diagram.
3. Conduct a large group discussion.
4. Summarize.

VARIATIONS:
1. Assign as homework.

2. The questions on page 294 may be used as a basis of the large group discussion rather than as an individual assignment.

3. Following Step 2, students could be placed into small groups to share their diagrams and discuss the interpretation questions on page 294.

KEY POINTS:
1. What is the relationship between dependency and power?

2. We may have a tendency to overestimate our level of dependency and the extent of our powerlessness, especially if we fall victim to the Misconceptions about Power in Box 9.1 on page 295.

SPECIAL NOTE: This diagram is used again in the application activity for this competency on page 309 of the text.

CHAPTER 8	BROKER ROLE
COMPETENCY 1	BUILDING AND MAINTAINING A POWER BASE

Assessment: A Power/Dependency Analysis of Your Position
Process Guide

PURPOSE: This activity allows students to examine the ideas of power from the perspective of the interdependence of most relationships and the use of power within those relationships. By comparing their diagrams, they can identify factors unique to each individual situation, and explore differing perceptions of dependency.

STEP 1. Introduce the activity by directing students to the instructions on page 293 of the text. Explain that they will have the opportunity to view power from the perspective of dependence/ interdependence, and how that dependence can work both for and against them.

STEP 2. Have students complete the diagram and respond in writing to each of the questions on page 294.

STEP 3. Conduct a large group discussion. Discuss their responses to the interpretation questions and ask for volunteers to draw their diagrams on the board and explain. Some discussion questions may include:

   A. How did you define dependence in order to complete the activity?

   B. Do you feel that you are in a position of high or low dependence? Does this position change? If so, why and under what circumstances?

   C. Do any of the people or situations reflected in your diagram tend to make you feel powerless? How? Do you think that you may tend to make others feel powerless? If so, under what circumstances?

   D. Do you feel that your position of dependence can be changed? If so, how?

   E. To what extend does the dependency reflected in your diagram agree with the Misconceptions about Power (Box 9.1)? Are these truly misconceptions? Are they popular or deeply rooted in your organization? If so, why?

STEP 4. Summarize by asking students what they consider to be the main points of this activity.

CHAPTER 8	BROKER ROLE
COMPETENCY 1	BUILDING AND MAINTAINING A POWER BASE

Analysis:
"I Hope You Can Help Me Out": Don Lowell Case Study
Activity Flow Sheet

PURPOSE: This activity allows students to analyze a case, exploring the uses of power and strategies for maintaining one's power base.

KEY POINTS: Eight Influence Strategies, influence versus manipulation, and the ethics of power.

TIME ESTIMATE: 45 minutes.

FORMAT: Individual activity, followed by work in 4-5 person groups and large group discussion.

SPECIAL NEEDS: None.

SEQUENCE:
1. Introduce the activity.
2. Students to prepare a written response to questions.
3. Place class members into 4-5 person groups.
4. Direct the groups to discuss their responses to questions 2-8.
5. Conduct a large group discussion.
6. Summarize.

VARIATIONS:
1. Students may read the case and respond in writing as homework, followed by steps 3 through 6 in class.

2. While the instructions suggest that the homogeneous groups be formed according to student responses to question 2, a point could be made to form heterogeneous groups instead. This option has the advantage of sparking lively debate in the small groups. There is some merit, however, to allowing the homogeneous groups to strengthen their position, and have the lively debate in the large group discussion.

KEY POINTS:
1. Power is the potential to influence.

2. Decisions on what to influence are often value issues, sometimes with ethical dimensions.

3. Understanding one's power/dependency relationships and one's power base helps increase one's options.

CHAPTER 8	BROKER ROLE
COMPETENCY 1	BUILDING AND MAINTAINING A POWER BASE

Analysis:
"I Hope You Can Help Me Out": Don Lowell Case Study
Process Guide

PURPOSE: The Don Lowell case study a typical instance of a request to use one's influence to do someone a favor. Students analyze this case, exploring the uses of power and the strategies for maintaining and/or using one's power base. Using the influence strategies discussed in the learning activity, students plan a strategy for achieving positive results. Students focus on the discussion question: What would you decide to do and why? A very interesting discussion can be generated about values and choices, and what is appropriate in a situation like this.

STEP 1. Introduce the activity by directing students to the case and directions on pages 302-304 of the text. Indicate that in this activity they will see how sources and bases of power sometimes switch in different situations.

STEP 2. Direct students to prepare a written response to questions 1 and 2 on page 304.

STEP 3. Place class members into small groups of 4-5 students each. Have the groups composed of students who gave the same response to question 2. Hopefully you will have at least:

   A. One group of those who would not get involved, and in no way try to influence the admission process.

   B. One group of those who would help only by clarifying the mother's need for admission.

   C. One group of those who would do everything within their power to get the mother admitted.

STEP 4. Direct the groups to discuss their responses to questions 2-8. Remind them to be as specific as possible. Have them discuss concrete methods and approaches that are being used by each character in the case study, as well as the methods and techniques they feel could be used to produce positive results given the decision they made in question 2.

STEP 5. Conduct a large group discussion, with the groups presenting their different perspectives and positions to the entire class.

Clarify that this activity involves two parts:

A. A value decision based on one's own perceptions of the situation and values relating to the uses of power.

B. Planning a strategy to reduce negative consequences and/or increase consequences of that decision.

For example, the groups which would not try to influence the mother's admission need to focus on how not to alienate Frank and how to avoid negative consequences.

The groups which would do anything to get the mother admitted need to focus on strategies to influence Sheila Hogan and to ensure that Frank "remembers" his promise.

STEP 6. Summarize, using the key points on the activity flow sheet and students' main ideas. Reiterate the positive and negative aspects of power in this situation.

CHAPTER 8	BROKER ROLE
COMPETENCY 1	BUILDING AND MAINTAINING A POWER BASE

Practice: The Big Move
Activity Flow Sheet

PURPOSE: This activity is a simulation, allowing role players to demonstrate the use of particular kinds of power. Students also have the opportunity to identify and rate the effectiveness of the power exhibited by each player.

KEY POINTS: Five sources of power.

TIME ESTIMATE: 60 minutes.

FORMAT: Small group role play activity in 6-person groups, followed by large group discussion.

SPECIAL NEEDS: Role play name tags or name cards, and the opening statement for each player (follows process guide).

SEQUENCE:
1. Introduce the activity.
2. Divide students into groups of 6.
3. Allow 30 minutes for the role play.
4. Direct them to complete the questionnaire.
5. Conduct a large group discussion.
6. Summarize.

VARIATION: Conduct the role play as a fishbowl activity, allowing the other class members to observe and to fill out the Assessing Power-Oriented Behaviors Questionnaire Sheet (page 308).

KEY POINTS:
1. Both personal and positional power were practiced.

2. The most effective power-orientations are a product of the person, the position, the situation, and the context.

See **SPECIAL NOTE** at end of Process Guide.

CHAPTER 8	BROKER ROLE
COMPETENCY 1	BUILDING AND MAINTAINING A POWER BASE

Practice: The Big Move
Process Guide

PURPOSE: This activity is a simulation, allowing role players to demonstrate the use of particular kinds of power. Students also have the opportunity to identify and rate the effectiveness of the power exhibited by each player. As such they practice giving and receiving feedback on the role.

STEP 1.. Introduce the activity by directing students to the instructions on page 304-308 of the text.

STEP 2. Divide students into groups of 6. Extra participants can serve as observers. Have students in each group choose one of the six roles to play, and give out the name tags and opening statements. Remind them to read their role description, but to refrain from reading the descriptions of others.

STEP 3. Allow 30 minutes for the role play, although suggest that they stop sooner if they feel that the exchange has come to closure for the small group.

STEP 4. Direct them to complete the questionnaire and engage in small group discussion.

STEP 5. Conduct a large group discussion. Additional questions may include:

   A. How did you feel during the role play? Did you feel that you were "in control" and held a strong power base? Why or why not?

   B. Did the power behavior that you were given in your role match your real life power orientation, or was it one you seldom rely upon?

   C. Do you feel that options were available to you? How did you develop them?

STEP 6. Summarize. Ask students what they learned from this activity that will enable them to deal more effectively with power in relationships and in organizations.

SPECIAL NOTE: This activity may take over 60 minutes. As a fishbowl, it can be particularly effective if you have astute performers who can demonstrate the use of particular kinds of power. While this activity takes a long time but certainly involves the class and can be used at a time in the course when the instructor wants heavy involvement. What may be helpful at this point is that this chapter, being late in the text, may be covered late in the course. If so, students may be experienced role players by the time they get to this activity. If there have been good discussions in class on the sources of power, this activity can be an exceptional experience for students.

THE BIG MOVE: Opening Statements for Role Play

Manager: Client Financial Services:

"As you know, I have been with the department since its founding, 10 years as manager. I have always been committed to the success of the department and the productivity and reputation of the client financial services unit is excellent."

--------------------[cut along this line]--------------------

Manager: Accounting:

"I have been manager of the accounting department for several years. You know me as an objective, no-nonsense person who has the facts at hand or can get them in most situations."

--------------------[cut along this line]--------------------

Manager: Purchasing:

"I have been here for 25 years. As manager of purchasing I have worked closely with all of you. You know that I have been responsible for getting many of the equipment purchases, materials, etc. that you have needed. I don't mind telling you right out that I think moving is foolish and I'm against it."

--------------------[cut along this line]--------------------

Manager: Stock and Bond Transfer:

"I realize that I have not been with the department for very long. You know, however, that I come here with extensive corporate experience. Obviously I favor the move as part of our necessary and revitalizing expansion effort."

--------------------[cut along this line]--------------------

Manager: Policy Department:

"The policy department has worked hard during the past few years to increase service options to clients. We are especially pleased to manage these increases while maintaining a new cost-reduction program. The two awards we received mean a lot, and we continue to work hard to achieve excellence."

--------------------[cut along this line]--------------------

Manager: Personnel:

"As manager of the personnel unit, I have been giving a great deal of thought to this move and its implications. While I have been manager for only 8 months, I have taken the position very seriously and make every effort to know the staff and our staffing needs."

CHAPTER 8	BROKER ROLE
COMPETENCY 1	BUILDING AND MAINTAINING A POWER BASE

Practice (Option 2): It's About Your Smoking
Activity Flow Sheet

PURPOSE: This activity helps students to think about their present level of power, and to practice using their power in order to convince someone to quit smoking.

KEY POINTS: Influence strategies and sources of power.

TIME ESTIMATE: This can go on for an indeterminate amount of time!

FORMAT: Individual activity outside of class followed by large group discussion.

SEQUENCE:
1. Introduce the activity.
2. Review briefly major concepts about their power bases.
3. Instruct students to complete the assignment by a specified date.
4. Ask for volunteers to share their experiences.
5. Conduct a large group discussion and summarize.

VARIATION: After step 2, students may be divided into small groups for the purpose of giving one another ideas and suggestions.

KEY POINTS:
1. Power/powerlessness is not unchanging. Contrary to what we may sometimes feel, we can enlarge our power base.
2. Efforts to use our power, even for a good cause, need to be very carefully considered.
3. Individuals ultimately have the only power over their own behavior.

NOTE: This activity may best be used as an option for student and not required.

CHAPTER 8	BROKER ROLE
COMPETENCY 1	BUILDING AND MAINTAINING A POWER BASE

Practice (Option 2): It's About Your Smoking
Process Guide

PURPOSE: This activity helps students to think about their present level of power, and to practice using their power in order to convince someone to quit smoking.

STEP 1. Introduce the activity by directing students to the instructions on page 308-309.

STEP 2. Review briefly the major concepts of power and dependency. Note the feelings of powerlessness that often accompanies dependency.

STEP 3. Instruct students to complete the assignment by writing by a specified date.

STEP 4. On the due date, ask for volunteers to share their experiences and insights with the class.

STEP 5. Conduct a large group discussion and summarize.

CHAPTER 8	BROKER ROLE
COMPETENCY 1	BUILDING AND MAINTAINING A POWER BASE

Application: Changing Your Power Base by Changing Your Influence Strategy
Activity Flow Sheet

PURPOSE: This activity helps students to think about their present level of power, using the concepts and skills learned in this competency. They also develop a plan for enlarging their power base.

KEY POINTS: Influence strategies and sources of power.

TIME ESTIMATE: 30 minutes.

FORMAT: Individual activity followed by large group discussion.

SPECIAL NEEDS: Students will need their diagram from the assessment activity on page 293 of the text.

SEQUENCE:
1. Introduce the activity.
2. Review briefly major concepts.
3. Instruct students to complete the assignment by a specified date.
4. Ask for volunteers to share their action plans.
5. Conduct a large group discussion and summarize.

VARIATION: After step 2, students may be divided into small groups for the purpose of giving one another ideas on which actions to plan.

KEY POINTS:
1. Power/powerlessness is not unchanging. Contrary to what we may sometimes feel, we can enlarge our power base.

2. Efforts to empower ourselves are enhanced by analysis and careful planning.

CHAPTER 8	BROKER ROLE
COMPETENCY 1	BUILDING AND MAINTAINING A POWER BASE

Application: Changing Your Power Base
Process Guide

PURPOSE: This activity helps students to think about their present level of power, using the concepts and skills learned in this competency. They also develop a plan for enlarging their power base. This activity is valuable in its application as a life skill, because it essentially allows students to feel empowered and in control.

STEP 1. Introduce the activity by directing students to the instructions on page 309. Remind them to use their diagram from the assessment activity for this competency.

STEP 2. Review briefly major concepts of power and dependency. Note the feelings of powerlessness that often accompanies dependency.

STEP 3. Instruct students to complete the assignment by writing a 3-5 page report and submitting it by a specified date.

STEP 4. Ask for volunteers to share their action plans with the class.

STEP 5. Conduct a large group discussion and summarize. Additional discussion questions may include:

   A. Why do some people at times resist the suggestion that they may have more power, or able to marshall more power, than they realize? What are some of the barriers to realizing our own empowerment?

   B. What are some of the consequences of feeling powerless?

   C. Do you believe that individuals can increase their power in organizations? Why or why not? Do some organizational structures make self-empowering efforts more difficult than other organizational designs?

   D. What is it about this activity that is empowering - even before any planned action is taken?

   E. How are these empowering skills valuable to one's life and relationships?

A note from one of the authors: A helpful discussion in Power, Influence and Authority is found in Cohen and Bradford's *Influence Without Authority* (N.Y.: Wiley, 1990). See

CHAPTER 8	BROKER ROLE
COMPETENCY 2	NEGOTIATING AGREEMENT AND COMMITMENT

Assessment: Are You a Novice or Expert Negotiator?
Activity Flow Sheet

PURPOSE: This activity allows students to consider the extent to which they are comfortable with negotiating in a variety of circumstances. This activity not only permits a quick self-rating, but also demonstrates the various settings to which negotiation skills apply.

KEY POINTS: Principles of *Getting to Yes*; also relates to assertive communication skills.

TIME ESTIMATE: 30 minutes.

FORMAT: Individual activity, work in groups of 4-6, followed by large group discussion.

SPECIAL NEEDS: None.

SEQUENCE:
1. Direct students to the activity and instructions.
2. Instruct them to write their responses to the questions.
3. Place students into small groups of 4-6 individuals.
4. Conduct a large group discussion.
5. Summarize.

VARIATION: In the interest of time, the activity can proceed from the individual response to the large group discussion, omitting step 3.

KEY POINTS:
1. Negotiating skills are applicable to a wide variety of circumstances.

2. Negotiating skills have much in common with assertive communication skills.

3. Note that combative/aggressive techniques are not considered consistent with polish negotiation skills.

4. Using negotiating skills in various situations helps us to feel empowered good about ourselves, especially in organizational settings.

CHAPTER 8	BROKER ROLE
COMPETENCY 2	NEGOTIATING AGREEMENT AND COMMITMENT

Assessment: Are You a Novice or Expert Negotiator?
Process Guide

PURPOSE: This activity allows students to consider the extent to which they are comfortable with negotiating in a variety of circumstances. This activity not only permits a quick self-rating, but also demonstrates the various settings to which negotiation skills apply. With this activity, students can understand that negotiation is an important life skill, not merely a remote concept to learn.

STEP 1. Direct students to the activity and instructions on pages 309-310 of the text.

STEP 2. Instruct them to write their responses to the questions in the margins or on separate paper. Remind them to add any items which they think may be significant.

STEP 3. Place students into small groups of 4-6 individuals. Direct them to discuss their answers, and to prepare a group response.

STEP 4. Conduct a large group discussion based on the groups' responses.

    A. How comfortable do you feel in asking for special consideration, or asking for a better deal?

    B. When is it appropriate/inappropriate to push the limits? When does asking for special consideration work? When doesn't it work?

    C. How can you apply negotiating skills to your personal relationships?

    D. How does effective use of such skills relate to our feeling good about ourselves? Usually people feel more empowered and better about themselves if they attempt a negotiation and fail, as opposed to not attempting one at all.

STEP 5. Summarize, using students' main points as well as the key points from the activity flow sheet.

CHAPTER 8	BROKER ROLE
COMPETENCY 2	NEGOTIATING AGREEMENT AND COMMITMENT

Analysis:
Conflict in the Cafeteria: The Broker as Mediator
Activity Flow Sheet

PURPOSE: This activity allows students to role-play a mediation situation, using negotiating skills covered in the learning section.

KEY POINTS: Organizational culture and four principles for *Getting to Yes*.

TIME ESTIMATE: 40 minutes.

FORMAT: 4 person groups, followed by large group discussion.

SPECIAL NEEDS: None.

SEQUENCE:
1. Divide the class into 4-person groups.
2. Clarify assignments and directions.
3. Conduct the first role play (5-10 minutes).
4. Discuss and debrief.
5. Conduct second role-play (5-10 minutes).
6. Discuss and debrief.
7. Conduct large group discussion.
8. Summarize.

VARIATION: This activity lends itself to a fishbowl format, permitting points to be made to the class during the activity.

KEY POINTS:
1. Informal mediation is an important skill for managers to have and use. However, we believe managers should mediate sparingly and allow people the chance to work out problems on their own first.

2. Organizational culture affects mediation situations.

3. Culture and personality differences, even among people of very similar backgrounds, will influence the dynamics of the bargaining.

CHAPTER 8	BROKER ROLE
COMPETENCY 2	NEGOTIATING AGREEMENT AND COMMITMENT

Analysis:
Conflict in the Cafeteria: The Broker as Mediator
Process Guide

PURPOSE: This activity allows students to role-play a mediation situation, using negotiating skills covered in the learning section. Sometimes what happens is that a manager will find herself/himself in the role of mediator involved in conflict resolution or getting a few people at cross purposes to work out their differences. This is a mediator role. The simulation gives them the opportunity to practice some of the skills of mediator, using the role of a failure mediator, and that of a success mediator.

STEP 1. Divide the class into 4 person groups. If one or two individuals remain, they may be placed as observers.

STEP 2. Clarify assignments and directions. Each group should contain the following characters:

1. Tony Lodge (or Toni, if this character is played by a female).
2. Billie Deore (or Bill, if this character is played by a male).
3. Leslie/Lester MacIntosh as a "failure" third party.
4. Leslie/Lester MacIntosh as a "success" third party.

STEP 3. Conduct the first role play (5-10 minutes). Leslie/Lester MacIntosh as a "failure" third party is involved in this first role play. Remind students to position themselves in their groups so that the key players sit in close proximity.

STEP 4. Discuss and debrief. Possible questions may include:

A. Was a solution reached? How?

B. How satisfied were the role play participants?

C. What kinds of similar experiences have the students had in the past?

D. What are the long term implications of what happened in the cafeteria?

STEP 5. Conduct second role-play (5-10 minutes). Use the same directions as the first role play. The only difference is that the student playing Leslie/ Lester MacIntosh as a "success" third party replaces MacIntosh as a "failure" third party in the role play.

STEP 6. Discuss and debrief. Possible questions include:

A. How did this role play differ from the first?

B. Were Lodge and Deore satisfied with the result?

C. What might have been done differently to obtain better results?

STEP 7. Conduct a large group discussion. Possible discussion questions include:

   A. For the students who played Lodge and Deore: how did their feelings differ between the two role plays? Explore. In which role play did they feel that their feelings and dignity were the most respected? Why?

   B. For the students who played MacIntosh: what were your feelings in each role play? What difficulties did you encounter? In what ways do you see yourself as skilled in mediation, and in what ways do you feel that you need to improve?

   C. In what kinds of situations have you acted as a third party in an obvious misunderstanding? Why did you intervene as mediator in these situations? Why was an agreeable resolution important to you in these situations?

   D. In what kinds of situations would you be prepared to act as a third party in the future?

   E. Why is it difficult to make a verbal intervention in someone else's argument and not appear to be taking sides?

   F. How can you use your body language to indicate both interest and impartiality as you try to give help?

   G. If emotions are too high for one to talk directly to the other, can you use yourself as the channel through which one gives feedback to the other? How?

   H. What would be the very first step you would take if you found that each individual really understood the other and that there were no longer any misunderstandings, but that there was really a basic value difference present?

   I. What role did organizational culture play in this situation? Some examples include:

   1. Lodge felt that since it was originally his/her project, he/she should determine job assignments (i.e. norms regarding who is in charge of this situation).
   2. Issues surrounding equity across workers and managers.
   3. Gender role issues.

   J. How was power used in this activity?

   K. How was persuasion used in this activity?

STEP 8. Summarize the major points of the activity, and what students have pointed out.

CHAPTER 8	BROKER ROLE
COMPETENCY 2	NEGOTIATING AGREEMENT AND COMMITMENT

Practice: The Copy Machine Problem
Activity Flow Sheet

PURPOSE: Students practice the skills of bargaining and negotiation in a work-related simulation.

KEY POINTS: Four principles of *Getting to Yes*.

TIME ESTIMATE: 45 minutes.

FORMAT: Dyad activity, with several students set aside as mediators; followed by large group discussion.

SPECIAL NEEDS: None.

SEQUENCE:
1. Select 3-4 mediators. Divide rest of class into pairs.
2. Ask players to play their roles until they have an agreement.
3. Each pair should write up the policy.
4. Conduct large group discussion.
5. Summarize.

VARIATIONS: Conduct as a fishbowl activity.

KEY POINTS:
1. The copy machine is symbolic of a deeper status anxiety issue.
2. It is possible to use negotiating skills to find a solution when the positions seem mutually exclusive.
3. The bargaining strategy used to negotiate in one situation may affect future negotiations.

CHAPTER 8	BROKER ROLE
COMPETENCY 2	NEGOTIATING AGREEMENT AND COMMITMENT

Practice: The Copy Machine Problem
Process Guide

PURPOSE: Students practice the skills of bargaining and negotiation in a work-related simulation. While students may not expect to work in an office setting like that occurring in this simulation, all students can expect to encounter similar occasional conflicts of interest.

STEP 1. Select 3-4 students to act as mediators. Ideally these students will have shown an aptitude for bargaining in previous activities. Divide rest of class into pairs. One person in each group should play Doyle (or Donna) Buchanan, and the other student should play Mary (or Marty) Caputo.

FURTHER EXPLANATION: Part of the conflict is that one department with customers and needs continuous copies, and the other department does a lot of production copying (large batches) on occasion. Caputo's department suffers from status anxiety: they feel like they are treated as second class citizens because they don't deal face to face with clients. Some of this needs to come out in Caputo's reaction. Caputo feels that the entire department deserves an apology. The issue of the copying machine is a *symbolic* issue. If Buchanan just tries to solve the technical problem (which in this case is easy to solve), then progress will be limited. Buchanan probably needs to get beyond the technical issues and into the personal and social issues at hand.

NOTE: This leads to a very interesting discussion of whether a manager needs to deal with the personal and social issues The authors have found that among MBA students, opinion is very divided. Half the students argue that it's not the manager's problem: if Caputo and her/his people feel hurt, that's their problem. Buchanan, a peer of Caputo's, has no concern here. The other students argue that if it is a real issue, then it is Buchanan's problem and action is warranted. Perhaps Buchanan can do more listening, go back to his/her unit and try to advance the notion that "their work is important as ours." This small case can trigger some very interesting discussions about where the responsibilities of a manager begin and end.

STEP 2. Ask students to play their roles. The pairs should reach a compromise using some of the strategies discussed in this competency. If necessary, review some basic strategies before beginning the activity. until they have an agreement or call in mediators.

STEP 3. Each pair should write up the policy and a statement that they agree to uphold it. If the managers are unable to reach an agreement, they may request the assistance of a mediator.

NOTE: If conflict levels among the pairs seems to be low, it may be necessary to increase it in order to demonstrate the major points of the activity. Managers may be told that performance evaluations are heavily dependent upon speed of service. Therefore, it is important to get copies made as quickly as possible.

STEP 4. Conduct large group discussion after all groups have reached a decision or 30 minutes have passed (whichever comes first). Possible discussion questions may include:

   A. What bargaining strategies did people use?

   B. What roles did the mediators play in the bargaining process?

   C. How powerful were the mediators?

   D. What arguments were most successful in persuading the other party to compromise?

   E. How did you "read" the nonverbal communication of the manager you were negotiating with?

   F. What strategies of influence did you use?

   G. How was power used in solving your dispute?

   H. Given what happened in your negotiation, would you approach a future bargaining session with the same individual?

   I. How would you describe the negotiating climate with respect to:

      1. Whether or not human nature is believed to be good, bad, or mixed.
      2. Past, present, and future time orientation.
      3. Individualism, teamwork, or hierarchical ordering of relationships.

STEP 5. Summarize the major points of the activity, using students' main ideas and the key points from the activity flow sheet.

CHAPTER 8	BROKER ROLE
COMPETENCY 2	NEGOTIATING AGREEMENT AND COMMITMENT

Application: Negotiating Positions on the Freedom Scale
Activity Flow Sheet

PURPOSE: This activity allows students a choice of one of three ways to apply principles discussed in the learning section.

KEY POINTS: Principles of *Getting to Yes* and the Freedom Scale

TIME ESTIMATE: in class set up time: 15 minutes; outside of class: 2-3 hours over the next 2 weeks; in class follow up discussion: 15-20 minutes.

FORMAT: Individual activity.

SPECIAL NEEDS: None.

SEQUENCE:
1. Introduce the activity.
2. Review with them the three possible activities.
3. Discuss the significance of option #3.
4. Set a due date for the written work of the activity.
5. Conduct a large group discussion and summarize.

KEY POINTS:
1. Negotiating skills have wide personal and organizational applications.

2. People manage up as well as down. The freedom scale and negotiating skills enable us to perform such managing well.

3. Negotiating skills are a needed and learned activity. As with writing skills, good negotiating skills are not an inborn trait.

CHAPTER 8	BROKER ROLE
COMPETENCY 2	NEGOTIATING AGREEMENT AND COMMITMENT

Application: Negotiating Positions on the Freedom Scale
Process Guide

PURPOSE: This activity allows students a choice of one of three ways to apply principles discussed in the learning section. The third option is a particularly powerful activity for understanding Onchen's freedom scale.

A note from one of the authors: A number of people have found the freedom scale to be useful in essential ways. The freedom scale is taken from William Onchen's *Managing Management Time*. Prior to the book, Onchen published the scale in what has become the most popular article ever printed in the *Harvard Business Review*, receiving the greatest number of reprint requests.

STEP 1. Introduce the activity by directing students to page 323-324 of the text.

STEP 2. Review with them the three possible activities, and discuss which they might like to choose.

STEP 3. Note that option 3 is particularly significant. The freedom scale is a powerful device for clarifying roles with one's boss, peers and subordinates. The authors have found it to be, in consulting and training, the most effective schema to use for role clarification in terms of accountability, reporting back, and negotiating a relationship. It takes ambiguity and potential conflict out of the relationship.

A note from one of the authors: Onchen makes the important point that when we are evaluated, it is usually based on our performance as subordinates. Ironically, we receive little training in how to be an effective subordinate because we are evaluated by "superiors".

STEP 4. Set a due date for the written work of the activity.

STEP 5. Conduct a large group discussion, allowing students to summarize what they have learned after completing the assignment.

CHAPTER 8	BROKER ROLE
COMPETENCY 3	PRESENTING IDEAS EFFECTIVELY

Assessment:
The Presenter's Touch: You May Have It and Not Know It
Activity Flow Sheet

PURPOSE: This activity allows students to assess the extent to which they may already have strong presentation skills.

KEY POINTS: Establish that most people are better communicators than they realize.

TIME ESTIMATE: 10 - 15 minutes.

FORMAT: Individual activity followed by large group discussion.

SPECIAL NEEDS: None.

SEQUENCE:
1. Introduce the activity.

2. Stress the importance of honesty in this assessment.

3. Point out that most people have better oral communication skills than they realize.

4. Conduct a large group discussion and summarize.

KEY POINTS:
1. Many characteristics contribute to good presentation skills.

2. Effective presentations skills are not a matter of talent; they are learned behaviors.

3. Presentation skills are very important to managerial competencies.

4. Good oral communication skills is an even more vital skill than written communication in most American companies surveyed.

CHAPTER 8	BROKER ROLE
COMPETENCY 3	PRESENTING IDEAS EFFECTIVELY

Assessment:
The Presenter's Touch: You May Have It and Not Know It
Process Guide

PURPOSE: This activity allows students to assess the extent to which they may already have strong presentation skills. This questionnaire highlights characteristics that many students may not have associated with presentation skills.

STEP 1. Introduce the activity by directing students to the questions and instructions on page 324-325.

STEP 2. Stress the importance of honesty in this assessment.

STEP 3. Point out that most people have better communication skills than they realize.

STEP 4. Conduct a large group discussion and summarize. Additional discussion questions may include:

   A. Did your score on the questionnaire correspond with the level of presentation skills that you tend to attribute to yourself? What surprised you about this activity?

   B. Why do you think that many people feel that they have fewer presentation skills than they actually may have?

   C. Why are good presentation skills important to the managerial role?

   D. Through what means can people most effectively improve their presentation skills?

CHAPTER 8	BROKER ROLE
COMPETENCY 3	PRESENTING IDEAS EFFECTIVELY

Analysis: Applying SSSAP
Activity Flow Sheet

PURPOSE: This activity allows students to analyze presentations according to their own experience. Additionally, they learn to identify the principles of SSSAP explained in the learning section.

KEY POINTS: Switzler's SSSAP: Set, Sequence, Support, Access, Polish

TIME ESTIMATE: In class to set up: 10 minutes; outside of class: 90 minutes; in class follow up discussion: 15-20 minutes.

FORMAT: Individual activity followed by large group discussion..

SPECIAL NEEDS: None.

SEQUENCE:
1. Direct students to the activity on page 333 of the text.

2. Remind students to be as unobtrusive as possible during the presentation.

3. Students should be alerted to the possible effect of their interest in the content of the presentation, in terms of their assessment of the presentations' effectiveness.

4. Instruct students to write a 1-2 page report.

5. Conduct a large group discussion and summarize.

VARIATION: This individual activity could be assigned for completion in small groups or teams. A cautionary reminder: Care must be taken to prevent groups of students from attending lectures, classes, and other campus events, and being disruptive to the presenter by being obviously making an assessment of the presenter's style.

KEY POINTS:
1. Effective speakers vary widely in the way they adhere to SSSAP and other principles.

2. Effective speakers often present a mix of skills and their own personalities.

3. Most speakers' performance can be improved in some way; however, that realization may not prevent them from delivering an excellent presentation.

CHAPTER 8	BROKER ROLE
COMPETENCY 3	PRESENTING IDEAS EFFECTIVELY

Analysis: Applying SSSAP
Process Guide

PURPOSE: This activity allows students to analyze presentations according to their own experience. Additionally, they learn to identify the principles of SSSAP explained in the learning section.

STEP 1. Direct students to the activity on page 333 of the text. Discuss with students various options of presentations they may attend. Perhaps a lecture is being scheduled in the community or on the campus that may interest them. Again, remind them of the preference **not** to use a televised presentation.

STEP 2. Remind students to be as unobtrusive as possible during the presentation.

STEP 3. Students should be alerted to the possible effect of their interest in the content of the presentation, in terms of their assessment of the presentations' effectiveness.

STEP 4. Instruct students to write a 1-2 page report commenting on the SSSAP principles and the questions on page 333. Set a deadline for this report to be handed in.

STEP 5. Conduct a large group discussion on the day that the reports are due. Discuss the questions on page 333. Summarize students' major points. Addition discussion questions may include:

   A. What was the relationship between your interest in the topic and your assessment of the presentation?

   B. To what extent does your feeling of liking the presenter as a person (from what you can ascertain in the presentation) affect your judgment of the effectiveness of presentation?

   C. Do you think it is possible to "separate the medium from the message?" Why or why not?

| CHAPTER 8 | BROKER ROLE |
| COMPETENCY 3 | PRESENTING IDEAS EFFECTIVELY |

Practice: You Be The Speaker
Activity Flow Sheet

PURPOSE: This activity provides students with the valued opportunity to prepare a presentation and to receive supportive feedback from peers. It also allows students to practice giving supportive feedback to others.

KEY POINTS: SSSAP

TIME ESTIMATE: 90 minutes.

FORMAT: Individual presentations to 4-6 person groups.

SPECIAL NEEDS: Sufficient copies of the Peer Feedback Form (follows process guide).

SEQUENCE:
1. Direct students to read the instructions on page 333.

2. Divide students into 4-6 person groups.

3. Remind students of the proprieties of giving constructive feedback to others.

4. Allow sufficient time in class for the presentations and feedback.

5. Conduct a large group discussion and summarize.

KEY POINTS:
1. Note that SSSAP can be used effectively in written communication as well as in oral communication.

2. SSSAP provides needed and helpful guidelines to preparing oral presentations about any subject.

3. Constructive feedback from peers is enormously helpful. This is a resource which we can tap at any time.

4. SSSAP is useful in helping people helping people learn to describe, create, and criticize.

CHAPTER 8	BROKER ROLE
COMPETENCY 3	PRESENTING IDEAS EFFECTIVELY

Practice: You Be The Speaker
Process Guide

PURPOSE: This activity provides students with the valued opportunity to prepare a presentation and to receive supportive feedback from peers. It also allows students to practice giving supportive feedback to others.

STEP 1. Direct students to read the instructions on page 333. Discuss with them various options of topics they might choose on which to prepare presentations.

STEP 2. Divide students into small groups. The size of the groups is a function of how much time you wish to allow. The larger the groups, the greater the feedback, but the longer the activity will take. Note that the time allotted for the group work will be 6 minutes per group member, plus a few extra minutes.

STEP 3. Remind students of the proprieties of giving constructive feedback to others. They may wish to give the speaker a chance to be self-critical before offering their comments.

Further, suggest that they might want to avoid being definitive and using phrases such as: You should have. . . or, You were wrong to. . . Instead, in giving constructive feedback, it is best to be more tentative, using such phrases as: I might be wrong but to me this seems. . . or, You might want to consider. . . or, I know I have a hard time with this, but. . .

STEP 4. Allow sufficient time in class for the presentations and feedback.

STEP 5. Conduct a large group discussion and summarize. Additional discussion questions may include:

A. Before this activity you had a level of self-assessment regarding your presentation skills. Has this activity altered that assessment? If so, how and to what extent?

B. What surprised you in doing this activity?

C. What were your feelings when you gave feedback to your peers?

D. What was the most difficult aspect of completing this activity? Why?

E. How did you find SSSAP to be helpful to you?

PEER FEEDBACK FORM

Speaker's name: _____ **Date:** _____

Feedback giver's name: _____

List things that worked, that were effective, about the speaker's presentation:

List some suggestions for improvement:

Speaker's name: _____ **Date:** _____
Feedback giver's name: _____

List things that worked, that were effective, about the speaker's presentation:

List some suggestions for improvement:

CHAPTER 8	BROKER ROLE
COMPETENCY 3	PRESENTING IDEAS EFFECTIVELY

Application: You Be the Critic
Activity Flow Sheet

PURPOSE: This activity allows students to evaluate the effectiveness of their oral presentation skills. Through a written evaluation, they can identify areas in which they need to give more attention to this skill.

KEY TOPICS: SSSAP

TIME ESTIMATE: In class set up: 10 minutes; time to plan and deliver the presentation; in class follow up discussion: 15-20 minutes.

FORMAT: Individual activity followed by large group discussion.

SPECIAL NEEDS: Students must make an oral presentation in the near future.

SEQUENCE:
1. Introduce the activity.

2. Discuss with students when and where they may make the oral presentation.

3. Assign a date for the submission of the written report.

4. Conduct a large group discussion and summarize.

VARIATION: Divide class members into teams, having them prepare more lengthy oral presentations than the 6-minute presentations in the practice activity. With this option, delete written peer feedback.

KEY POINTS:
1. Self-evaluation is an invaluable resource to improving one's competencies.

2. In self-evaluation it is just as important to point out your strengths as it is to point out areas of needed improvement.

CHAPTER 8	BROKER ROLE
COMPETENCY 3	PRESENTING IDEAS EFFECTIVELY

Application: You Be the Critic
Process Guide

PURPOSE: This activity allows students to evaluate the effectiveness of their oral presentation skills. Through a written evaluation, they can identify areas in which they need to give more attention to this skill.

STEP 1. Introduce the activity by directing students to the instructions on page 308. Note that it may be necessary to provide opportunities for students to make oral presentations, or perhaps to make this an optional activity.

STEP 2. Discuss with students when and where they may make the oral presentation. Opportunities could be provided by using the small group format (as with the practice activity) with two differences: written peer feedback not required, and the increasing the length of the presentations. Students might choose from among a number of topics relating to the content of this course.

STEP 3. Assign a date for the submission of the written report.

STEP 4. On the day when students hand in their written reports, conduct a large group discussion and summarize. Discussion questions may include:

    A. What surprised you about doing this activity?

    B. What specific self-evaluation strategies did you utilize?

    C. How did the principles of SSSAP help you in your presentation?

CHAPTER 9 — INNOVATOR ROLE

The Innovator Role, along with the Broker Role, comprises the Open Systems Model of the Competing Values Framework. As such this managerial role is often associated with the organization's interaction with and response to the external environment. Managers in the innovator role find themselves engaged in creative problem solving, monitoring external trends, advocating new ideas, and responding to any environmental changes that may affect the organization.

Like other managerial competencies, the innovator role competencies reflect skills that are helpful to students in their daily lives, and which they may already be using to some extent. Living with change and managing change are important life skills, considered essential to emotional well-being. Mastery of these competencies enhances our ability to embrace life with eager anticipation and enthusiasm, and decreases any tendency to see ourselves as victims of events. Creative thinking is a skill which many people have but tend to underestimate in themselves. Hopefully this chapter may help students more fully believe in their creative abilities.

The competencies of the innovator role present a number of paradoxes to managers. It has been argued that the phrase "organizational change" is an oxymoron. While we may disagree with that view, the point of organizational resistance to change is noted. Organizations tend to be stable with many change-resistant characteristics in their design and operations. Yet change is becoming increasingly pervasive as well as salient. Managers in the innovator role need to operate within the paradoxes of adaptability and stability, or encouraging employee creativity while getting the work done.

It is important for students to understand that as organizations change to meet the demands of the future, definitive models for change do not exist. That is to say, we has yet to observe an organization which manages change perfectly. Everyone is learning to manage in the face of uncertain and opposing demands.

The competencies of the Innovator Role: The three competencies in this role and their corresponding topics in the learning activities are:

Competency 1: Living with Change
Topics: Planned and unplanned change
            Helping ourselves and others deal with unplanned change
            Using the organizational culture to deal with unplanned change
            Using your leadership style to deal with unplanned change
                    Manager as conductor
                    Manager as developer

Competency 2: Thinking Creatively
Topics: Developing creative thinking skills in yourself and others
                    Domain-relevant skills
                    Creative-relevant skills
            Barriers to creative thinking
            Task Motivation
            Brainstorming and NGT
            Importance of Creative Thinking in Organizations

Competency 3: Creating Change
Topics: Common processes associated with organizational change
Understanding resistance to planned change
Designing change
Force Field Analysis
Implementing change
Three approaches to managing change
    Rational-empirical approaches
    Normative-reeducative approaches
    Power-coercive approaches
Effective management of change

Conceptually the innovator role is not limited to these competencies. Other competencies have been identified as:

Effective risk taking in organizations
Fostering a creative work climate
How to manage organizational transitions
How to manage a failed innovation
How to see problems as opportunities
Understanding the present and forecasting the future
Recommending changes in organizational policy

The Innovator Role and current issues: Change issues involved in this role bear direct relationship to some workplace issues of the 1990's and beyond. The U. S. work force is becoming increasingly culturally diverse. Yet most of us do not have experience in culturally diverse organizations. With no models to follow, how can we learn to manage cultural diversity?

Furthermore, as organizations find themselves operating an increasingly dynamic and fast-paced environment, they experience an intensifying need to draw on employees' creative resources in order to keep up. One of the intensifying challenges of the coming decades is ensuring human survival on this planet. It is argued that this challenge, shared by all, can be meet by people in organizations which value and advance creativity.

Some questions to consider in this chapter are:

1. How can an organization foster creative thinking among employees while maintaining a coordinated work flow and ensuring task completion?

2. Under what circumstances is it undesirable for organizations to encourage employee creativity?

3. While this chapter presents change as largely resisted by employees, is this accurate? What kinds of changes are welcomed by employees and resisted by upper management?

4. What is the relationship between fostering employee creativity and productivity?

CHAPTER 9 — INNOVATOR ROLE
COMPETENCY 1 — LIVING WITH CHANGE

Assessment: Personal Acceptance of Change
Activity Flow Sheet

PURPOSE: This activity allows students to assess the extent to which they tend to accept change in their lives.

KEY TOPICS: Helping ourselves and others to deal with unplanned change. Leads into a discussion of the differences between planned and unplanned change.

TIME ESTIMATE: 25 minutes.

FORMAT: Individual activity followed by large group discussion.

SPECIAL NEEDS: None.

SEQUENCE:
1. Introduce the activity.

2. Direct students to write down their answers to the discussion questions on page 338.

3. Conduct a large group discussion.

4. Summarize.

VARIATION: After students have completed the scale items, place them into dyads to discuss the discussion questions with a partner. The discussion questions are particularly important to this activity; if students do not write out their responses, it is important that they be allowed to discuss them thoroughly.

KEY POINTS:
1. People often resist change at the time it occurs, but find themselves accepting it later. Often people are happy that the change occurred.

2. People are adaptable, and have considerable capacity for accepting change in their lives.

3. Our ability to accept change depends somewhat on prior experiences with change, but we can increase this ability with attention and conscious effort.

3. The ability to accept change is an important life skill.

CHAPTER 9	INNOVATOR ROLE
COMPETENCY 1	LIVING WITH CHANGE

Assessment: Personal Acceptance of Change
Process Guide

PURPOSE: This activity allows students to assess the extent to which they tend to accept changes in their lives. The questions permit students to indicate their level of resistance to events at the time the event occurred. Students then contrast that resistance with their ability to accept the same changes over time.

STEP 1. Introduce the activity by directing students to pages 337-338 of the text. Explain that this is a reflective activity, and suggest that they take their time in re-creating their feelings during the experiences indicated. Note that it is in their interest to be honest and emotionally thorough in their responses.

STEP 2. After students have completed the scale, direct them to write down their answers to the discussion questions on page 338.

STEP 3. Conduct a large group discussion based on their scores and their responses to the discussion questions. Additional questions may include:

  A. Who had the largest difference between their two columns? Who had the smallest? How would you contrast your experiences?

  B. Some people not only resist change before it happens, but *refuse to accept* the change after it has occurred. Why do you think they refuse to accept changes? NOTE: Sometimes people feel that refusal to accept change is a way to continue to object to it. In other words, if a person truly objects to the change, and then accepts it, then such acceptance may indicate that their initial objections were weak or not well-founded.

  C. Why is the ability to accept change considered an important life skill?

  D. What can people do to become more accepting of change in life?

STEP 4. Summarize the discussion of their major points.

CHAPTER 9	INNOVATOR ROLE
COMPETENCY 1	LIVING WITH CHANGE

Analysis: Resistance to Change
Activity Flow Sheet

PURPOSE: This activity allows students to analyze their affective response to a work situation where change is resisted.

KEY TOPICS: Using your leadership style to deal with unplanned change.

TIME ESTIMATE: 20 minutes.

FORMAT: Individual activity followed by large group discussion.

SPECIAL NEEDS: None.

SEQUENCE:
1. Introduce the activity.
2. Instruct students to submit a short written response..
3. Conduct a large group discussion.
4. Summarize the major points of the discussion.

KEY POINTS:
1. Organizational changes may have emotional consequences for individuals who are affected by those changes.

2. The emotional consequences may be unintended by those who designed the changes.

3. The feelings of individuals are legitimate and are not open to challenge. That is to say, to assert to someone that they "should" or "should not" feel what they feel verges on nonsense and may only compound the situation. It would be appropriate, however, for someone to be told that their emotional response was not the intention of the organizational change.

SPECIAL NOTE: Students will need their responses in order to complete the following practice activity, page 346-347 of the text.

CHAPTER 9	INNOVATOR ROLE
COMPETENCY 1	LIVING WITH CHANGE

Analysis: Resistance to Change
Process Guide

PURPOSE: This activity allows students to analyze their affective responses to a work situation where change is resisted. By completing the questions in the first person, students can better understand some of the emotional dimensions associated with facing unplanned change.

STEP 1. Introduce the activity by directing students to pages 345-346 of the text. Explain that in this case, they play the role of a manager who is affected by an organizational change.

STEP 2. Instruct students to respond to the emotional dimensions of the experience, and to submit a short written response to question 3 on page 346.

STEP 3. Conduct a large group discussion. Note the following:

  A. Ask students what their responses were.

  B. Acknowledge that for students to share their feelings is risk-taking and requires considerable courage.

  C. It may be necessary to discuss the inappropriateness of commenting negatively on someone else's feelings.

  D. Note how none of us appreciate being told that we should not feel a certain way. Such admonishments seldom make the emotions disappear, but often merely compound the situation with additional undesirable emotions.

  E. Note the importance of dealing with others' feelings in organizational settings.

STEP 4. Summarize the major points of the discussion, noting the key points listed on the activity flow sheet.

CAUTION: Notice that the purpose of this activity is **not** to arrive at a solution, but merely to describe the emotional components of the situation. As such, *placing students in groups for discussing the questions is not advised.* In such groups there may be a tendency for students to feel that they "should" or "should not" feel certain ways, and to compare their emotional responses to those of the other group members. Such an outcome could be very dysfunctional.

CHAPTER 9	INNOVATOR ROLE
COMPETENCY 1	LIVING WITH CHANGE

Practice: Resistance to Change Revisited
Activity Flow Sheet

PURPOSE: This activity allows students to use what they learned from the analysis activity to initiate change in such a way as to mitigate any negative emotional consequences for others.

KEY TOPICS: Using your leadership style to deal with unplanned change

TIME ESTIMATE: 20 minutes.

FORMAT: Individual activity followed by large group discussion.

SPECIAL NEEDS: Student responses to the analysis activity on page 345-346 of the text.

SEQUENCE:
1. Introduce the activity by referring students to their responses to the analysis activity.

2. Direct students to the instructions on page 346 of the text.

3. Have students respond in writing to the questions.

4. Conduct a large group discussion.

5. Summarize.

VARIATION: Place students into 4-5 person groups, as upper management teams, to respond to the questions.

KEY POINTS:
1. Awareness of possible emotional consequences of our actions can be helpful as we seek to design those actions.

2. Note that the issue is often not IF the change will be made, but HOW it is presented to those who are affected by it. Often negative feelings can be avoided with appropriate implementation planning.

CHAPTER 9	INNOVATOR ROLE
COMPETENCY 1	LIVING WITH CHANGE

Practice: Resistance to Change Revisited
Process Guide

PURPOSE: This activity allows students to use what they learned from the analysis activity to initiate change in such a way as to mitigate any negative emotional consequences for others. The emphasis is not on IF the change will occur, but HOW.

STEP 1. Introduce the activity by referring students to their responses to the analysis activity.

> Remind them that in the analysis activity, they played the role of a manager who was subject to unplanned change. In that role students were able to identify some possible emotional dimensions of the experience for the manager.

> Explain that in this activity, they are to act as the manager's manager and change agent.

> In light of the emotional dimensions which they explored in the analysis, how would they now handle the change?

STEP 2. Direct students to the instructions and questions on page 346-347 of the text.

STEP 3. Have students respond in writing to the questions.

STEP 4. Conduct a large group discussion. Ask the students for their answers to each question, and record them on the chalkboard. Additional questions may include:

> A. Would your answers have been different if you had not completed the analysis activity? Explain.

> B. How can the skills reflected in this activity apply to making changes in your personal life?

STEP 5. Summarize noting the key points from the activity flow sheet, as well as the major points made by students.

CHAPTER 9	INNOVATOR ROLE
COMPETENCY 1	LIVING WITH CHANGE

Application: Diagnosing Your Organizational Culture
Activity Flow Sheet

PURPOSE: This activity allows students to identify the components of the culture of an organization in which they are/were involved.

KEY TOPICS: Using organizational culture to deal with unplanned change

TIME ESTIMATE: In class set up time: 10; outside of class: 60 minutes; in class follow up discussion: 20 minutes.

FORMAT: Individual activity followed by large group discussion.

SPECIAL NEEDS: None.

SEQUENCE:
1. Introduce the activity.

2. Point out that identifying the elements of one's organizational culture is not a simple task.

3. Help students identify an organization for this assignment.

4. Set the date that the paper is due.

5. Conduct a large group discussion and summarize.

VARIATION: If the students select the same organizations, then they may be divided into teams for the purpose of diagnosing the culture.

KEY POINTS:
1. The components of organizational cultures are often difficult to identify.

2. Organizational cultures are significant to the quality of individuals' experience within the organization.

3. Organizational cultures are subject to change.

CHAPTER 9	INNOVATOR ROLE
COMPETENCY 1	LIVING WITH CHANGE

Application: Diagnosing Your Organizational Culture
Process Guide

PURPOSE: This activity allows students to identify the components of the culture of an organization in which they are/were involved. This activity provides a valuable opportunity for students to " dig beneath the surface" of organizational life.

STEP 1. Introduce the activity by referring students to the questions on page 347. If necessary review with students the concept of organizational culture and its components. Explain that this activity assists them in diagnosing such a culture.

STEP 2. Point out that identifying the elements of one's organizational culture is not a simple task; cultures comprise the basic assumptions of our lives, and as such, may be difficult to identify.

STEP 3. If necessary help students identify an organization for this assignment.

STEP 4. Set the date that the paper is due.

STEP 5. On the date the papers are due, conduct a large group discussion of their responses to the 4 questions on page 347. Summarize the major points made by students. Additional discussion questions may include:

   A. What surprised you about this assignment?

   B. Did you find that organizational cultures are difficult to uncover and describe? What makes them difficult to describe?

CHAPTER 9	INNOVATOR ROLE
COMPETENCY 2	THINKING CREATIVELY

Assessment: Are You A Creative Thinker?
Activity Flow Sheet

PURPOSE: This activity allows students to understand that they are probably more creative than they may realize.

KEY TOPICS: Creative thinking; barriers to creative thinking. Leads into a discussion of characteristics of creative individuals.

TIME ESTIMATE: 20-30 minutes.

FORMAT: Individual activity followed by large group discussion.

SPECIAL NEEDS: None.

SEQUENCE:
1. Introduce the activity.

2. Direct them to write out responses to the three questions (repeated in the process guide).

3. Conduct a large group discussion.

4. Summarize their major points.

VARIATION: After step 2 students could be placed into dyads for the purpose of discussing the interpretation questions.

KEY POINTS:
1. Creative abilities are not the sole domain of an elite group of artistically talented individuals. Virtually all individuals have some measure of creative ability.

2. Creative ability can be developed and increased.

3. The first step to increasing one's creative ability is to acknowledge one's creative potential.

4. Creativity is useful for the manager, both in dealing with people issues and in addressing nonstandard problems or issues.

5. Many people have characteristics that they have held as undesirable, but which actually are indicative of creative ability.

CHAPTER 9	INNOVATOR ROLE
COMPETENCY 2	THINKING CREATIVELY

Assessment: Are You A Creative Thinker?
Process Guide

PURPOSE: This activity allows students to understand that they are probably more creative than they may realize. The items often refer to attitudes and behaviors which students may not have previously associated with creativity.

STEP 1. Introduce the activity by directing students to the questions on pages 347-348. Explain that these questions will help them gauge their creative abilities.

STEP 2. Direct them to write out their responses to the following three interpretation questions after they complete the questionnaire:

1. Which of these behaviors and attitudes did you previously think of as reflective of creative ability? Which surprised you? Was there any pattern to the items that surprised you? What might that be?

2. Are any of the items you checked behaviors or attitudes you regard as undesirable? If so, think about why you see them as undesirable. How might you redefine these behaviors or attitudes so that you could channel some of your untapped creative energies into productive use?

3. Overall, how creative do you think you are?

NOTE: Research indicates that the major difference between creative people and uncreative people is that creative people *think* they are creative.

STEP 3. Conduct a large group discussion based on their responses to the interpretation questions. Additional discussion questions may include:

A. How creative are your close friends? What have they done that leads you to regard them as creative?

B. How creative can you be at school and in your work?

C. How many of you know of children who are sometimes creative? How many uncreative children do you know?

D. Why do people stop being creative? What messages do people receive while growing up that give them the feeling that they are not creative?

E. How does creativity get forced into hiding as people move into adulthood? How can it reappear?

STEP 4. Summarize the major points made by students, as well as the key points on the Activity Flow Sheet.

CHAPTER 9	INNOVATOR ROLE
COMPETENCY 2	THINKING CREATIVELY

Analysis: Creativity and Managerial Style
Activity Flow Sheet

PURPOSE: This activity allows students to reflect on how someone's managerial style can affect the extent to which employees will see themselves as creative.

KEY TOPICS: Developing creative thinking in others; task motivation

TIME ESTIMATE: 40 minutes.

FORMAT: Individual activity, work in 4-5 person groups, followed by large group discussion.

SPECIAL NEEDS: None.

SEQUENCE:
1. Introduce the activity.
2. Direct students to write down the name of the individual.
3. Instruct students to respond to the items.
4. Have students write their responses to the discussion questions.
5. Place students in 4-5 person groups.
6. Conduct a large group discussion.
7. Summarize.

VARIATION: Omit the small group discussions and proceed directly from step #4 to step 6.

KEY POINTS:
1. One's managerial style can have a significant influence on employees' perception of their creative abilities, as well as on their demonstrated creative activities.

2. Reflection on how others' managerial styles have affected us can assist in our understanding of how we may wish to tailor our own managerial styles.

CHAPTER 9	INNOVATOR ROLE
COMPETENCY 2	THINKING CREATIVELY

Analysis: Creativity and Managerial Style
Process Guide

PURPOSE: This activity allows students to reflect on how someone's managerial style can affect the extent to which employees will see themselves as creative.

STEP 1. Introduce the activity by having students identify an individual for whom they have worked, either in or out of a workplace setting.

STEP 2. Direct students to write down the name of the individual, and to recall experiences with that person.

STEP 3. Instruct students to read the directions and respond to the items on page 357 of the text.

STEP 4. Have students write out their responses to the discussion questions on page 357 of the text.

STEP 5. Place students in 4-5 person groups, with the charge to generate a list of strategies in response to question 5.

STEP 6. Conduct a large group discussion based on the groups' listings.

STEP 7. Summarize the key points on the Activity Flow Sheet as well as the points generated in the discussion.

CHAPTER 9	INNOVATOR ROLE
COMPETENCY 2	THINKING CREATIVELY

Practice: Creative-Relevant Skills
Activity Flow Sheet

PURPOSE: This activity provides exercises that are fun to do, and which enhance students' abilities to associate previously unrelated concepts and to think differently about things.

KEY TOPICS: Creative-relevant skills.

TIME ESTIMATE: 40 minutes.

FORMAT: Individual activity and large group discussion.

SPECIAL NEEDS: None.

SEQUENCE:
1. Introduce the activity.

2. Give students 3 minutes to list uses of the paper clip.

3. Give students 3 minutes to list names of the restaurant.

4. Conduct a brief large group discussion.

5. Give students 5 minutes to complete the developing mental imagery exercise.

6. Conduct a brief large group discussion.

7. Give students 10 minutes to describe three problems and to apply an analogy to each one.

8. Conduct a large group discussion.

VARIATIONS:
1. Assign a short paper for the Using Analogies exercise, responding to the instructions on page 359. Be sure to specify a length and due date.

2. For steps 2 and 3, place students into 3-4 person groups or teams, charged with the generation of as many responses as possible. Give the groups 5 minutes for each exercise.

KEY POINTS:
1. With a little effort and practice, creative skills can be developed and increased.

2. Often activities which enhance our creative skills are also fun.

CHAPTER 9	INNOVATOR ROLE
COMPETENCY 2	THINKING CREATIVELY

Practice: Creative-Relevant Skills
Process Guide

PURPOSE: This activity provides exercises that are fun to do. The exercises are designed to enhance students' abilities to associate previously unrelated concepts and to think differently about things. With these exercises students have permission to break out of usual barriers to creative thought, and receive practice in doing so.

STEP 1. Introduce the activity by directing students to the exercises on pages 358-359 of the text. Explain that these are activities which are fun, for which there are no right or wrong answers.

STEP 2. Give students 3 minutes to list uses of the paper clip. Call time if necessary.

STEP 3. Give students 3 minutes to list names of the restaurant. Call time if necessary.

STEP 4. Conduct a brief large group discussion on breaking established thinking barriers, and generate a master list of the paper clip uses and the restaurant names.

STEP 5. Give students five minutes to complete the developing mental imagery exercise.

STEP 6. Conduct a brief large group discussion. Ask them what they found difficult to do and why.

STEP 7. Briefly recall to students of the uses of analogies. Give them 10 minutes to identify and describe three problems and to apply an analogy to each one.

STEP 8. Conduct a large group discussion. Ask for volunteers to share their problems and applied analogies. List on the board any new analogies generated.

CAUTION: It may be necessary to guard against students who may compare themselves unfavorably with other students in the completion of these exercises. Some people may be very creative, but are just not adept at thinking of a lot of different things "on the spot." Furthermore, there are volumes of activities that accomplish the same purpose; this text had space only for a few. Don't let students become discouraged. Expanding one's creativity should be an affirming experience.

CHAPTER 9	INNOVATOR ROLE
COMPETENCY 2	THINKING CREATIVELY

Application: New Approaches to the Same Old Problem
Activity Flow Sheet

PURPOSE: With this activity students identify a problem which they have, and apply their creative skills to redefining it.

KEY TOPICS: Creative-relevant skills.

TIME ESTIMATE: In class set up time: 15 minutes; outside of class: 60 minutes; in class follow up discussion: 20 minutes.

FORMAT: Individual activity followed by large group discussion.

SPECIAL NEEDS: None.

SEQUENCE:
1. Introduce the activity.

2. Read the directions with them.

3. Set a date for the submission of the papers.

4. On the submission date, conduct a large group discussion and summarize.

KEY POINTS:
1. Creative thinking skills can defuse the troublesome nature of a problem.

2. In order to apply creative skills effectively to a problem, one must sincerely want to arrive at a solution to the problem.

3. Taking a different approach to a troublesome problem can generate information which may make the problem more manageable.

CHAPTER 9	INNOVATOR ROLE
COMPETENCY 2	THINKING CREATIVELY

Application: New Approaches to the Same Old Problem
Process Guide

PURPOSE: With this activity students identify a problem which they have, and apply their creative skills to redefining it.

STEP 1. Introduce the activity by referring students to the directions on pages 359-360 of the text. Explain that their benefit from this activity will increase in proportion to the difficulty of the problem that they choose.

> **NOTE:** Sometimes the most troubling and urgent problems students have are personal, the details of which they may be hesitant to divulge in an assignment. Nor would they want this problem subjected to grading. Yet this activity may be most beneficial when considering such problems. If you do not plan to grade this assignment on its content (but only on its completion), you could have students complete the paper for their own use, submitting to you a short summary and response to question #8.

STEP 2. Read the directions with them, adding any explanation as necessary.

STEP 3. Set a date for the submission of the papers.

STEP 4. On the submission date, conduct a large group discussion. Ask for volunteers to share their experience. Generate from the class a master list of strategies in response to question 8.

CHAPTER 9	INNOVATOR ROLE
COMPETENCY 3	CREATING CHANGE

Assessment: Changes in My Organization
Activity Flow Sheet

PURPOSE: This activity demonstrates to students the point that the substance of a change is different from the methods through which it is implemented.

KEY TOPICS: Designing change, implementing change, and three approaches to managing change.

TIME ESTIMATE: In class set up time: 10 minutes; outside of class: 45 minutes; in class follow up discussion: 20 minutes.

FORMAT: Individual activity followed by large group discussion.

SPECIAL NEEDS: None.

SEQUENCE:

1. Introduce the activity.

2. Read the questions with the students, adding additional explanation as necessary.

3. Set a due date (preferably the next class session) for the students' papers.

4. One the due date, conduct a large group discussion.

KEY POINTS:

1. It is important to distinguish between the substance of a proposed change and its implementation procedures.

2. The procedures for implementing change affect people's perception of the substance of the change, in terms of value, feasibility, and desirability.

3. A proposed change within an organization can be needed beyond dispute, but if its implementation is haphazard and not carefully planned, the proposed change can become vigorously opposed, and ultimately fail.

SPECIAL NOTE: Students use this activity in order to complete the first part of the practice activity on page 374 entitled "Force Field Analysis."

CHAPTER 9	INNOVATOR ROLE
COMPETENCY 3	CREATING CHANGE

Assessment: Changes in My Organization
Process Guide

PURPOSE: This activity demonstrates to students the point that the substance of a change is different from the methods through which it is implemented. Students compare two changes in an organization: one which is successful, and one which is unsuccessful. Students attribute the extent of success to either content of the change or to implementation procedures.

STEP 1. Introduce the activity by directing students to the instructions on page 360. If necessary assist them in identifying an organization with which they have been affiliated.

STEP 2. Read the questions with the students, adding additional explanation as necessary. Perhaps you could point to your college or university as an organization, identifying and comparing a successfully implemented change and an unsuccessfully implemented change. Examples may range from changes in admissions standards to changes in degree programs.

> **NOTE:** It may be the case that whether or not an implemented change is successful is a judgment call. For instance, some previously all-women's colleges have become coeducational. Although apparently successful, some individuals regard such changes as unsuccessful over the long term because of concerns for declining enrollments. The important thing for this activity is for students to use their judgment as to whether an identified change is successful.

STEP 3.. Set a due date (preferably the next class session) for the students' papers.

STEP 4. On the due date, conduct a large group discussion. Additional questions may include:

> A. How difficult is it to separate the substance of a change from the method of implementing it?

> B. How does the method of implementing a change affect our perception of the value of the change?

CHAPTER 9	INNOVATOR ROLE
COMPETENCY 3	CREATING CHANGE

Analysis: Reorganizing the Legal Division
Activity Flow Sheet

PURPOSE: This activity gives students an opportunity to analyze a case that explores issues related to frequently occurring changes in an office.

KEY TOPICS: Designing change, implementing change, and effective management of change.

TIME ESTIMATE: 45 minutes.

FORMAT: 4-5 person groups followed by large group discussion.

SPECIAL NEEDS: None.

SEQUENCE:
1. Divide students into 4-5 person groups.
2. Introduce the activity.
3. Conduct a large group discussion.
4. Summarize the major points of the groups.

VARIATIONS:
1. Depending upon the size and nature of the class, the small groups may be omitted, and the entire activity conducted as a large group discussion.

2. The case may be assigned as homework, requiring written responses to each question throughout the case.

KEY POINTS:
1. We can expect all changes to have driving forces and resisting forces.

2. It is important to understand the forces which lead to change and those which lead to resistance to change.

SPECIAL NOTE: This activity forms the basis for the second part of the practice activity "Force Field Analysis" on page 374 of the text.

CHAPTER 9	INNOVATOR ROLE
COMPETENCY 3	CREATING CHANGE

Analysis: Reorganizing the Legal Division
Process Guide

PURPOSE: This activity gives students an opportunity to analyze a case that explores issues related to frequently occurring changes in an office. This case demonstrates forces that lead to change and the forces that lead to resistance to change. Students determine what specific problems exist, what strategies they might use to solve the problem, and examine a strategy for facilitating change.

STEP 1. Divide students into 4-5 person groups.

STEP 2. Introduce the activity by directing students to the case and questions on pages 371-374 of the text. Direct them to read each section individually and, as a group, discuss the questions which follow the section. Remind them NOT to proceed to reading the next section of the case individually.

STEP 3. Conduct a large group discussion of the four discussion questions on page 374. Ask students to be as specific as possible in their responses when describing what steps Paul should take.

STEP 4. Summarize, using the main points of the groups and the key points from the activity flow sheet.

CHAPTER 9	INNOVATOR ROLE
COMPETENCY 3	CREATING CHANGE

Practice: Force Field Analysis
Activity Flow Sheet

PURPOSE: This activity allows students to practice the method of force field analysis as applied to the assessment activity (page 360 of the text) entitled "Changes in My Organization" as well as to the analysis activity (page 371-374) entitled "Reorganizing the Legal Division."

KEY TOPICS: Force field analysis

TIME ESTIMATE: In class set up and small group activity: 30 minutes; outside of class writing: 30 minutes; in class follow up discussion: 20 minutes.

FORMAT: Small group activity followed by individual activity and large group discussion.

SPECIAL NEEDS: Responses to the following activities: the assessment on page 230 and the analysis on pages 371-374.

SEQUENCE:
1. Introduce the activity by directing students to the instructions on page 374 of the text.

2. Divide students into 4-5 person groups.

3. Conduct a large group discussion.

4. As individuals, have them conduct a force field analysis on the change they identified in question 4 of the assessment activity (page 360 of the text).

5. Assign a short paper, mapping their force field analysis and responding to the questions in the directions on page 374.

6. Conduct a large group discussion and summarize.

VARIATION: Steps 4 and 5 may be completed as homework.

KEY POINTS:
1. Force field analysis is a useful tool for considering implementing an organizational change.

2. It may not always be necessary to use every step in a force field analysis procedure. Sometimes we can short-cut our approach to match the need.

CHAPTER 9	INNOVATOR ROLE
COMPETENCY 3	CREATING CHANGE

Practice: Force Field Analysis
Process Guide

PURPOSE: This activity allows students to practice the method of force field analysis as applied to the assessment activity (page 360 of the text) entitled "Changes in My Organization" as well as to the analysis activity (page 371-374) entitled "Reorganizing the Legal Division." In this activity students complete a force field twice.

STEP 1. Introduce the activity by directing students to the instructions on pages 371-374 of the text. Explain that in this activity, they are to conduct two force field analyses: one on the previous case (Reorganizing the Legal Division) and one on a change they would make in their organization, as identified in question #4 of the assessment on page 360. Have students gather any relevant materials from these activities.

STEP 2. Divide students into 4-5 person groups. Give them 30 minutes to complete the force field analysis for the Legal Division case, and to respond to the discussion questions on page 374.

STEP 3. Conduct a large group discussion. Map the force field analysis on the chalkboard, based on the responses from the groups. Discuss their responses to the discussion questions.

STEP 4. Direct students out of their groups. As individuals, have them conduct a force field analysis on the change they identified in question #4 of the assessment activity (page 360 of the text).

STEP 5: Assign a 3-5 page paper, mapping their force field analysis and responding to the questions in the directions on page 374.

STEP 6. Conduct a large group discussion and summarize. Ask students to explain the benefits of a force field analysis in implementing change.

CHAPTER 9	INNOVATOR ROLE
COMPETENCY 3	CREATING CHANGE

Application: Planning a Change
Activity Flow Sheet

PURPOSE: This activity allows students to plan a change which is important to them.

KEY TOPICS: Designing change and implementing change.

TIME ESTIMATE: In class set up time: 10 minutes; outside of class writing: 30 minutes; in class follow up discussion: 20 minutes.

FORMAT: Individual activity followed by large group discussion.

SPECIAL NEEDS: None.

SEQUENCE:
1. Introduce the activity.

2. Assign a short paper and assign a due date for the paper.

3. Conduct a large group discussion and summarize.

KEY POINTS:
1. Sometimes we want change, we do not resist change, and still we find it difficult due to what appears to be the overwhelming nature of the change.

2. Setting target dates makes a proposed change more manageable, and assists us in bringing it to fruition.

CHAPTER 9	INNOVATOR ROLE
COMPETENCY 3	CREATING CHANGE

Application: Planning a Change
Process Guide

PURPOSE: This activity allows students to plan a change which is important to them. By giving target date guidelines, the proposed change becomes more manageable for students.

STEP 1. Introduce the activity by directing students to the instructions on page 375 of the text. Encourage students to choose a change which is important to them, which they want to make, but which has been difficult for them to start. You may need to assist them in choosing a change for this activity. It may be necessary to caution students against planning something which is too grandiose or unmanageable, such as "Hitting the lottery before graduation so I can take early retirement."

STEP 2. Assign a short paper describing the experience and assign a due date for the paper. Tell them to respond in writing to the questions on page 375.

    NOTE: It may be the case that for some students, the most beneficial application of this activity would be to a personal problem. However, they may not wish to submit their work on such a problem for a grade. You may wish to have them turn in an abbreviated paper which discloses that they have completed the assignment without disclosing the nature of the problem they are working on.

STEP 3. Conduct a large group discussion. Summarize, using students' main points as well as the key points from the activity flow sheet.

CHAPTER 10   INTEGRATION AND THE ROAD TO MASTERY

Chapter 1 of the text presents a perspective of integrating the eight managerial roles into an overall historical and theoretical framework. Chapters 2 through 9 introduce students to competencies in each of the eight managerial roles and provide activities which enhance students' ability to integrate each role into their working and personal lives. Now chapter 10, as the conclusion, provides students with strategies, enabling them to integrate all of these roles with balance and discretion, acknowledging the intricate and dynamic inter-relationships.

This chapter challenges students to *do* something about what they have learned during this course. Chapter 10 provides students with the framework to construct and develop a plan whereby they will experience improvement in their levels of mastery of the key managerial roles. By doing this, chapter 10 advances the expectation that students are able to apply these competencies, thus affirming the value of their course work for many years to come, and perhaps for the duration of their careers.

It is important that students focus on mastery as a process and a journey. None of the authors consider themselves to be "master managers" in the sense that they "have arrived." Rather, the meaning of mastery is the ability to self-examine, to grow from experience, and to develop judgment and discernment in the application of competencies to appropriate situations.

Inherent in mastery is developing a sense of oneself. One cannot be a "copy-cat master manager." Management is simply too individual-specific. Two managers faced with identical situations, may find that dissimilar responses are appropriate because they themselves have diverse styles and different relationships with their employees. Again a central paradox is apparent: while we learn from other managers and increase our competency abilities, there is no role model of the one perfect master manager for us to copy. Each person can be said to have a master manager inside, waiting to be improved and developed, and each person's master manager is different.

Topics included in this chapter are:

    The road to mastery
        Stage 1: novice
        Stage 2: advanced beginner
        Stage 3: competency
        Stage 4: proficiency
        Stage 5: expert
    The profile of a master manager
    How masters see the world
    The possibility of self-improvement
        Agenda for self-improvement
            Learn about yourself
            Develop a change strategy
            Implement the strategy
            The results

CHAPTER 10 — INTEGRATION AND THE ROAD TO MASTERY

Assessment: Reexamining Your Profile
Activity Flow Sheet

PURPOSE: This activity allows students to respond again to the course preassessment discussed in chapter 1 of the text, page 26, and compare their current profile with their initial profile. It is likely that this profile will vary from their original one.

KEY TOPICS: The profile of a master manager; the possibility of self-improvement.

TIME ESTIMATE: In class set up time: 10 minutes; outside of class: 45 minutes; In class follow up discussion: 30 minutes

FORMAT: Individual activity followed by large group discussion.

SPECIAL NEEDS: Students will need either the software package with access to a computer, or a hard copy of the instrument (see Part 4, Chapter 1 of this **Instructional Guide** for instructions and a hard copy of the questions). Students will also need their profiles from when they initially responded to the course preassessment.

SEQUENCE:

1. Introduce the activity.

2. Be certain that each student has all of the materials necessary to respond to the course preassessment.

3. Conduct a large group discussion after they have finished with the instrument and have their new profiles

4. Summarize.

KEY POINTS:

1. Everyone has areas where they may need to improve.

2. The road to mastery is a life-long journey, not a destination.

3. We can learn the managerial competencies which we lack, given time, effort, and opportunity.

SPECIAL NOTE: **This activity is needed for completion of the practice and application activities in this chapter.**

| CHAPTER 10 | INTEGRATION AND THE ROAD TO MASTERY |

Assessment: Reexamining Your Profile
Process Guide

PURPOSE: This activity allows students to respond again to the course preassessment discussed in chapter 1 of the text, page 26, and compare their current profile with their initial profile. It is likely that this profile will vary from their original one. This activity demonstrates for students improvement in managerial competency as a result of the experiences associated with the course, and also highlights areas of needed improvement.

STEP 1. Introduce the activity by reminding students of the course preassessment and the profile they developed at the beginning of the course. Direct students to the instructions on page 380 of the text.

STEP 2. Be certain that each student has all of the materials necessary to respond to the course preassessment.

STEP 3. Conduct a large group discussion after they have finished with the instrument and have developed their new profiles. In addition to the questions on page 380-381, additional discussion questions may include:

   A. What did you find surprising about your new profile? Do you think it is accurate?

   B. As you compare your new profile with the original from the beginning of the course, where do you find the most dramatic changes? How do you account for these changes?

   C. As you look at the profiles of some of your classmates, do they match your impressions of these individuals? Why or why not?

STEP 4. Summarize the major points of the discussion, including the key points from the activity flow sheet.

CHAPTER 10 — INTEGRATION AND THE ROAD TO MASTERY

Analysis: The Transcendence of Paradox
Activity Flow Sheet

PURPOSE: This activity allows students to analyze the cases of two well-known managers in terms of mastery level.

KEY POINTS: Paradox; integration of seemingly opposite approaches

TIME ESTIMATE: 30 minutes.

FORMAT: Individual activity, then 4-5 person groups, followed by large group discussion.

SPECIAL NEEDS: None.

SEQUENCE:
1. Introduce the activity by directing students to the instructions on pages 398 of the text.

2. Direct students to individually respond to the questions, and to write down their thoughts.

3. Place students into 4-5 person groups. Allow 20 minutes for discussion.

4. Allow groups to report and conduct a large group discussion.

5. Summarize the discussion.

VARIATIONS:
1. Step 2 can be completed as homework, with instructions to write out their responses to the three questions on page 398.

2. The small group discussion can be omitted by proceeding directly to a large group discussion.

KEY POINTS:
1. Performance in any one managerial role at the expense of attention to the competencies of the other roles can lead to failure and disappointment. This is the case even if one's performance in that one role is extraordinary.

2. Integration of seemingly opposite roles is an important skill.

CHAPTER 10 — INTEGRATION AND THE ROAD TO MASTERY

Analysis: The Transcendence of Paradox
Process Guide

PURPOSE: This activity allows students to analyze the role in terms of contradictions and integration of opposites. This activity demonstrates the importance of balance and discretion in playing the managerial roles.

STEP 1. Introduce the activity by directing students to the cases and instructions on pages 398 of the text. Give them 15 minutes to read the and jot down notes in response to the questions.

STEP 2. Place students into 4-5 person groups. Have group members compare their responses to the three questions, and to develop a group response to those questions.

STEP 3. Conduct a large group discussion. On the chalkboard, list group responses to the three questions.

STEP 4. Summarize the discussion. Use the cases to illustrate the key points on the activity flow sheet.

CHAPTER 10   INTEGRATION AND THE ROAD TO MASTERY

Practice: The Evaluation Matrix
Activity Flow Sheet

PURPOSE: This activity allows students to consider their level of comfort and expertise with the eight managerial roles, and to summarize their thinking on a chart.

KEY POINTS: The profile of the master; agenda for self-improvement.

TIME ESTIMATE: 45 minutes.

FORMAT: Individual activity followed by large group discussion.

SPECIAL NEEDS: Their self-assessment profiles from the assessment activity on page 398.

SEQUENCE:
1. Introduce the activity.

2. While they may wish to jot notes in the matrix on page 398-399, suggest that they may wish to enlarge it, or even to duplicate one for each model of the Competing Values Framework in order to accommodate all of their comments.

3. Emphasize to students that this matrix is for their use after the course is completed.

4. Conduct a large group discussion after students have completed their matrix and summarize.

KEY POINTS:
1. It is important to plan for one's self-improvement development in the managerial roles.

2. The matrix takes the task of self-improvement and breaks it down into manageable steps.

3. Mastery of the managerial roles is a continuing process.

CHAPTER 10	INTEGRATION AND THE ROAD TO MASTERY

Practice: The Evaluation Matrix
Process Guide

PURPOSE: This activity allows students to consider their level of comfort and expertise with the eight managerial roles, and to summarize their thinking on a chart. The chart also specifies self-improvement steps that students can pursue after this course is completed.

STEP 1. Introduce the activity by directing students to the Evaluation Matrix on page 398-399 of the text. Explain that once completed, this matrix provides a summary of where they are with regard to the managerial roles. It also provides an organized plan for self-improvement, with specific steps that can be pursued after the course is over.

STEP 2. While they may wish to jot notes in the matrix on page 398-399, suggest that they may wish to enlarge it, or even to duplicate one for each model of the Competing Values Framework in order to accommodate all of their comments.

STEP 3. Emphasize to students that this matrix is for their use after the course is completed. They may wish to update it on an annual or a semi-annual basis. However, since it is for their use and benefit, encourage them to be thorough and honest in their responses.

STEP 4. Conduct a large group discussion after students have completed their matrix. Ask for volunteers to share their experiences and observations with this activity. Summarize the points made by the students as well as the key points on the activity flow sheet.

CHAPTER 10   INTEGRATION AND THE ROAD TO MASTERY

Application: Your Strategy for Mastery
Activity Flow Sheet

PURPOSE: This activity allows students to write a paper in which they construct a plan for managerial self-improvement and the development of mastery.

TIME ESTIMATE: In class set up time: 15 minutes; outside of class: 3 hours; in class follow up activity: 30 minutes.

FORMAT: Individual activity and large group discussion.

SPECIAL NEEDS: Materials from the activities in this course, especially the assessment and practice activities from this chapter.

SEQUENCE:

1. Introduce the activity by directing students to the instructions on page 399 of the text.

2. Specify the requirements of the final paper.

3. Conduct a large group discussion.

KEY POINTS:

1. In order to begin efforts to master managerial competencies, it is first necessary to identify one's competency strengths and which competencies require improvement.

2. Long-term major self-improvement efforts require careful planning.

3. Do not be discouraged. Resist the temptation to avoid those roles which you do not happen to like. Read books which elaborate the meaning of those roles, and come to appreciate their value and significance in overall managerial mastery.

| CHAPTER 10 | INTEGRATION AND THE ROAD TO MASTERY |

Application: Your Strategy for Mastery
Process Guide

PURPOSE: This activity allows students to write a paper in which they construct a plan for managerial self-improvement and the development of mastery. In this effort, students draw from the activities of the entire course.

STEP 1. Introduce the activity by directing students to the instructions on page 399 of the text. Explain that this activity permits them to construct a comprehensive and thorough improvement plan which will be useful to them in their future endeavors.

STEP 2. Specify the requirements of the final paper: length, due date, etc., and respond to their questions.

STEP 3. Conduct a large group discussion regarding the value of such planning, and the benefit they stand to derive from this activity. Summarize and mention the key points from the activity flow sheet.